T0295590

Museum Resilience

Museum Resilience

Adaptive Planning for a New Era

Susan Guyette

ROWMAN & LITTLEFIELD
Lanham • Boulder • New York • London

Published by Rowman & Littlefield
An imprint of The Rowman & Littlefield Publishing Group, Inc.
4501 Forbes Boulevard, Suite 200, Lanham, Maryland 20706
www.rowman.com

86-90 Paul Street, London EC2A 4NE

British Library Cataloguing in Publication Information Available

Library of Congress Cataloging-in-Publication Data
Names: Guyette, Susan, author.
Title: Museum resilience : adaptive planning for a new era / Susan Guyette.
Other titles: Adaptive planning for a new era
Description: Lanham : Rowman & Littlefield, [2024] | Includes bibliographical references. | Summary: "Focused on multiple-scenario planning method, Museum Resilience gets to the 'how' for expanding inclusivity and decolonization efforts, as well as adapting in a time of visitation and financial challenges. Unique features of the book include explaining worldview differences, value-based planning techniques (adaptive and multiple-scenario), the specifics of expanding museum income through collaborations, and ways of developing learning programs that support cultural continuance. The author has field-tested these methods for 30 years (over 50 plans completed), blending her graduate degrees in Cultural Anthropology and Urban and Regional Planning to design methods for cross-cultural planning. Integral to the book are planning processes for museums to use with communities in addressing these issues. Each chapter contains an annotated 'Further Readings' feature, useful for textbook readers. Another feature of the book is the integration of examples concerning potential roles museums can take in opening environmental awareness. The author is an experienced leader in culturally diverse issues, focusing on value-based planning and designing techniques that work across cultures" — Provided by publisher.
Identifiers: LCCN 2023058516 (print) | LCCN 2023058517 (ebook) | ISBN 9781538189153 (cloth) | ISBN 9781538189160 (paperback) | ISBN 9781538189177 (ebook)
Subjects: LCSH: Museums and community. | Museums—Planning. | Museum techniques.
Classification: LCC AM7 .G88 2024 (print) | LCC AM7 (ebook) | DDC 069/.068/4—dc23/eng/20240205
LC record available at https://lccn.loc.gov/2023058516
LC ebook record available at https://lccn.loc.gov/2023058517

∞™ The paper used in this publication meets the minimum requirements of American National Standard for Information Sciences—Permanence of Paper for Printed Library Materials, ANSI/NISO Z39.48-1992.

To Gershon

Acknowledgment

As the world shifts into a new era, one with increased challenges, the voices of wisdom, both past and present, are here to guide us. First, I would like to extend my appreciation to the many communities who welcomed me to work with them, sharing their cultural visions. The methods in this book evolved with community input from dozens of cultures. How joyful it is to see you thriving and moving forward in these challenging times!

My appreciation is extended to those generous mentors who set me upon a path dedicated to cultural value-based work. I am especially grateful to Charlotte Heth, David Warren, Walter Dasheno, Gregory Cajete, Alfonso Ortiz, and Beatrice Medicine for their generosity of time in my early mentoring.

The Roaming Writers of Santa Fe, my devoted writing peers—Pat Murphy, Jeanne Simonoff, Jennie Ayers, Regina Ress, Melanie Faithful, Morgan Farley, and Marguerite Sterns—offered critique and encouragement. Charles Harmon, my editor at Rowman & Littlefield, is thanked deeply for his kindness, belief in the value of this work, and support along the path to publication.

Dr. Jessie Ryker-Crawford, my department chair at the Institute of American Indian Arts (IAIA), contributed invaluable feedback, inspiration, and enthusiasm. Her vital work teaching Museum Studies at IAIA gives hope to a new generation of students reinventing museum concepts to fit their cultures.

Deep gratitude is extended to Ann Lowe for her graphic assistance, as well as to Susan Waterman and Kathleen Dexter for editing assistance. Allison Colbourne is thanked for providing research assistance at the Museum of Indian Arts and Culture's library. Emily Stovel, former officer in the New Mexico Association of Museums, is appreciated for discussions on museum relevance and community integration. Gail Chehak, Tribal Relations and Outreach Manager at the American Indian Alaska Native Tourism Association (AIANTA), afforded me the opportunity, through conference presentations and participation on the Education Committee, to test the idea of museums as a hub for community tourism.

Former Governor George Rivera and Melissa Talachy comprised the team working on development of the Poeh Cultural Center and Museum (Pueblo of Pojoaque). My work with them stimulated an understanding of community-integrated approaches. Committed staff of the Poeh Museum and Cultural Center—Karl Duncan, Steve Fadden, Lynda Romero, and Reuben Martinez continue to evolve this national model of a community-integrated museum.

Successes of the New Mexico MainStreet program and my involvement as a technical assistance provider illustrated the potential of a community-integrated method. The model developed for this significant region of traditional cultural retention reinforces an integrated preservation, cultural practice, and economic development model.

I honor extended family members—Esther Bell, Albertine Phillips, Pat Phillips, Florence Theriault, and my mother, Edna Guyette—for nurturing me in our extended family and providing the foundation of culture and community. My grandparents, Joseph and Annie Theriault, taught me connections to the Earth and the importance of self-sufficiency, family, and values crucial to guide twenty-first-century involvement.

Above all, there is the beloved who provided ongoing support, encouragement, writing comradery, editing, listening, and unwavering inspiration—my husband, Gershon Siegel. Our sons, Austin Spafford and Ezra Braun Sage, remind me continually of the changing world and our need to adapt—quickly.

My inspiration comes from Mother Earth, our teacher, bringing forth hope for a new dawn of increased perception regarding the mutual benefits of cultural sharing, plus recognition of the solutions already here. Our part is to listen.

Acknowledgment

Contents

Contents   **xiii**

Preface

At the time of this writing, the call for effective museum strategies to reach audiences became suddenly more complex. How, in times of unexpected quarantine and the quandary of continued financial support, would museums continue to deliver programs and services at all? This disruption opened the door to a new way of thinking about cultural institutions connecting and planning for uncertain futures.

As this catalyst unlocked the discussion of a new growth potential, one of thriving instead of just surviving, the discussion expanded to ways of seeking greater inclusivity and improved access. New behaviors of museum visitors are pressing digital engagement, loyalty, and giving, based on changing public needs. And new technologies in an increasingly digital world give hope not only for visitation with fewer environmental impacts but also to expanded inclusivity and hybrid possibilities reaching a broader range of audiences. Giving voice to culture takes on a deeper dimension.

The call for inclusivity highlights the importance of preserving cumulative worldwide knowledge—broadening the array of solutions to global challenges. To ensure continuity of invaluable cultural knowledge for the coming generations, a balance of activities and resources to preserve the past and teach in the present is important. Cultural ecology is the study of human adaptations to social and physical environments. Honoring this cumulative wisdom, especially for understanding interwoven connections in the natural world, brings a diverse pool of knowledge widely available.

Innovative planning methods presented in this book, stemming from adaptive scenario planning, emphasize multiple futures possible and decision-making pathways. Resilience is strengthened with this path, and all sizes of museums benefit from inclusivity solutions. Museums of the future are likely to expand their functions within a sustainable framework embracing culture, economy, and the natural world—if not only from the standpoint of necessity for survival. As a plus, the broadened community connection attracts a higher likelihood of financial support.

In my experience as a community planner, I notice the frequent disconnect of museums from a range of other community needs and programs. Most communities are multi-ethnic, yet in-depth participation from all cultures is rare. Still, depth is essential for cultural groups to find museum programs useful education for their own groups, in addition to the potential for cross-cultural collaborations. To be representative, this cultural connection must relate to deeper aspects of community and teach through supportive practices. New technology opens ways for the community-integrated museum to become a center for documentation and practice based on cultural priorities.

This book challenges many mainstream concepts relating to museum development—highlighting multiple ways of viewing a museum's purpose. Planning methods developed through four decades of my work with museums and culturally diverse communities emphasize ways of working with existing museums to redirect toward a more dynamic learning environment. For example, encouraging the re-examination of collections is likely to initiate a rich discussion.

I encourage you to have a curiosity about the potential of including new cultural worldviews and culturally based approaches. Indigenous methodologies are not solely for Indigenous people. The wisdom of time-honored traditions may spark new community perspectives across cultures. Consider this an exciting new age for a paradigm shift by including the preservation of global planetary wisdom. Museums fostering forward-movement discussions focused on solutions will contribute an invaluable resource for planetary well-being—for inclusivity embraces nature.

Building or maintaining a public space such as a museum will mandate a wise use of resources. We are entering a new era with a call for interpretive and financial sustainability. Asking inclusive questions will be key; the planning processes in this book will be valuable for developing flexibility and deep listening to changing community needs. Community integration described in this book is practical, exciting, and twenty-first century.

My intention with this book is to present a planning method applicable for changing conditions while encouraging an inclusive process. The following pages lead to the path.

Susan Guyette, Ph.D.
Santa Fe, New Mexico, USA

Introduction

Globally, there is a strong sense of something essential becoming lost. Heritage, cultural values, and sustainable economy, as well as ways of relating to, and co-existing, in nature are topics of conversation in the community museum movement. Museums, as places of cultural expression, bring people together. In this view, addressing inclusivity is more than counting numbers; it is rather about co-creating a new future on Mother Earth.

Relative to this pivotal era, diverse interpretations of history and topics further our understanding of cultural differences and similarities. By presenting diverse views of culture, a museum fosters a sense of belonging and connectedness—reflecting Stephen Weil's iconic call "from being something to being for somebody."[1] Respecting different cultural worldviews and multiple views of history are urgent steps for transformation in relation to the current climate crisis, as this text underscores. We are all related.

Financial sustainability is a growing concern in the museum world. Support through tax dollars is decreasing while reliance on earned income and donors is increasing. The more engaging a museum's programs are to the local community, the greater the potential for grants, financial sponsors, and paid services, such as offering training or sales of authentic items in the museum store.

Sound business practices are increasingly necessary. As the COVID-19 pandemic taught, organizations with "pre-existing conditions"—such as lack of community connection, absence of a diversified funding base, and rigid administrative structures—struggled or closed. Reliance on one source of income is no longer a viable option; diversifying and creating a broad safety net through community connection adds strength and stability to any museum. In this era, the United States is rich in museums, with over 35,000 estimated by the IMLS (Institute of Museum and Library Services).[2] This represents a major national cultural source for equitable representation. The time is now to thrive, not just to survive.

Why plan in the face of uncertain times? Adaptive planning increases the flexibility to alter direction in changing times. Ecologists are discovering that disturbance in ecological systems, rather than remaining the same over time, increases their ability to adapt or rebalance. Viewed in this way, sustainability is closely tied to the ability to rebalance. Resilience and sustainability are intertwined in the process of adaptation.

The only contemporary certainty is uncertainty, calling for multiple-scenario thinking. Questions commonly asked include the following: Will the global economy recover or decline? Will communicable diseases limit programmatic options for museums? Will resources for the arts and museums continue to be available? Will luxury spending be reduced? Will changes in weather patterns prevent visitation? Will the travel industry continue to grow or hold at present levels? How will technology innovations support virtual visitation options? Will environmental concerns come to the forefront of contemporary issues? In the face of uncertainty, proactive planning enables a museum to shift direction on short notice.

This recent era of restricted mobility underlined a time to re-envision museums as places of living culture and community activity vital for adapting to changing times. What this signifies varies from culture to culture. The transition from focusing on objects to thinking of places for cultural continuance relates to a museum's mission, exhibits, collections, and interpretation. Resilient museums often reflect the heartbeat of a community—the place emanating life, continuity, and cultural expression.

Intergenerational teaching is regenerative, a feature of culture best to recover in relation to surmounting societal and environmental crises. The community-connected museum is a center for gathering: a place to celebrate culture; a place to honor the keepers of traditions; a place to interact and share cultural knowledge; a place to teach cultural classes and language; a place to encourage intergenerational interaction; a place for educational activities; and a resource for earned livelihood. Fostering connections to nature, furthering public education through community-determined messages, providing space for community-focused events—all are activities encouraging participatory approaches.

Community may be defined by a geographic boundary or by an awareness of belonging. Community members share an emotional connection, as expressed through shared culture, history, common places, time together, similar experiences, and the sense of making a difference where participation satisfies the members' needs.[3] Inclusivity advocate Mark Winne points out the importance of community dynamics: how community is defined has real implications for who makes decisions and who is affected by those decisions.[4]

Regarding the future of museums, community integration is essential for the paradigm shift from object-focused to people-focused, serving at the intersection of multiple cultural needs. The reimagining of museums as cultural institutions holds potential for creativity, multiple community benefits, and new resources for rapidly changing times. A call for an inclusive shift, echoed for at least the past three decades,[5] is now coming to a focus, as reflected in the imperative *Change is Required: Preparing for the Post-Pandemic Museum.*[6]

RETHINKING PURPOSE

As global economic conditions shift, many museums are rethinking their purpose. Community museums are most often small museums with limited resources. Yet, larger museums may also transform their spaces into centers where people celebrate cultural continuity and community with expanded purpose and resources. The small museum orientation with community activities and spaces, such as changing exhibits, is applicable to the larger museum setting as well, tapping both virtual and physical options.

This book presents a methodology applicable to both museums and cultural centers. Museums of the future are likely to expand their functions within a flexible framework embracing culture, economy, and ecology. And cultural centers may consider a limited collection intended for teaching purposes.

Emerging trends in museum visitor interests include:

- An emphasis on the experiential;
- Increasing online and interactive programming;
- Multigenerational engagement;
- Teaching programs for community members to support cultural retention;
- Interactive and tactile educational experiences;
- Connections to other community needs, such as job creation, with the museum serving as a referral hub; and
- Connections to local ecology and education on global environmental conditions.

In an economic climate of shrinking resources, museums are concerned about financial stability. Will museum support be cut from local government budgets if seen as a luxury? A practical approach to sustainability requires a long-term connection to the economics and ecosystems of a community as a part of culture.

THE COMMUNITY-INTEGRATED MUSEUM

Connecting a museum to community priorities and everyday life expands financial opportunities, both through potential partnerships and access to a broader range of funders. Honoring diversity of beliefs and lifeways—the strength of sustainability and resilience—increases both options and wisdom. The following diagram reflects the steps for planning outcomes explained in this text.

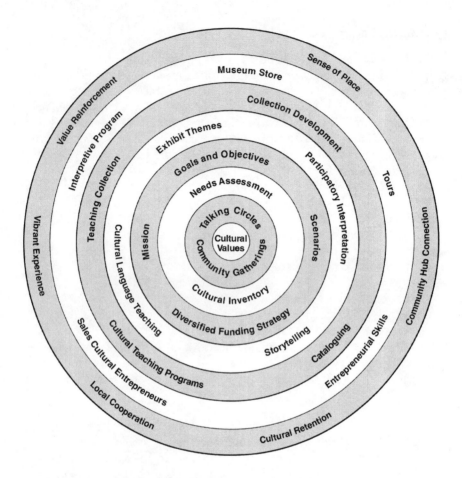

Museum Store
Sense of Place
Collection Development
Value Reinforcement
Interpretive Program
Exhibit Themes
Goals and Objectives
Participatory Interpretation
Tours
Teaching Collection
Needs Assessment
Talking Circles
Cultural Values
Community Gatherings
Scenarios
Cultural Language Teaching
Mission
Community Hub Connection
Vibrant Experience
Cultural Inventory
Diversified Funding Strategy
Sales Cultural Entrepreneurs
Cultural Teaching Programs
Storytelling
Cataloguing
Entrepreneurial Skills
Local Cooperation
Cultural Retention

TOWARD AN INCLUSIVE PARADIGM

Cultural continuity is one focus of a community-integrated museum, essential for co-creating a new future. A community-centered rather than visitor-centered approach is exciting for museum visitors—furthering the opportunity to see how the community is connecting past, present, and future. Planning criteria for addressing DEAI—diversity, equity, accessibility, and inclusivity—are integrated throughout this text. The DEAI task force of the American Alliance of Museums[7] is bringing forth leadership by identifying museum strategies for moving from awareness and commitment to assessment and training, then to implementation and accountability.

Inclusivity is more than "letting everyone in"— rather, it is "letting the museum out" through a commitment to represent different worldviews in intentional practice. Multiple contrasting interpretations of history not only best tell of past events but also impart context for understanding present views.

This text presents a new paradigm for the community-integrated museum to address cultural reach, experiences, and inclusivity.

CULTURAL REACH

- Welcomes the visitor in a unique, culturally specific way
- Interprets from the lens of cultural and local values
- Encourages inclusive participation beyond museum walls
- Improves access to collections for the purpose of cultural continuity
- Reflects sustainability factors in cultural context.

EXPERIENCES

- Provide a community-integrated, interactive visitor experience
- Employ a broader range of multi-modal technologies
- Improve access to collections for the purpose of cultural continuity plus
- Interface with other segments of a community-wide system for education, economics, and environment.

INCLUSIVITY

- Highlights local issues and solutions
- Presents multiple interpretive views
- Furthers nature connection and action
- Uses an adaptive approach to planning, emphasizing multiple scenarios, collaborative decision-making, and an ability to quickly shift direction plus
- Connects to global issues.

Museums recalibrating to include inclusive histories, with interpretation from the cultures involved, is a wise intention.[8] Taken to the next step, effective interpretation bridges past and present to the future, reflecting a continuum for a dynamic view of culture. In a rapidly changing cultural milieu, this continuity is guided by the wisdom of past experience.

EXPANDING CULTURAL INCLUSIVITY

All communities share a culture, or a belief system, and often, several belief systems are reflected in culturally diverse communities. In the American/ Western view, culture with a capital "C" connotes representations of fine art or formal music events and is otherwise referred to as "high" culture. In contrast, the customs, lifeways, and cultural arts or crafts of everyday life are referred to as culture with a small "c." Traditional communities are keenly aware of this hierarchical bias and the need for a paradigm shift to represent everyday culture and all peoples. As Laura-Edith Coleman reminds us in *Understanding and Implementing Inclusion in Museums*, American museums are currently exclusive and exclusive spaces.[9]

Several distinct groups are present in most communities, yet not all may be represented at the museum. In recent decades, the tendency to develop museums to interpret from a particular ethnic or special interest viewpoint has been increasing. While this is sometimes a necessary trend for interpretation, the proliferation of museums is expensive to maintain. Moving toward the concept of the "incluseum"[10] puts the focus on aspects of relationships, social justice, representation, and access, as well as institutional change.

In times of rapid change, traditional communities are concerned about cultural survival. The importance of maintaining cultural diversity in a multi-ethnic world is pressing, as diverse knowledge of cultural ecology and biodiversity represents an array of possible solutions to the currently unfolding environmental crises. The concerns are not only about "us"—one creature among many, and the cultural knowledge of how to interact in our ecosystems—but also about a highly intra-connected web of species and plant life.

In the twenty-first century, a vital question to ask is, "What is the contemporary responsibility of a museum as a cultural institution to broaden wisdom, especially in relation to cultural knowledge of health and environmental stewardship"? "Will climate crisis be relegated to science museums when actions are guided by cultural beliefs?" Concern for adaptive strategies in this time of immense change is rapidly coming to the forefront. And insight provided by history museums may provide the critical foundation for preserving a cumulative body of cultural knowledge essential for a positive ecological future.

Questions addressed in this book highlight the preciousness of cultural diversity: "What are the considerations central to both the tangible and the intangible aspects of culture?" and "How can a community museum or cultural center interface with social justice issues concerning culture, economy, biological diversity, and climate change?"

These are not only trying times but also exciting times. The richness of our pooled cultural knowledge, considered both locally and globally, is best expressed by anthropologist Wade Davis:[11]

> Together the myriad of cultures makes up an intellectual and spiritual web of life that envelops the planet and is every bit as important to the well-being of the planet as is the biological web of life that we know as the biosphere. You might think of this web of life as an "ethnosphere," a term perhaps best defined as the sum total of all thoughts and intuitions, myths and beliefs, ideas and inspirations brought into being by the human imagination since the dawn of consciousness. The ethnosphere is humanity's greatest legacy. It is the product of our dreams, the embodiment of our hopes, the symbol of all we are and all that we, as a wildly inquisitive and astonishingly adaptive species, have created.

Considering the potential for connectedness between museums, offering a broad array of learning experiences through different cultural perspectives is an exciting prospect. In this way, supporting the everyday cultural goals of community strengthens cumulative cultural retention efforts globally. When cultural groups know their history—how items were used and their symbolic meanings—they are inspired to learn their culture. Generations interacting weave the social network, giving strength to culture and community. Participatory planning facilitates the discovery of these local goals.

There is considerable urgency for involving youth. Digital resources developed by museums are in demand due to the increase in homeschooling. Many culturally diverse communities are deeply concerned about the widening gap between generations and the lack of cultural learning. The broader the generational gap, the more difficult it is to fill the gaps in the transfer of knowledge. Cultural loss is a serious concern.

Connecting a museum's sustainability to a community's sustainability is worthwhile for many reasons. The benefit is not solely for museum sustainability but for sustaining cultural knowledge as well. For example, a museum can become the focal point for referrals to cultural entrepreneurs. Creating employment in this way encourages learning, optimally in classes held at the community-based museum, with archives and collections available for supervised study.

These principles also apply to the museum connection in a larger urban network. Museums can become hubs, connecting a sizeable network of services, attractions, and activities to encourage both locally based enterprise and visitor services. The arts and cultural district movement in the United States reflects this intention of cohesion.

STRENGTHS OF ADAPTIVE PLANNING

Adaptive, value-based museum planning examines the scenarios of possible futures, given the yet unknown trends in visitation, the economy, environmental conditions, and popular interests shifted by cultural change. For this reason, an inclusive organizational foundation is created that encourages resilience, or the ability to improve decision-making, adjust, and be sustainable with change. Central to adaptive planning is an analysis of current trends and strategies for alternative scenarios. Strengthening a local network is another outcome of linking through a flexible approach to planning.

Adaptive scenario planning:

- Uses participatory approaches, necessary for representing multiple viewpoints and multi-generational interests;
- Sees the museum plan as a management tool;
- Examines multiple scenarios;
- Considers multi-modal options;

- Furthers connection, forming a community network for ongoing participation; and
- Provides a means of feedback to the community.

Such an approach goes beyond inviting communities to programs. Directions determined with participation further an interface with other community programs. Community connection integrates cultural richness into museum programming. Yet, this is more than just an invite. Rather, connection implies that the museum will use resources—human, collections, and space—to support the goals of the community. In serving the needs of a school, this might look like offering interpretation for children, classes in the cultural arts, or an exhibit of children's art in a changing exhibit space. The use of modern technologies furthers the potential for increased discussion facilitating community connection.

USING THIS BOOK

Rethinking a museum is a valuable process for community reach, encouraging connections to multiple audiences. The link between museums and cultural continuance can be strengthened in this process. Particularly in small communities, museums may be the only space available where culture can be taught.

To be representative and tell stories accurately in the twenty-first century, a museum must represent multiple perspectives and cultures, as well as modalities of interpretation. Reinterpreting history and events is a necessary part of expanding inclusion and accuracy. This is a part of what Stephen Jenkinson calls the moral ecology of our times.[12]

Another central function of a museum is to further cultural understanding. New roles as the focal place for receiving visitors and as a hub for community-wide referrals, extend an introduction to local cultures. In a global context, the significance of both cultural and bio-diversity is key to maintaining the strengths of diversity—for actions stem from cultural beliefs.

This book provides specific steps for expanding community relevance and inclusivity in museum programs. The first chapter illustrates the past-present-future connections necessary for cultural expression as well as differences in worldviews for perceiving those links. Planning methods for increasing resilience are introduced in Chapter 2. The process of multiple-scenario planning in Chapter 3 leads to organizational flexibility and economic stability in times of rapid change. Then Chapter 4, on rethinking collections, connects the purpose of a collection to past, present, and future needs, as well as links to local programs.

Chapter 5, on bringing life to exhibits, introduces multi-cultural and multi-modal ways of communicating in an exhibit. The discussion on interpretation is continued with strategies for introducing diverse messages into exhibits and telling relevant stories. In Chapter 6, the potential for developing inclusive learning or teaching programs within cultural context is explored. The connection between a museum and generating employment for community members is described in Chapter 7.

Ways of connecting to community by becoming a hub for an arts and culture district are addressed in Chapter 8, as well as introducing the idea of a museum welcoming. This community-integration theme is followed by engagement in tourism, particularly through the creative economy—the topic of Chapter 9. By increasing community integration, the potential for diversifying sources of museum income expands, as illustrated in Chapter 10—furthering the feasibility of sustainable financial support. The final chapter provides methods for evaluating success and redirecting in relation to resilience.

A new era is at the forefront for museums, stimulating and yet challenging! Difficult choices concerning present uses of space, both physical and virtual, as well as preservation and meeting future needs—are topics facing museums in contemporary times. Yet, there are solutions to improve access for present needs while curating in the best possible way for the future.

Context for past, present, and future presents a dynamic view of culture. Interpretation of multiple histories not only best tells of past events but also imparts context for understanding the present. Taken to the next step, effective interpretation bridges past and present to the future, reflecting a continuum. In a rapidly changing cultural milieu, this continuity is guided by the wisdom of past experience.

NOTES

1. Weil, Stephen. "From Being about Something to Being for Somebody: The Ongoing Transformation of the American Museum." *Daedalus*, Vol 128, No 3, 1999: 229–58.
2. Institute of Museum and Library Services. 2014. www.imls.gov.
3. Adapted from "Group Think," by David McMillan and Davis Chavis, *New York Times Magazine*, April 22, 2018.
4. Winne, Mark. *Food Town USA*. Washington, DC: Island Press, 2019.
5. Karp, Ivan, Christine Mullen Kreamer, and Steven D. Lavine. *Museums and Communities: The Politics of Public Culture*. Washington, DC: Smithsonian Institution, 1992.
6. Decter, Avi, Marsha Semmel, and Ken Yellis. *Change is Required: Preparing for the Post-pandemic Museum*. Lanham, MD: Rowman & Littlefield, 2022.
7. American Alliance of Museums. *DEAI Report*. 2022. www.aam-us.org.
8. Moore, Porchia, Rose Paquet, and Aletheia Wittman. *Transforming Inclusion in Museums: The Power of Collaborative Inquiry*. Lanham, MD: Rowman & Littlefield, 2022.
9. Coleman, Laura-Edith. *Understanding and Implementing Inclusion in Museums*. Lanham, MD: Rowman & Littlefield, 2018.
10. Paquet Kingsley, Rose. "Inclusion in Museums: A Matter of Social Justice." *Museum Management and Curatorship*, Vol 31, No 5, 2016: 474–90.
11. Davis, Wade. *The Wayfinders*. Toronto, ON: House of Anansi Press, 2009.
12. Jenkinson, Stephen. *Come of Age: The Case for Elderhood in a Time of Trouble*. Berkeley, CA: North Atlantic Books, 2018.

1

Past, Present, Future

Museums at the crossroads of community relevance are asking vital questions: Will museums of the future interpret a cultural heritage of the past? Will their programs be central for carrying forward a living diversity of traditions? How will museums become more community integrated and inclusive? What are the possible uses of new technology to reach broader audiences? And how will financial support be diversified to ensure a safety net? Inclusion is about a future valuing diverse worldviews.

Rethinking the purpose of museums makes sense given the range of urgent needs worldwide, as immense societal change and restructuring take place. This is an exciting era with the ability to create far-reaching online resources. A central theme of this book relates to options for a community museum to become a cultural lifeline and tell important stories. Questions regarding the extent of collections—whether to collect at all, needs for gathering or teaching places, and the potential for interpretation of community connection to local ecosystems—are at the foundation of a sustainable museum model.

Every museum plays a role in the future of cultures. Considered in a holistic way, museums are connected to, and reflect, the culture or cultures they represent. What will become a new niche for museums in these turbulent times? Equity and inclusivity are not just romantic notions but rather necessities for recognizing the already-existing solutions embedded in our global collective wisdom.

Culture is regarded in this book as central to all sustainability, as cultural values are at the core of everyday actions. The dangers of assimilation into a global, Western monoculture are real, foreshadowing global cultural loss. Why is this important? Every museum may contribute to preserving the pool of knowledge essential to ways of living in balance within our communities and on Earth.

These are the conscious choices of museums; a shift locally can hold global consequences. Why is the focus on local so important? Acting locally in museum activities connects a group to a sense of place. Knowledge of relationships in the local ecosystem is usually held by wisdom keepers and will become invaluable in caring for, as well as surviving in, a specific locale. As Daniel Wildcat points out in *Red Alert*,[1] addressing such perceptions about interconnected webs of life is essential for supporting local ecosystems.

Inclusion is about co-creating a new future, drawing on the strengths of diverse worldviews and contributing through a new cultural lens. For inclusion is not about writing exhibit text and translating into other languages. The museum with a good cultural fit considers cultures and worldviews, plus mission, as part of interpretive goals. This chapter gives glimpses of worldview perceptions, with Indigenous examples in relation to nature.

This call is coming from many cultures. Native American (Ho-Chunk Nation) Amy Lonetree adeptly refers to the necessary transition of many mainstream museums from a "temple" to a "forum."[2] Museums grounded in the consciousness of the world around them realize the limited options, particularly in small communities, for spaces to host gatherings related to social, environmental, and economic justice—as well as the link between nature and social issues.

Several movements in the museum field, particularly with ethnic communities, concern worldview interpretation and inclusivity. The term *decolonization*, described by Lonetree in relation to Indigenous museums,[3] focuses on redirection of the museum's purpose to serve urgent needs. In Native American communities, this direction is often referred to as re-indigenization.

The DEAI movement addresses diversity, equity, accessibility, and inclusivity throughout museum management. The term decolonization is now extended as BIPOC to include Black, Indigenous and People of Color. As Brandie Macdonald emphasizes, decolonizing is a process of collaboration.[4]

Since decolonizing is a common new conversation, an important question to address is "What is colonization?"[5] One original purpose of a museum—to house the spoils of conquest—led to the design of museums for the storage of collections without interpretation from the conquered culture. This is one aspect of colonization. Referring to a living people in the past tense is another example of colonization.

Teaching the cultural arts and language, improving access to collections, implementing community-determined interpretation, and representing multiple worldviews are all unique features of the community-interactive museum.[6] Decolonization is guided by the responsibility to ensure respectful and reciprocal relationships.[7] Respect in this process involves deep listening, understanding the depth of different viewpoints, and serious consideration of alternatives.

Robert Janes, author of *Museums in a Troubled World*, issues a call for museums to contribute to the social, cultural, and economic vitality of the local area.[8]

Will museums be confined to an ever-increasing reliance on consumption, entertainment and pedagogy, or will they engage in more substantial issues and interests?

There is a difference between people-focused and community-focused. All museums involve people and strive to offer visitor education. People-focused comes from the cultural orientation toward the individual. In most cultures of the world, community and family are the primary points of reference.[9] This distinction is fundamental to the adaptive planning approach taken and the museum's ability to serve as a hub. For example, museums, as participants in the creative economy, often are the link to preventing out-migration in communities losing population due to unemployment and shrinking resources.

Community-integrated museums are places of cultural learning and sharing rather than facilities with a primary emphasis on objects. While objects may be important to learning, they are not the main focus. Museums connected to local needs are a reflection of culture and are rich in interpretation. In addition to furthering cultural understanding, resilient museums connect to the community as a whole—supporting cultural retention, job creation, and restoring relationships within the natural world. Recognizing ways of connecting is central to expanding adaptive strategies for a new era. As you guide a community-based process, look at the following adaptive approach.

Chart 1.1. Inclusivity Factors and Change

The importance of preserving cultural diversity is coming to the forefront of these discussions. Connecting cultural diversity to biodiversity defines our shaping role in nature, based solidly upon positive belief systems. The call to fully develop purposeful museums is a continued thread in this method-based book. By taking public service commitment a step further, wherever the starting place, a museum can support locally determined directions in cultural practice.

Collections will continue to be important, for preserving historical record and representations of cultural items for study are essential to cultural continuity—one purpose for collections. Yet, to provide a balanced approach to collections, important questions need to be asked: "Why are we collecting?" and "For whom are we collecting?"

The second question sometimes gets lost in the process. "For whom?" is interrelated with an improved system for access. Putting the collection to work for community priorities not only underlies shifts in collection policy but also concerns the design of an accessible (yet protected) collections storage area and online three-dimensional images for study.

Cultural beliefs underlie all actions. Museums incorporating living traditions can be a bridge for community and cultural expression. Increasing resiliency is a direct response to changing societal needs and visitor interests. In preparing for the planning process, internal discussions may focus on the following issues.

PLANNING PROCESS

A COMMUNITY-INTEGRATED APPROACH

- What are our intentions, redefined, in a rapidly changing world?
- What is the purpose of collecting objects?
- How can communities best tell their stories?
- How will wisdom-rich traditional cultures survive?
- How will the museum be resilient in times of rapid change?

TANGIBLE AND INTANGIBLE CULTURE

Museums are places for cultural expression. In this book, the term *culture* refers to lifeways, customs, beliefs, values, language, and views of the environment.[10] Intangible culture refers to lifeways and customs, whereas objects are often referred to as tangible culture. The benefits of teaching and interpreting tangible culture by including intangible cultural heritage include raised self-esteem, community esteem, cultural pride, and environmental awareness, plus expanding minority and women's opportunities.

In perspective, the history museum developed as a place to preserve tangible treasures garnered in times of war. Today, differences in emphasis on material culture exist between cultures. Some are more object-oriented; others place a higher value on intangible culture. For these communities, conserving the past in relation to present and future cultural needs is central to the mission of the museum.

As the concept of a museum is evolving from being object-oriented (tangible items representing culture) to the more process-oriented, intangible aspects of culture, community integration becomes a priority. A collection's emphasis on tangible culture represents but one worldview, and many cultures do not place an emphasis on collecting, in any aspect of life, except the essential.

However, preserving and interpreting objects can become urgently significant if made accessible to originating communities. The shift from object-oriented to culture-oriented is a new framework for the twenty-first century. A growing shift away from the object focus reflects a growing interest in how communities are restoring cultural traditions and living sustainable lifestyles—often based on regaining wisdom of the past.

A majority of museum texts focus on the tangible. This planning guide gives equal attention to the intangible and to the intersection between the two, bringing life to a museum as a place for interaction as well as preservation. Balance in approach, through community involvement, is central to adaptive planning.

The bridge from tangible to intangible can be achieved through participatory techniques. Central importance to a museum may not be objects but rather the stories of how they relate to culture and cultural continuance. Stories gathered are the medium, the in-between spaces of intangible and digital heritage—to include art, architecture, archaeology, and oral history.[11] Since cultural boundaries are limits on the type or depth and amount of information appropriate to share, defining limits through community interaction is vital during the interpretive process.

The benefits of collaboratively preserving cultural objects, or "treasures," include community members earning income through the heightened appreciation and selling of the cultural arts. Additionally, strengthening or recovering a connection to the natural world through the sustainable use of natural materials may be a key outcome for communities. Both tangible and intangible aspects of culture relate to the "triple bottom line" variables of sustainability—culture, economy, and ecology.

For example, the proper storage of collection items is often critical for recovering culture. The questions now being asked include, "Which items are important for reaching our cultural goals?" and "How many items can we afford to curate properly?"

Interpretation connects objects in a cultural story to visitors' lives. A story told well intrigues the visitor and involves the community. An accessible teaching collection, either physical or through photography, enhances the story, as well as the cultural teaching necessary for continuance.

UNDERSTANDING VALUES AND WORLDVIEWS

The cultural arts expressed in object form reflect values and belief systems. A tendency to perceive a topic from the ethnocentric perspective of one's own culture is a natural tendency, while gaining an understanding of how to see others through an expanded cultural lens enables museum staff to connect to other cultures. The central purpose of the cultural value-based planning processes in this book is to open doors for mutual understanding.

Why is understanding diversity important to our future on Earth? In this section, Indigenous examples are given to illustrate contrast in worldviews. According to the United Nations, there are over 476 million Indigenous people living in ninety countries around the world, accounting for 6.2 percent of the global population. Of those, there are more than 5,000 distinct groups.[12] In North America, there are 574 federally recognized Native American tribes in the United States and another 630 First Nation communities in Canada.

The potential for a community-integrated museum to interpret diverse worldviews relies on community and regional connection. Seeing a topic from only one cultural viewpoint encourages cultural bias through perceiving objects and events from one set of values, historical context, or meaning. Interpretation becomes very limited with this perspective and loses the potential richness of cultural diversity.

Insight into other worldviews is the key to making in-depth rather than superficial connections, particularly in the bridge from focus-on-object to cultural interpretation. One technique for contrasting different worldviews is to show two or more interpretations of an event or a cultural relationship, juxtaposed side by side. The "I get it" moment often comes with contrast. A well-designed exhibit and interpretive program is exploratory into this shared perceptual space.

Worldview is sometimes referred to as world space since reactions and interactions are based on diverse beliefs. Ken Wilber[13] refers to world space as a particular degree of shared depth. The inclusive exhibit and interpretive program explores this shared perceptual space. As a basis for improved communication or interaction, sharing serves the museum visitor's relational ability to understand and interact with other cultures, subcultures, and ethnic groups. The following sections on differences in values and time perception illustrate the importance of worldview to cultural understanding.

IDENTIFYING COMMUNITY VALUES

Culture is a way of life, with values guiding every action taken. Cultural values connect people. For a museum to be truly effective in encouraging cultural practice, there must be connections to all segments of the community. In times of potentially shifting directions, values form the foundation for decision-making.

Why is this perspective important? In a community-integrated sense, the future of cultural practice and retention is critical to community, family cohesion, health, economy, and job creation—all aspects of culture.

Museum statements relating to values often intend to convey institutional values or guiding principles. This chapter suggests a different starting place—with the value sets representative of groups within the community. Then, institutional values can be derived to reflect community values. Identifying local values underlying the strengths of diverse cultural approaches as part of the planning process creates a solid foundation for moving forward together.

Value-based adaptive planning discovers:

- Diverse beliefs in a community, connecting groups in the planning and implementation processes;
- Different cultural approaches to involvement;
- Recognition of the cultural values expressed in those approaches;
- The type of meeting or gathering structure appropriate to the cultures involved;
- Ways of gaining intergenerational input;
- Pathways for creating alternative scenarios;
- A feedback loop back to the community; and
- Cultural practices for honoring contributions and appreciating participation.

Values are the foundational ways of the past, guiding us into the future, even in times of uncertainty. Asking the community about central values sets the foundation for further evolving an inclusive museum. Once an assessment of values present in the community is complete, the next step is to highlight traditions and values the community team does not want to lose.[14]

Traditional communities pass down values, beliefs, and information from generation to generation. The following values are an example identified in a strategic planning process for a small rural museum.

Mainstream American	Indigenous, Hispanic, other traditional
Individual	Community
Nuclear family	Extended family
Competition	Cooperation
Accumulation	Generosity
Consumption	Conservation
Hierarchical	Balance

Chart 1.2. Contrasting Value Sets

By identifying values related to cultural arts, family, community, and entrepreneurial livelihood, a solid foundation is formed for moving forward. The museum, moving forward congruent with strategic direction expressed in the vision and mission, is a community hub for potential cultural revitalization and opportunity for cultural entrepreneurs.

THE PAST-PRESENT-FUTURE CONTINUUM

How the past is perceived in relation to the present and the future varies among cultures. The presentation of culture can either stereotype people in the past time period or reflect an ongoing, adapting, vital culture. These groups usually have not disappeared; rather, cultural change is an ongoing process. This practice commonly occurs with Native Americans, First Nations, Mayans, and Toltecs, as examples.

Even if population numbers have declined, usually, the culture has continued on some level or has become integrated into surrounding cultures. All of these situations show potential for cultural revitalization; to create focus, the planning processes in this book include the desire to "bring back" traditions.

Ways of viewing the past can vary widely from culture to culture. An Indigenous elder I worked with in the mid-1970s[15] referred to "the generations coming behind us," while looking over his shoulder to a position behind him. In his worldview, people face and see the past in the present as they move into the future. The future is moving behind, not to be known but to be guided by wisdom.

This orientation stresses moving into the future with learned cultural wisdom—keeping an eye on the past. Seven-generations thinking acknowledges three generations before and thinks mindfully up to three generations to come. This multiple-scenario perspective, often reflected in Indigenous cultures, takes into consideration alternative impacts of current actions on future generations. Such an outlook is also present in many other Indigenous cultures, including the Maori in New Zealand.

In the view that traditional arts are linked to ancestors, symbolism and continued presence, there is a richness of connectedness to the past-present-future continuum. Languaging reveals orientation in worldview. Consider the Western European expressions "facing the future," or "moving forward."

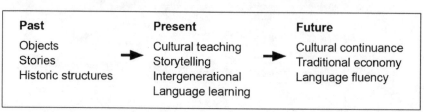

Past	Present	Future
Objects	Cultural teaching	Cultural continuance
Stories	Storytelling	Traditional economy
Historic structures	Intergenerational	Language fluency
	Language learning	

Chart 1.3.   The Past-Present-Future Continuum

BEING AND BECOMING

While the Western/European sense of time is linear, or following one point in time after another, the majority of cultures in the world see time as cyclical—evolving and reinforcing with recurring cycles. Charts 1.4 and 1.5 illustrate cultural variations in perceptions of time. In the Western/European worldview, time follows a linear path to the future, with less emphasis on keeping an eye on the wisdom gained from the past. Progress tends to be measured in future innovation and economic growth. Decolonizing involves linking the linear mind to the non-linear process of relating.

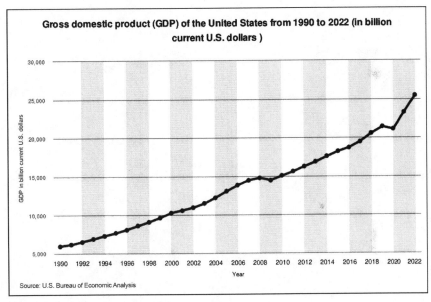

Chart 1.4. Linear vs. Cyclical Time
Western/European Linear View
Source: U.S. Bureau of Economic Analysis, Gross Domestic Product, 2023.

INDIGENOUS CYCLICAL

Peoples with strong ties to the land and agricultural lifestyles tend to think more in terms of life by the cyclical seasons. For this reason, ties to nature are strong within the cyclical worldview. As Pueblo scholar Gregory Cajete emphasizes in *Native Science*,[16] the tribal universe is a circle of learning, life, and relationship, inclusive of all the important information needed to make life decisions. We learn from animal behavior how to survive in our ecosystems. The following circle of perception illustrating a nature-based worldview is from the Wabanaki peoples[17] of the Northeastern United States.

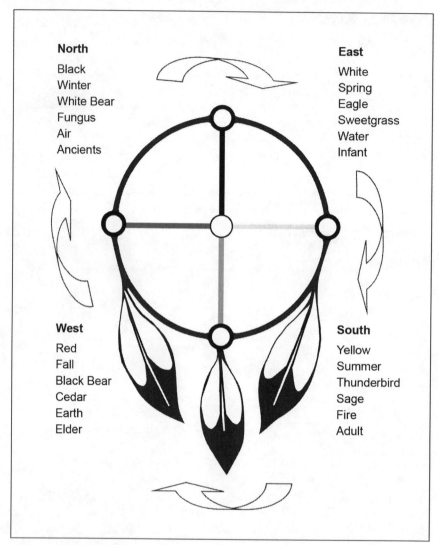

North
Black
Winter
White Bear
Fungus
Air
Ancients

East
White
Spring
Eagle
Sweetgrass
Water
Infant

West
Red
Fall
Black Bear
Cedar
Earth
Elder

South
Yellow
Summer
Thunderbird
Sage
Fire
Adult

Chart 1.5. Wabanaki Concept of Life By the Seasons

This circle of life, often known as the four directions or the medicine wheel, includes stories of colors, seasons, spirit animals, medicine, elements, and life stages in a continual renewal of life—based on cyclical experience and connection in nature. This worldview leads to a deep perception of natural interrelationships in perceiving life by the seasons in the natural world.

The past-present-future connection as a process affords a circle of lessons and insights. The concept of cyclical time is illustrated by Cara Romero, an

Indigenous photographer, as "everywhen."[18] Understanding inter-relationships with our past and how it shapes our present world is at the center of interpretation and context.

ANIMATE AND INANIMATE WORLDVIEWS

An animate view of the universe is seen as alive, "all my relations." For example, in many Pueblo Indigenous (US) worldviews, the clouds and the rocks are seen as animate and alive—the opposite of being seen as objects in Western worldviews. As emphasized in *The American Indian Mind in a Linear World* by Donald Fixico, this view of aliveness sees a "respectful" view of nature, regarding the natural environment on a social and kinship basis.[19] Animate views of nature see the interconnected web of life as essential to maintain intact, for the well-being of every part of the web.

Inanimate views tend to objectify and lead to hierarchical thinking of the world. This view in regard to nature sees natural resources as objects "to be used up." Inanimate views of nature tend to look at the "parts" more than the relationships. Recovering the kinship worldview leads to seeing interrelationships.

DISSECTING AND INTEGRATING

The Western/European worldview tends to break concepts into smaller and smaller parts. This dissecting of the universe seeks to understand natural phenomena by searching for the detail. What is lost? When analysis tends to be the primary method, the weakness lies in never really discovering all of the parts. The interrelationships, the webs of connectedness, and the understanding of how the whole fits together become obscured by focusing on the parts.

In contrast, an emphasis on the whole is observational in method and tends to take the bigger-picture approach of understanding the total result of connectedness. This integrating process focuses on relationship outcomes and the benefits of seeing the whole. "How can exhibit interpretation relate to the whole, the interrelationships, and to environmental context?" is an inquiry likely to lead to solutions for the pressing dilemmas of these times.

EGALITARIAN VERSUS HIERARCHICAL

An underlying egalitarian view of kinship with all of the animate world respects humans as not existing "apart" or "above" but rather as equals in worldview. We learn from watching animals and honoring their strengths, becoming aware of healing practices and use of medical plants, for example. Similarly, seeing other races in the egalitarian view honors the knowledge and experience of each, forming a global pool of wisdom. Recognizing and respecting these diverse cultures in the coming years of environmental crisis carries the potential for solutions to pressing issues.

A hierarchical view of the world places humans at the top of a chain rather than as one part of the circle of life. Colonialism is a hierarchical view.

LANGUAGE STRUCTURE REFLECTS WORLDVIEW

Most Indigenous languages are process-oriented, emphasizing ongoing relationships. These languages are well-adapted to expressing processes, an essential orientation for understanding the natural world and reciprocal relationships in nature. The closest in the English language is the use of gerunds or words with an "-ing" ending.

In the subject-verb-object sentence structure of English, objectifying is more easily realized. What to do in composing exhibit labels or scripts in English? Using more gerunds is useful. Maybe the time has come to become more inventive with English to describe processes and relationships.

Changing our languaging about nature by not talking about our relationship *to* nature but rather *in* nature reflects our worldview position as being a part of nature—not separate. Seeking to understand processes rather than results and being observant of intra-relationships *in* nature furthers positive solutions and interpretation.

WORLDVIEW CONCEPTS

Being and becoming as part of an intricate, intra-connected web of life becomes the focus in an animate world. The following planning process is useful for community groups in the discovery of worldview similarities and differences. The intersections of the two lead to common ground for moving forward.

PLANNING PROCESS

DISCOVERING WORLDVIEW CONCEPTS

- Which values are representative of different cultural groups in the community?
- Where are the overlaps in values and differences?
- What are local views regarding the past?
- How can local beliefs about the future be best described?
- In what ways can cultures come together to interpret these worldviews and connections in the local ecosystem?
- How can linear and cyclical views of time be contrasted and integrated into museum themes?

- How do past, present, and future connect to tell a story important to the community?
- What elements in the environment are seen as alive?
- How will we work together to create a community network based on cultural understanding and inclusivity?
- What pace is comfortable for moving forward?

When the starting place for planning is inclusive, depth evolves in the museum concept.

TERMS CARRYING CULTURAL BIAS

Avoiding insensitive terms laden with cultural bias is important for involving all local cultures. The following terms commonly used by museums carry cultural bias, often unknowingly, to those designing an exhibit or other museum programs:

Developing: This connotes a hierarchy of practices and knowledge, often based on Western/European technological expertise. Acknowledging and honoring the wisdom carried in the ancient technology of Earth-based cultures is an example of overcoming the bias inherent in this term.

Civilized: This implies a hierarchical view of cultures, usually representing Western/European at the top as the culture to strive for as the ideal.

Progress: This is a hierarchical and technologically skewed term often considered disrespectful of the strengths inherent in all cultures.

Primitive: This term expresses a hierarchy, with non-Western/European cultures viewed as simpler, not recognizing the cultural complexity in the belief systems surrounding objects, spirituality, sustainable economic systems, and understanding of ecological relationships.

Myth: This term connotes a story that is not true, failing to see the symbolic tie to culture, people, history, and relationships.

Use of these terms without a full understanding of bias is often automatic, made without an understanding of cultural context. Referring to a people in the past tense tends to enable hierarchical thinking.

How does one overcome a slant to one point of view? Presenting different interpretations of the same object enriches perception. For example, contrasting the scientific explanation with cultural interpretation or story not only provides interesting content but also teaches about different worldviews. Or, contrasting the interpretations of two or more cultures teaches the existence of multiple views, leading to cultural understanding and tolerance.

Decolonizing efforts are keenly aware of these biases.

FORM, SCALE, AND TIMING

In the process of reimagining museums, another dimension of flexibility is added by looking beyond the linear view of development. Three variables useful for incorporating different worldviews and values—form, scale, and timing—are factors leading to a sustainable approach.[20]

To maintain a good cultural fit, new initiatives may be introduced while retaining *forms* of local cultures. Included in the planning process, the following factors help to identify the uniqueness of a particular community.

- Cultural values
- Multiple cultural communication styles
- Assessments to determine cultural/art/creative economy issues and needs
- Community collaboration models
- Architectural style and floor plan conducive to the activities identified in the planning process

Interfacing with arts councils, becoming a hub for an arts and culture district, and serving as a referral network for the community's tourism are ways of shifting form by interfacing in tandem with changing local needs.

Appropriate *scale* increases the potential for success. Scale may be defined in relation to available capital, management expertise, and lowered environmental impacts. Capacity building is a key consideration in determining scale and pace rather than striving for the typical American larger outcome. Slower, gradual, and linked development leads to a larger and more solid community foundation. Options include:

- Starting out small and expanding by phasing, for a small museum;
- Not seeing space limitations as a barrier but rather looking for temporary spaces at outreach locations;
- Seeking online options;
- Starting with a small project, demonstrating a high level of interest, and building an addition for expansion; and
- Including outdoor space options—e.g., ethnobotany tours, art shows, cultural festivals, and exhibit pop-ups.

The third variable—*timing*—relates to building community capacity. When new directions are planned in stages, occurring when communities are receptive, infrastructure is in place, and capital is available—then local confidence increases.

Ways of being aware of the ideal timing for both the museum and community partners include:

- Building rapport with local organizations, groups, and local government;
- Trying pilot programs, evaluating success, then securing funding for the larger program; and
- Using training programs and internships to expand locally available expertise.

Using these three variables in the planning process—form, scale, and timing—considers both participant and museum readiness. This provides a foundation for gradual shifts in community-determined directions.

REIMAGINING MUSEUM PURPOSE

Increasing museum relevance with a strong local connection requires presenting the multiple viewpoints of those being represented. Reducing bias in interpretation is one concept central to that intention. Methods are suggested in this book for multiple ways of viewing a museum's purpose—away from the mainstream approach of collections as the primary direction and to the viewpoint of utilizing the collection to support internal cultural goals. Looking at the positive, decolonizing a museum opens new prospects for community integration.

Respect for cultures is a value at the foundation of museum services. Decolonization as a process honors cultural values, represents community voices in interpretation, and supports cultural continuance. Such an approach generates actions that are respectful, ethical, empathetic, and useful.[21] These factors assist the museum consultant and the community as well as a means of moving forward to redirect a museum. "How can colonization reverse through museum programs?" is a frequently asked question. In summary, the direction of decolonization includes thirteen critical factors:

1. ***Recognizing Basic Cultural Differences:*** Culture is a way of life, with values guiding every action taken. For a museum to be truly effective in encouraging cultural practice, there must be connections to all segments of the community. Values are the foundation or the way of the past that guide us into the future. For any museum project to be culturally meaningful, respect for these values must be integrated into every step forward.[22]
2. ***Connecting Museum Programs to Cultural Identity:*** Shifting the museum focus away from a sole emphasis on history and toward living cultures and cultural revitalization is the current trend. History *is* important as part of a past-present-future continuum. Cultural longevity depends on the ability to sustain cultural knowledge.[23]
3. ***Shifting Away from Objects to a Community-Oriented Focus:*** A transition from "object-oriented" thinking to places for cultural continuance is becoming an important trend for community-based museums. As the

keepers of diverse traditions are advancing in age, this shift is urgent. A strong focus on interpretation facilitates the shift.

4. **Identifying Past-Present-Future Continuum Messages:** Community-integrated museums include culturally appropriate spaces for teaching language, cultural arts, and other traditions. Their designs reflect traditional building forms and the kinds of spaces needed to teach the cultural arts.

5. **Defining a Unique Welcoming:** A welcoming is an invitation to enter a cultural worldview, a unique space, or a different time period. Use of a different language or dialect signals entry into a different perspective. Several worldviews may be represented. Welcoming sets the tone of this emergence, this insight into new perspectives or new learning styles.

6. **Maintaining Cultural Privacy:** Respecting wisdom within the community is important when defining cultural boundaries for sharing. Whether information is appropriate to share or whether selling items is appropriate in the museum setting are important considerations to identify.

7. **Encouraging Revitalization through Culturally Appropriate Design:** Examples of culturally specific design features include the following: a welcoming area, the inclusion of a circular storytelling area, a children's activity area, classrooms tailored to the teaching of specific cultural arts (including storage for large items and supplies, access to water, and display areas for projects), space for art shows, and a museum store to sell the work of cultural entrepreneurs.

8. **Communicating Cultural Messages:** Exhibitions further visual and interpretive access to collections; therefore, interpretation is the bridge from collections to exhibits. Multifaceted interpretation is exciting to the viewer and inspires cultural learning.

9. **Improving Collections Access:** Many museums are rethinking the original purpose of their collections and access issues. For example, an ethnic-specific view of collection purpose often differs markedly from a mainstream American museum. Rather than a focus on objects (tangible culture), a community-determined mission is likely to focus on cultural learning and the significance of objects to cultural continuity (or intangible culture).

10. **Storytelling as Interpretation:** Interpretation is the meaning, explanation, or story integral to a display of objects. While objects are of interest to visitors, interpretation brings life to the cultural story. Cultural committee members—the keepers of cultural knowledge—are an excellent resource to provide the content for interpretive materials.

11. **Linking to Job Creation:** All cultures, historically, have a traditional economy. Forms that worked for thousands of years can become a foundation for a current-day economy, specific to each community. One role of the museum linking to creative economy is to serve as a referral and training hub, vitally important to fostering a small-scale, linked approach to

economy. Why is this so important? Interfacing museum goals with local or tribal government goals is often key to ongoing support for the museum—in addition to generating jobs locally.

12. **Increasing Financial Sustainability:** With the trend of decreasing support through tax dollars, museum sustainability is a key issue. Drawing an audience for museum programs involves reaching local residents as well as out-of-state visitors to the region. Linking the museum to the tourism industry is essential for audience development and increasing the potential for museum income. In relation to sustainability in the broader sense, preserving the cultural, economic, and ecological knowledge of how to live on Earth in a way that lasts over time—conserving resources—is central to these teachings. Museums are able to open the pathway through interpretive programs.

13. **Understanding Intra-relationships within Ecosystems:** The connection to specific places and spatial situations in unique ecosystems is part of the nature-culture nexus.[24] For this reason, local connections and understanding are critical to foster in this era.

When these elements of a successful program work together, a positive cultural future is created, youth are inspired to learn, and families work together from a common historical connection. The rich tapestry of cultural knowledge reflected in the museum is interwoven with everyday activities, reflecting the uniqueness of each community. As global awareness of living in reciprocal relationships with our ecosystems increases, interest in understanding the wisdom of diverse cultures is coming to the forefront of the general public.

CULTURE AS EVOLVING

A worldview is a cultural lens. A particular view representing a belief system, a perception of the universe, differs from culture to culture. This aspect of interpretation furthers the cultural understanding so needed for cultural groups to live harmoniously and learn from each other's strengths. Appreciation for our commonalities and differences is then fostered.

To continue trying to find solutions to planetary crises using the same, dissecting worldview is not likely to produce sound results. Globally, cultures perceive the need for an interdependent, connected way of perceiving their place in relation to each other and the ecosystems that support them. The rise of sister museums is evidence of this trend.

Seeking visitors appreciate alternative ways of interacting and understand the importance of maintaining diversity as a common pool of knowledge. One intention of your planning process may be to re-examine the new-century purpose of the museum in a rapidly changing world. Moving away from the viewpoint of the last few centuries, of culture being static versus presenting culture as always evolving, is a productive approach for changing times.

Context for past, present, and future presents a dynamic view of cultures evolving. Interpretation of history not only best tells of past events but also imparts context for understanding the present. Taken to the next step, effective interpretation bridges past and present to the future, reflecting a continuum. Best to engage with the current environmental crisis, to learn from diverse cultural lifeways, and to assist communities with collaborative interpretation.

As the following chapters illustrate, understanding differences in worldviews is foundational for bringing together an inclusive plan.

FURTHER READING

Cajete, Gregory. *Native Science: Natural Laws of Interdependence*. Santa Fe, NM: Clear Light Publishers, 2000.

This classic on Native American perspective explains Indigenous science as a way of understanding, experiencing, and feeling the natural world. Gregory Cajete points to parallels and differences between the Indigenous science and Western science paradigms, addressing topics including history, primal elements, social ecology, animals in stories and reality, plants and human health, cosmology and astronomy. In the Indigenous view, human observers are in no way separate from the world and its creatures and forces. Because all creatures and forces are related and thus bear responsibility to and for one another, all are co-creators. The science and worldview of the continent's First Peoples offer perspectives that can help us work toward solutions.

Chilisa, Bagele. *Indigenous Research Methodologies*. Thousand Oaks, CA: Sage Publications, 2019.

This text is applicable cross-culturally and useful for illuminating diverse perspectives, particularly those of women, Africans, minority groups, former colonized societies, Indigenous peoples, historically oppressed communities, and people with disabilities. Topics cover the history of research methods, ethical conduct, narrative frameworks, interviewing, evaluation, and participatory methods. Chapters focus on decolonizing, indigenizing, and integrating these methods and applications to enhance participation of Indigenous peoples as knowers and foster collaborative relationships.

Moore, Porchia, Rose Paquet, and Aletheia Wittman. *Transforming Inclusion in Museums: The Power of Collaborative Inquiry*. Boulder, CO: Rowman & Littlefield, 2022.

Presenting a new paradigm for understanding inclusion grounded in a museum worker perspective, this text examines advantages and disadvantages in practice, as well as the integral concerns of racial equity and social justice. Questions raised throughout this book invite readers to reflect on how their own experiences can add to, and expand on, new ways of thinking about inclusion in museums.

Murawski, Mike. *Museums as Agents of Change: A Guide to Becoming a Changemaker*. Lanham, MD: Rowman & Littlefield, 2021.

Museums everywhere have the potential to serve as agents of change. This progressive text opens the vital discussion on how individuals can radically expand the work of museums to live up to this potential by addressing the relevant issues in communities. How can we work together to build a stronger culture of equity and care within museums? There are important questions for all of us to be thinking about more deeply as citizens and community members, move us to become voices, and demand that our museums take action toward positive social change and bring people together into a more connected society.

NOTES

1. Wildcat, Daniel. *Red Alert: Saving the Planet with Indigenous Knowledge*. Golden, CO: Fulcrum, 2009.
2. Lonetree, Amy. *Decolonizing Museums: Representing Native America in National and Tribal Museums*. Chapel Hill, NC: The University of North Carolina Press, 2012.
3. Ibid.
4. Macdonald, Brandie. "What Keeps Me Awake at Night: A Letter on Decolonization." In *Change is Required: Preparing for the Post-pandemic Museum*, Avi Decter, Marsha Semmel, and Ken Yellis (eds.), pp. 117–21. Lanham, MD: Rowman & Littlefield, 2022.
5. Lonetree, *Decolonizing Museums*.
6. Wilson, Shawn. *Research is Ceremony: Indigenous Research Methods*. Halifax, Nova Scotia: Fernwood Publishing, 2008.
7. Smith, Linda Tuhiwai. *Decolonizing Methodologies: Research and Indigenous Peoples*. New York: Zed Books Ltd, 1999.
8. Janes, Robert. *Museums in a Troubled World: Renewal, Irrelevance or Collapse?* New York: Routledge, 2009.
9. HeavyRunner, Iris, and Joann Sebastian Morris. "Traditional Native Culture and Resilience." *CAREI Research/Practice* Vol. 5, No. 1, 1997.
10. Guyette, Susan, and David White. "Reducing the Impacts of Tourism through Cross-Cultural Planning." In *The Culture of Tourism and the Tourism of Culture: Selling the Past to the Present in the American Southwest*, Hal Rothman (ed.), pp. 164–84. Albuquerque, NM: University of New Mexico Press, 2003.
11. Onciul, Bryony, Michelle Stefano, and Stephanie Hawk, eds. *Engaging Heritage, Engaging Communities*. Suffolk, UK: The International Centre for Cultural and Heritage Studies, 2017.
12. https://www.un.org/en/fight-racism/vulnerable-groups/indigenous-peoples.
13. Wilber, Ken. *Sex, Ecology, Spirituality: The Spirit of Evolution*. Boston: Shambhala, 2000.

14. American Association of Museums. *National Standards & Best Practices for U.S. Museums.* Washington, DC: American Association of Museums, 2008.
15. Personal communication Willie Jumper, Cherokee elder, Cherokee Nation, 1974.
16. Cajete, Gregory. *Native Science: Natural Laws of Interdependence.* Santa Fe, NM: ClearLight Publishers, 2000.
17. http://www.muiniskw.org/pgCulture2b.htm.
18. Romero, Cara. Everywhen: Indigenous Photoscapes. www.cararomerophotography.com.
19. Fixico, Donald. *The American Indian Mind in a Linear World: American Indian Studies and Traditional Knowledge.* New York: Routledge, 2003.
20. Guyette, Susan. *Sustainable Cultural Tourism: Small-Scale Solutions.* Santa Fe, NM: BearPath Press, 2013.
21. Lonetree, *Decolonizing Museums.*
22. Guyette, *Sustainable Cultural Tourism.*
23. Kovach, Margaret. *Indigenous Methodologies: Characteristics, Conversations, and Contexts.* Toronto: University of Toronto Press, 2021.
24. Wildcat, *Red Alert.*

2

The Adaptive Planning Process

What is unique about adaptive planning? An adaptive approach encourages the capacity to shift direction. This is different from the intention to control outcomes.[1] Rather, organizational self-reflection and exploring the wisdom of time-honored traditions opens flexibility. Adaptive planning recognizes that change will happen, focuses on integrative networks, and increases security in economically uncertain times. An emphasis on process is strongest when inclusive—gaining strengths and problem-solving abilities from different cultural worldviews.

All museums are facing economic uncertainty. Federal grants, local tax support, donations, earned income, and even endowments depend on national or local economic conditions. Socially relevant issues may change suddenly, given local circumstances. Multiple-scenario planning offers techniques for switching rapidly and smoothly while diversifying sources of support.

Feeling listened to in a culturally respectful way forms the basis of inclusive participation. Moving toward this intention, participation is a process of community involvement with representative groups—sometimes referred to as "stakeholders"—or groups with a concern in the outcomes. Assembling a planning committee or a cultural committee to meet in-person or online is one way of ensuring inclusive representation and creating those partnerships so valued by funders.

When coming from a place of confidence in times of uncertainty, a new, adaptive paradigm for museum planning increases hybrid strategies, blending the old with the new. Community relevance now requires authentic engagement as well as the processes of learning, trust-building, and continuous communication.[2] Emergent voices tell us that risk is lessened over the long term by:

1. Increasing community connectedness and involvement with multiple stakeholders;
2. Recognizing stakeholder values, goals, and knowledge through co-learning;[3]
3. Collectively recognizing signs of change;

4. Using multimedia options;
5. Expanding or contracting beyond patterns of the past;
6. Focusing on incremental changes to increase flexibility;
7. Utilizing new technologies to increase outreach connection;
8. Keeping current with changes in funding trends;
9. Diversifying sources of financial support; and
10. Evaluating and redirecting as necessary.

In facing uncertainty, the pace of life tends to become more hectic. Including a broader reach of experience and insights within the community expands options and participation toward carrying forth solutions. Ways of balancing in-person and electronic data gathering are discussed later in this chapter. By broadening focus, community-integrative options expand possibilities for greater impact and funding. A three-year timeframe is the most effective for adaptive planning, with a five-year snapshot into the longer term.

How does adaptive planning differ from strategic planning? In the past—and likely to change due to global crises—strategic plans tended to be calculated by a straight-line time graph of current trends carried into the future. Planning assumptions are often generated without examining possible changes in social or environmental conditions.[3] The greater the extent of community integration, the wider range of inputs forms a network or a "net of support" for times of change. This method opens museum eyes to an extended future landscape by challenging current thinking and considering aspects that might have been overlooked previously.[4] Embracing diverse views is a matter of moving from "sharing power" to "empowering communities."

Strength exists in establishing networks for multi-pronged solutions. In the current milieu, much attention is given to the idea of partnerships. Focal questions to ask concern organizational ability to offer breadth to programmatic solutions—as well as interpretive participation relevant to changing conditions. "How will partners form a supportive network in times of crisis to redirect and thrive?" is a new central dilemma. Ask deep questions rather than becoming a partner on paper only.

To be locally relevant and adaptive, the planning process, inclusive of partners, starts in the community with stakeholders determining concerns, issues, needs, and expressed directions. Then, the planning process moves inward to the museum, to discover collaborations possible to meet priorities. Whether planning a museum's future direction, carrying out a previously defined mission, or defining a new mission to meet changing needs, a museum-outward participative process is essential for securing input.

On a cautious note, there may be cultural resistance to the idea of attempting to control the future, depending on the cultures involved. A rigid notion of control is not the intention of adaptive planning. Particularly where colonization is prevalent, emphasize that adaptive planning draws from diverse cultural

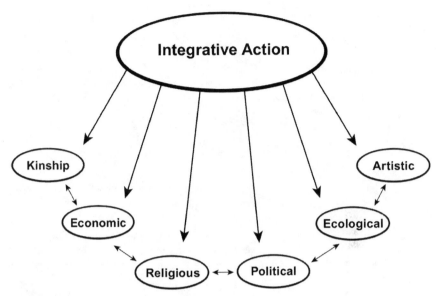

Chart 2.1. Community-Wide Integration

strengths and forms of cooperation. In a multicultural setting, drawing upon cumulative strengths and experiences increases resilience. Efforts to be truly inclusive will be appreciated.

This is an altogether different process than a museum planning an exhibit topic and then reaching out to the community to gather input on the topic determined internally within the museum. The community-first sequence is less likely to be driven by existing collections. In this chapter, the first steps of a participative method for a value-based planning process are presented. A method for informing community solutions in a culturally appropriate manner, as well as empowering local groups to make their own planning decisions, holds high potential for museum participation.

Adaptive planning involves thinking of options in advance and then developing programmatic alternatives. Perceiving a situation from multiple worldviews is also part of an adaptive strategy. And identifying long-term needs to preserve the very cultures that are represented is another.

How can the optimal scenario be discovered? Planning method strength lies in asking effective questions. Throughout this book, planning processes present guiding options for exploring these questions—based on a broad range of community settings for participative discussion. A cross-cultural planning approach is taken; therefore, not all of the questions may fit your museum. In-depth questions come from an understanding of the culture and rapport.

Gathering community input into a reframing of museum activities increases community integration. An in-depth, value-based approach, or a good "cultural fit," can be achieved and tailored to a specific community. A participatory process for evolving an adaptive paradigm follows.

PLANNING PROCESS

SEEING ADAPTIVE STRATEGIES

- Which new directions expand a past-present-future connection?
- Are there traditional stories about times of adaptation in the community?
- What are ways of fostering community involvement and linkages to other community programs?
- How will multiple communication styles represented in the community be incorporated into the planning process?
- How can we better recognize the richness of cultural diversity?
- Which messages and themes concerning cultural continuance are being determined within the community network?
- How does local preservation contribute to a broader bio-cultural knowledge base?

When cultures adapt over thousands of years, invaluable stories about processes of adaptation are likely to exist. Drawing from the wisdom of the past takes present cultures beyond waiting for the invention of new methods; merging ancient wisdom with new technologies holds potential for moving forward. In many Indigenous cultures, seven-generation planning and the use of prophesy guide the anticipation of impacts with long-term perspective. The stellar text *Reclaiming Indigenous Planning*, edited by Ryan Walker, Ted Jojola, and David Natcher, describes planning considerations of worldviews, beliefs, values, and attitudes in relation to ancestors, people, and community, as well as places.[5]

One central message of this book concerns the cultural options for a museum's decision-making and form. Critical to this process, adaptive planning expands the ways in which cross-cultural sharing can enrich potential approaches for all. Not one museum structure is right or wrong; the integrated approach must be tailored to specific cultures and museum intentions for the best overall cultural fit. "Best practices" typically carry hierarchical bias, a pitfall for achieving true inclusivity.

ADAPTIVE SCENARIOS

Although uncertainty is inevitable, creating a viable developmental vision supports continuance. Resilient thinking as a concept requires flexibility. Moving forward is strengthened when change is accepted and the ability to switch to an applicable scenario is quick. Through adaptive planning, a value-based and inclusive mission supports flexibility and the ability to shift. If a situation becomes unacceptable or unstable, transforming affords an opportunity for careful consideration of purpose.

In *Transformative Scenario Planning*, Adam Kahane[6] recommends a planning process based on understandings, relationships, intentions, and actions to address a problematic situation. For the new scenario, which opportunities and threats would we face and which of our strengths and weaknesses would be important? Advantages of multiple-scenario planning include:

- Emphasizing a decision-focused process;
- Creating flexibility, or the ability to redirect;
- Building confidence with a board or cultural committee, presenting alternatives reinforced with financial projections;
- Lessening the risk over the long term; and
- Increasing security in economically uncertain times.

A sole focus on mission, objectives, participants, timelines, and budgets often leaves out a broader range of possible intentions. And yet, with an updated set of intentions and different scenarios, the planning process will still need participants' input for the mission, objectives, timelines, and budgets to be a community-representative effort. Even project methods may be approached differently culture to culture. Scenarios of possible futures include a range of budget calculations.

Scenarios are stories in the sense that they describe the evolving dynamics of interacting forces rather than the static picture of a single end-point future.[7] Scenarios represent a range of outcomes, valuable to consider in an age of changing possible futures. This text recommends at least three options:

1. The current level scenario;
2. The retraction or minimal scenario (decreased resources or attendance); and
3. The optimal or expansion scenario (increased resources).

A fourth scenario, between current and optimal, may be useful for phasing-in new directions. The virtual museum may be an only option applicable when physical visitation is prohibitive. Designing museum programs with multimodal components creates a basis for focused expansion or retraction when conditions shift. Flow is key in the process to enable a timely shift, when necessary.

Decisions on cultural boundaries—the types of information appropriate to share and not share—come from internal discussions. In certain traditional cultures, these decisions are embedded in a religious framework. Avoiding exploitation of the sacred is a commonly held boundary—one to explore carefully in a museum-related planning process. For example, religious privacy

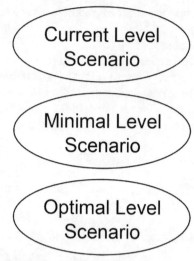

Chart 2.2. Potential Museum Scenarios

concerns are common in certain Native American, Hispanic Catholic, Jewish, and other traditions. Religious items in collections may be subject to limited viewing restrictions and privately held documentation. To the greatest extent a cultural group perceives the possibility of cultural privacy, there will be less hesitation to generate ideas for options.

Exploring culturally relevant topics opens up the discussion to all community groups. This is useful in determining priorities and adds interpretive value to the process. Moreover, seeing a balance of private and public spaces in museum building use encourages a sense of community belonging and increased community involvement. Rather than bringing forth a document that sits on a shelf, regard the museum plan as a management tool for an inclusive future.

DISCOVERING ADAPTIVE PATHWAYS

Integrating the museum planning process with the comprehensive planning of local government and plans of other organizations is central to enhanced adaptive capacity. Otherwise, participation in museum planning tends to be focused as input to a predetermined direction. An optimistic, supportive network is formed with a community-integrated process.

Step 1: Examine community-wide plans to discover local demographics, needs assessments, current strategies, local resources, and initiatives underway—essential for connecting to other local programs.

Step 2: Explore local and cultural styles of planning, participation, and conducting meetings.

Step 3: Expand community-level organizing by developing a representative planning or cultural committee to increase stakeholder participation as co-learning partners.[8]

Step 4: With participation, discover the cultural values present with ethnic groups and overlaps in these values that represent common ground for planning. Identify important issues being addressed and not addressed to determine indicators of adaptive capacity.

Step 5: Hold a series of planning meetings or use digital technology such as online surveys to identify needs, generate perceptions on possible scenarios, see collaborative decision-making processes, and identify adaptive pathways and distribute back to the community for feedback. Include partner organizations.

Step 6: Determine cultural interests of community groups, needed intersections, and a range of ways the whole will benefit by coming together.

Step 7: Facilitate internal museum-planning meetings to discuss resources, directions, and possible interface projects for incremental, transformative, or systemic results.

Step 8: Set priorities for cultural revitalization through classes, interviews, or demonstrations if there exists a determined need. This is an excellent opportunity to document wisdom keepers and community leaders for future interpretive projects.

Step 9: Continue to hold meetings or secure input digitally, as well as document programs and steps needed to continue the participative process with the community, building stakeholder cooperation.

Step 10: Share results extensively through gatherings or online platforms to further continue alignment and participation. All too often, community members never see participation results or have the option to review directions or programs derived from the planning process.

An inclusive process recognizing the potential for bringing together several cultural styles strengthens community cohesion. When this inclusionary process is followed, community members feel the listening, become true stakeholders, and will participate later in museum programs.

My earlier books, *Planning for Balanced Development*[9] and *Sustainable Cultural Tourism: Small-scale Solutions*,[10] address culturally-based methods for conducting surveys and assessments appropriate for developing museums and cultural centers. The connection between museums, cultural retention, entrepreneurial support, attracting visitors, and diversifying financial support is a cohesive approach.

EXAMINE COMMUNITY-WIDE PLANS

Museums do not exist in isolation. If prior assessments and studies are completed, summarize the findings, actions, resources, and limitations during the community discussion to lend continuity. This forms a solid foundation underlying museum potential for moving forward on culturally connected topics. Maintaining a sense of place, both historically and ecologically, is central to community well-being.

The museum fully integrated with local sustainability efforts considers culture, economy, and ecology—or the community as a whole. In overview, the primary types of plans to examine are summarized in Chart 2.3.

PLAN TYPE	CULTURAL INFORMATION INCLUDED
Comprehensive	Addressing a broad range of community topics called elements is essential for community-wide cooperation and resultant collaborations.
Cultural	Cultural plans promote inclusion, while encouraging diversity, knowledge held, and inter-cultural sharing. History and respect among groups are fostered through the planning process—the seeds of cooperation.
Economic Development	Recognition that the museum is a vital part of the local economy can improve resources available. Including cultural entrepreneurs and smaller-scale enterprises as links, results in the development of a more locally-grown economy.
Educational	Integrating cultural values, strengths, styles of learning, and cultural arts relates to exhibit development, access to collections and collaborations with other educational programs.
Land Use	Museum inclusion in land use plans can open possible interpretive venues beyond museum walls. Land as a cultural and historic resource, rather than as a commodity to be allocated, is valued in a broad range of cultures.
Health Care	Traditional health care practices of ethnic groups and preservation of medicinal plants are strengths for creating population resilience.
Transportation	Coordination with transportation providers can open access for tours linking to museum programs.
Tourism	Visitors are seeking experiences. Participation with the tourism industry leads to marketing options and the ability to be included on a regional tour.
Technology	As museums reach broader audiences on the internet, local broadband access, computer and mobile phone availability, plus inclusion in new technologies as they develop—expands the virtual possibilities for exhibits, speaker programs, and other educational programming.

Chart 2.3. Types of Community Plans for Inclusion

A discussion of types of community-wide plans, typical content, and their relevance to museum planning is discussed in Appendix B. If these plans are not completed locally, one emerging role of the museum as a cultural institution may be to encourage community-wide planning inclusive of culture, furthering a coordinated approach to community services. Or, a greater cultural interface in the community produces a likely inclusive outcome. As you examine the plan types, look for museum relevance, potential partners, and overlap content areas in the following planning process. This is a foundational step in preparing for community input.

PLANNING PROCESS

CONNECTING TO COMMUNITY PROGRAMS

- How could the museum support the community vision?
- Which planned goals and programs could the museum partner with to meet both community and museum needs?
- What will be the museum's role in preserving cultural diversity based on the presentation of cultural lifeways?
- Which exhibit topics would reflect cultural connection from the past to present and future?
- How can the connection between programs strengthen interpretation?
- Who are the leaders, elders, and cultural advisors able to assist with interpretive programs?
- How will the museum engage in the discussion of cultural, economic, and environmental change?
- Describe ways for the museum to further participate in the creation of new pathways for healthy families and earned livelihood.

ADAPTIVE PLANNING AND PARTICIPATION

One starting place for expanding or redirecting programming and resources is a participative process leading to the strategic plan—a valuable tool for assessing potential, focusing direction, and identifying resources. Then, after projects are defined, financial needs can be calculated and sources of income identified. Multiple-scenario planning is useful, projecting the optimal, likely, and minimal budgets for moving ahead.

If you are a planner or technical assistance provider from a culture external to the community and cultural privacy is required, ask participants to discuss these issues in private and then identify information appropriate for sharing with the public. By using this technique, cultural privacy is maintained and participants are likely to feel more comfortable with the planning process. These considerations are important for subsequently moving forward through action steps.

An intergenerational planning committee provides a valuable way of shaping the participatory process and giving voice to culture. Achieving truly representative participation depends upon the design of planning processes used and the avoidance of cultural bias. Presenting different worldviews furthers an understanding of diverse interpretations of history and formats for expressing culture. For example, the impact of colonialism as a fact of history and the current-day implications are often overlooked.

GATHERING COMMUNITY INPUT

Appropriate combinations of methods that will work often depend upon the size of the community and the cultures involved. The following are useful individually, or in multiple approaches, to gather input on needs and desired directions.

- Informal discussion
- Community meeting/gathering
- Focus groups interested in a topic
- Interviews
- Surveys conducted at a meeting, households, or a business
- Questions within another community survey, such as tourism or economic development
- Meetings, focus groups, and surveys conducted online
- Periodic feedback discussions

Ways of gathering planning data also need rethinking. In times of limited contact, such as communicable diseases, when in-person meetings are not feasible, alternative methods of gathering data may be substitutes for physical gatherings. Electronic data gathering opens a range of solutions, and it is ever-changing. With new software options, participation meetings are possible online, gathering data through surveys and chat box responses. Focus groups and surveys via the Internet are useful. Technology availability and community member experience are critical components in these decisions.

Smaller focus groups using online platforms allow discussion options. Emails to museum members and mailing lists of partner organizations are other options for sending surveys and providing opportunities to comment, along with encouraging reviews of the planning process. If a community has numerous households without computers, then mobile phones or mailed surveys could be used as data-gathering methods.

To increase response rate, remember to include a "perk" for responding. Conducting a raffle at the meeting, with the respondent receiving a raffle ticket upon return of the completed survey (in-person or online), is a result-producing technique. Ask participating artists or entrepreneurs to donate items. Providing a meal during the planning meetings creates an incentive and produces amazing outcomes. Childcare provides another successful draw. One advantage of the in-person survey over the online completion is the synergy during discussion.

Documenting participants' comments can occur in real-time plus after a recorded meeting. Remember, varying methods of gathering input open participatory alternatives. In optimal conditions, a combination of in-person gatherings plus electronic opportunities with online platforms is useful for reaching all age groups. For example, using mobile phones for youth input or in-person meetings for seniors are all contemporary options. Additionally, planning meetings held outdoors often inspire connections to nature.

MEETING FORMS

Meeting formats differ from culture to culture. And there is much to learn from each, enriching the larger participative process. Understanding the appropriate form for a meeting is crucial to determine before scheduling, as meetings may take different forms cross-culturally. For example, in mainstream planning practice, meetings tend to occur indoors, with participants sitting in rows. In many rural and Indigenous cultures, meetings involve getting together informally or less formally, to build consensus.

The mainstream American style of planning is usually highly structured with a set agenda and procedures to numerically quantify opinions, whereas numerous under-represented groups prefer a "gathering" with a slow discussion in a participatory circle, leading to consensus. Starting with an intention, or a prayer to call guidance from ancestors or a higher power, highlights the importance of the gathering to the benefit of the whole. This type of focus-creating activity heightens cooperation and tends to lessen negativity or complaints.

In many egalitarian cultures, a respectful meeting allows time for everyone present to speak. Multi-generational participation encourages a wide range of perspectives, and discussion at several intervals "fine tunes" the process. Observing patterns and connections is the positive outcome of listening to, and respecting, concerns.

Participants want recognition of their voice. Being open to all ideas and recording all, either on a visible board, paper flipchart, or a laptop with projector, are popular options for in-person meetings. Using index cards (paper or electronically) for participants to record their ideas and then posting them on a wall or a whiteboard lends the flexibility to move ideas according to topic groupings, or to remove them, as ideas are narrowed. If working electronically, several platforms offer tools, such as whiteboards, to display ideas. Breakout groups are also possible for further discussion. Consider the interaction potential.

One technique for setting priorities when ideas are posted is to guide participants in the use of colored dots placed by the ideas generated. This exercise lends an immediate sense of those idea clusters considered most important to the group while leading to a fun, consensus-building process. For the in-person meeting, encouraging physical movement enhances alertness.

In traditional communities, the interrelationships between ideas are complex and sometimes difficult to record. Drawings rather than long bulleted lists may be more effective since interrelationships are more easily seen visually by connecting ideas. Circles showing process and continuity are often preferred in traditional cultures.

Consider the following aspects of a meeting.

- Location, whether tied to the setting of other community activities, shapes the tone and quality of input. Locations where planning meetings are held, with some away from the museum, are essential for positive turnout and responsiveness.
- Formal structure or informal discussion style varies from culture to culture.
- Being attuned to the culture's idea of a productive time length furthers comfort with the planning process.
- Attention to cultural forms for gatherings, such as starting or ending with a prayer or intention, communicates respect for the meeting and, in some cultures, a connection to the guidance of ancestors.
- Making clear the intention of the meeting yet keeping a time available for related topics at the end focuses the conversation.
- Serving food communicates a sense of community and connection in many cultures. Potlucks are an option, if the budget is limited.
- Feedback to participants keeps them involved, whether for in-person or online meetings.

Maintaining cultural sensitivity and interaction through the planning process—including all groups or stakeholders—is well worth the investment of time. Not commodifying or objectifying items with cultural meaning becomes particularly crucial when the culturally significant arts are of concern. Some communities make adamant statements—"Culture is not to be exploited, not to be sold."

Frequently, objects hold deeper, symbolic meanings than the aesthetic value. True involvement allows the time for thorough internal community considerations. Giving the space for discussions that need to occur in private weaves the tapestry of cultural richness and strengths.

FRAMING THE QUESTIONS

Twentieth-century museum professionals tended to be trained from the history museum standpoint and of the mainstream–dominant cultural group. As Mike Murawski urges in *Museums as Agents of Change*,[11] museums are not neutral, and "interrupting White dominant culture in museums" will take re-conceptualizing museum purpose and method. For the new era, changing demographics and economic conditions necessitate an expanded viewpoint for framing the questions.

Leading questions, asked from a narrow conventional museum perspective, are not likely to elicit "thinking-outside-of-the-box" responses. Asking participants for their ideas on reshaping the museum may shake the status quo foundation while leading to innovative concepts. Open-ended questions allow a broader range of responses than multiple-choice ones—key for reducing cultural bias and opening a creative planning process.

Connecting to other community programs facilitates asking relevant questions while enlarging a support network for the museum. For some project topics, earmarked funding can be secured only by another program, yet the administration of the grant can be co-carried through the museum. Think of the gains possible with a deep, open discussion.

Positive cultural and art programs are effective means of raising self-esteem and fostering creative capability. Youth programs or substance-abuse prevention programs focusing on cultural immersion are examples. Others include language programs, tourism projects, traditional food knowledge, and senior programs. In some instances, particularly in rural areas, the museum may be one of the few venues where facility space is available as a hub for programming with community-wide service.

PLANNING PROCESS

PRESERVING FOR WHOM?

- How does our community define needs in relation to museums and cultural centers?
- How do cultural values relate to museum purpose?
- What is the importance placed on objects?
- How can cultural retention be fostered?
- How does physical design affect functional possibilities of the museum?
- Is cultural privacy a factor in redirecting a museum with increased community involvement?
- How can support for a cultural center or museum contribute to local sustainability?
- How can technical assistance be guided to reflect community values?

The museum's function in a culturally oriented program can vary from providing fiscal sponsorship to space to hold classes or the broader role of organizing and carrying out a project. Communicating cultural messages and interpretation are integral to the museum's unifying role.

In the early stages of planning, participation begins to focus the effort. Completing a preliminary plan outline, based on the key topic areas identified during participation, gives a general framework for further data gathering. Chart 2.4 outlines a sample adaptive scenario plan.

- Executive summary
- Introduction
- Purpose of the plan
- Overview of community and connections
- Community locations of planning sessions
- Adaptive planning method
- Stakeholders and participation
- Adaptive strategies, vision, mission, goals and objectives
- Overview of potential scenarios

Internal, community:

- Cultural values represented
- Key issues
- Youth programs
- Intergenerational involvement
- Language integration
- Cultural assessment and inventory
- Identification of priorities
- Methods for cultural revitalization
- Storytelling program
- Curriculum for teaching
- Facility needs for teaching
- Assessment of resources
- Methods identified to encourage cultural learning
- Specific projects designed to teach and increase involvement
- Job creation through arts, culture, and museum interface

External audience:

- Messages to communicate
- Documentation projects

- Exhibit themes
- Use of technology
- Policies
- Public programs and outreach
- Visitor services
- Facility requirements

Virtual Museum:

- Technology available and needed
- Training options
- Virtual exhibits
- Museum store online
- Social media
- Website
- Opportunities for feedback

Funding Sources:

- Federal/state
- Private foundations
- Membership program
- Earned income
- Marketing strategy

Action Plan:

- Scenario options
- Income strategy for each scenario
- Interface with local government
- Staff training
- Operating budget (projected income and expenses), 3 years for scenarios
- Timelines, persons responsible, and resources
- Annual evaluation criteria
- Annual report outline
- Conclusion

Chart 2.4. Sample Adaptive Scenario Plan Outline

In the ideal planning situation, the person preparing the plan is also familiar with the language preferred by specific funders, to maximize use of the
text describing plan assessments and projects directly while securing funding.
When community members perceive the likelihood of progressing beyond a
plan on paper, deep participation is inspired. Making the bridge from initial to
ongoing participation will depend upon building trust.

Participation as a process creates realistic, inclusive assessments while
building partnerships. These outcomes enhance internal capacity to overcome
the isolated style of development that tends to occur with museums. Then, a
narrowing of options becomes possible as participation progresses, needs are
perceived, and phased. One museum "community-extended-outward" outcome is what might be termed "community esteem," sensing internal capability
or the confidence to move forward. Watch their faces as people leave.

FURTHER READING

Decter, Avi, Marsha Semmel, and Ken Yellis, eds. *Change is Required: Preparing
for the Post-Pandemic Museum*. Lanham, MD: Rowman & Littlefield, 2022.
    In this book about the future of museums, options taken amidst upheavals
and disruptions show how a number of American museums have charted new
directions for themselves and their communities. Many museums have taken
a decisive turn to digital programming. Others have taken a turn toward community, developing new kinds of collaborations with their neighbors and local
audiences. Still others have moved issues of equity and justice—internally and
in the world—to the center of their institutional concerns.

Korn, Randi. *Intentional Practice for Museums: A Guide for Maximizing Impact*.
Lanham, MD: Rowman & Littlefield, 2018.
    An impact statement generated through intention practice addresses
audience relevance, the museum's distinct qualities, and staff members' pas-
sions. The process addresses the Plan quadrant (What impact do you want to
achieve?), the Evaluate quadrant (In what ways have you achieved impact?),
the Reflect quadrant (What have you learned? What can you do better?), and
the Align quadrant (How do we align our actions to achieve impact?). A cyclical
process is presented.

Simon, Nina. *The Participatory Museum*. Santa Cruz, CA: Museum 20, 2010.
    With accessible and engaging language, this book empowers museum pro-
fessionals to interact with visitors in new ways. A wide range of techniques for
increasing audience participation includes three ideas: 1) an audience-centered
institution; 2) visitors constructing their own meaning from cultural experiences; and 3) users' voices informing and invigorating both project design and

public-facing programs. Rich in examples, this text moves the reader to a new level of engagement.

Walker, Ryan, Ted Jojola, and David Natcher, eds. *Reclaiming Indigenous Planning*. Montreal: McGill-Queens University Press, 2013.
　　Centuries-old community planning practices offer a broad range of techniques for awareness-raising, seven-generations visioning, and participation in community planning processes. Examples are useful in the broader societal context for reclaiming and redirecting the political, sociocultural, and economic issues shaping lives.

NOTES

1. Wilkinson, Angela, and Roland Kupers. "Living in the Futures." *Harvard Business Review* (May 1, 2013). https://hbr.org/2013/05/living-in-the-futures.
2. Orduña, Armando. "Beyond the Handshake: Effective Steps in Community Engagement." In *Change is Required: Preparing for the Post-pandemic Museum*, Avi Decter, Marsha Semmel, and Ken Yellis (eds.), 57–62. Lanham, MD: Rowman & Littlefield, 2022.
3. Chermack, Thomas, Susan A. Lynham, and Wendy E. A. Ruona. "A Review of Scenario Planning Literature." *Futures Research Quarterly*, Summer 2001: 7–31.
4. Williams, Darryl. "Notions of Permanence, Visions of Change." In *Change is Required: Preparing for the Post-Pandemic Museum*, Avi Decter, Marsha Semmel, and Ken Yellis (eds.), pp. 63–68. Lanham, MD: Rowman & Littlefield, 2022.
5. Walker, Ryan, Ted Jojola, and David Natcher (eds.). *Reclaiming Indigenous Planning*. Montreal: McGill-Queen's University Press, 2013.
6. Kahane, Adam. *Transformative Scenario Planning: Working Together to Change the Future*. San Francisco: Berrett-Koehler Publishers, Inc., 2012.
7. Ralston, William, and Ian Wilson. *The Scenario Planning Handbook: Developing Strategies in Uncertain Times*. Mason, OH: South-Western Engage Learning, 2006.
8. Butler, J. R. A., E. L. Bohensky, W. Suadnya, et al. "Scenario Planning to Leap-frog the Sustainable Development Goals: An Adaptation Pathways Approach." *Climate Risk Management,* Vol 12, 2016: 83–99.
9. Guyette, Susan. *Planning for Balanced Development: A Guide for Rural and Native American Communities*. Santa Fe, NM: Clear Light Publishers, 1996.
10. Guyette, Susan. *Sustainable Cultural Tourism: Small-Scale Solutions*. Santa Fe, NM: BearPath Press, 2013.
11. Murawski, Mike. *Museums as Agents of Change: A Guide to Becoming a Changemaker*. Lanham, MD: Rowman & Littlefield, 2021.

3

Multiple-Scenario Method

Scenarios are stories of probable futures based on possible changing conditions. Several examples are changes in museum visitor interests, epidemics, natural disasters, weather issues, or uneven funding support. A rethinking of strategic planning to include adaptive, nonlinear techniques—while keeping the strengthening aspects of an assessment—retrofits this valuable planning method. Multi-scenario flexibility will be vital in the emerging future. And flow from one scenario to another underlines the ability to shift.

You may be asking, "How many scenarios: three, five, or seven?" The strength of this work lies not in the number but rather in the process of learning flexibility. To be truly of service to our communities is the basic human need calling us to continued existence.

Letting go of hierarchical thinking, individualism, having to be right, or proving a point requires releasing rigidity. Creative thinking seldom comes from inflexibility. Inquire: "What are the cultural connections that will improve overall well-being, cultural understanding of connections in nature, and bring us to cohesive actions that reduce the destruction of our community and our home, Mother Earth?" Respect for our home and for other cultural groups is a fundamental motivation for inclusivity.

Toward this end, working with complementary strengths and worldviews is valuable for a team approach in the community-integrated network. Rather than seeing strategic planning as the main methodology, this chapter recommends strategic planning methods, incorporating nonlinear approaches, and partnering for the assessment stage rather than as a linear projection. Strategic planning plus periodic evaluation forms the basis for perceiving needed shifts. Fostering community hope and a sense of discovery, while moving out of post-disaster conditions, is a fast-moving necessity.

GENERATING SCENARIOS

Well-researched scenario development is worth the time in terms of being able to adjust quickly, without off-guard surprise! The following are examples of mitigation conditions defined in planning processes.

1. **A shift in national or local interests**: Aiming for a balance of generational and audience segment interests—based on visitor surveys and market research—increases appeal to broader audiences. This allows for shifts if one or more audience segments are not able to visit.
2. **Concern for environmental issues:** Actions to heighten awareness are based on cultural beliefs and perceived priorities. Exploration into potential actions of individuals and cumulative community potential is quickly becoming a hot topic.
3. **Tourism visitation trends:** Reduced visitation potential due to travel restrictions or limited surplus personal income could lead to a lower national or regional draw. With less long-distance travel possible, the local community may seek closer-to-home activities designed to fit local interests and ecosystem concerns.
4. **Fluctuations in funding:** Following a diversified funding strategy with the inclusion of earned income reduces reliance on solely one or two sources. Widespread community benefits translate to an expanded range of funders.
5. **Visitation restrictions:** Developing a balanced approach to in-museum services, outdoor spaces for activities, and online outreach increases ability to continue services. Outdoor screens or performance areas meeting distancing requirements are possibilities to consider.
6. **Internet presence:** Online exhibits, learning activities, interpretive tours, speaker programs, and cultural arts courses allow for a rapid shifting of focus when physical visitation is limited. The caveat: This scenario may favor the economically secure. Many rural and lower-income families do not have computers. Using mobile device applications to complement computer-based programs widens access possibilities. Also, drive-up Internet access stations for those households not able to pay for Internet access are a value-added service. Working collaboratively with schools is another option for expanding reach.

When planning during stressful times, three principles are recommended for museums in the ground-breaking book, *Change is Required*:[1] 1) community-centered design; 2) prioritized care representing diversity, or museums embracing the opportunity to be partners in caring with other community organizations; and 3) museum staff members from the community bringing forth ethnic and generational representation. Inclusivity is enhanced when these principles are followed.

PLANNING PROCESS

VISIONING SCENARIOS

- Does planning incorporate the visioning processes of local cultural groups?
- Do scenarios reflect the values and priorities of a range of cultural and age groups represented?
- How will community lifeways be enhanced through cultural retention and environmental stewardship?
- Are funding alternatives broadened through partnerships?
- Do alternatives for programs projected allow for multiple scenarios?

Seen as a process, this framework is useful for tweaking perceptions of shift points and possibilities. The following chart is a tool for evaluating the viability of several scenarios.

EVALUATION CRITERIA	Scenario 1 BUSINESS AS USUAL	Scenario 2 MINIMAL	Scenario 3 SUSTAINABLE GROWTH
Epidemics	Exhibits, educational programs	Online and outdoor programming	Connection to local economy, cultural retention
Financial stability	Museum store open, increases in local inventory	Museum store online	Local entrepreneurial training and sales
Weather disasters	Interpretive programs, virtual tours	Online exhibits, Programming/ Use of more accessible venues	Expanded tours to heighten awareness, inclusion in small-scale itineraries, outreach in nature
Cultural benefits	Interpretive programs, documentation	Small or changing exhibits/ travelling exhibits	Cultural art shows, classes—opening opportunities for cultural continuity
Inclusivity stakeholders	Outreach to diverse stakeholders and addressing internet access options	Outreach to diverse stakeholders and increasing internet access options	Collaborative programs with community partners, inclusion of multiple world views and perspectives

Figure 3.1. Scenario Decision-Making Matrix

Impact Factors	Impact	Rate Change	Uncertainty Level
Shift in national/local interests (e.g. information vs. experiences)	Medium	Slow	Medium
Tourism visitation trends	High	Medium to fast	High
Fluctuations in funding available (e.g. tax dollars, grants)	High	Medium	Medium
Visitation restrictions (epidemics, crime, limited personal budgets)	High	Fast	High
Internet reliability	Medium	Slow	Medium

Figure 3.2. Scenario Impact Factors

Once possible scenario areas are identified, decision-making processes become clearer. A representative team is likely to see strengths and collaborative ways of designing a recovery net. Flexibility will then be more likely, leading to resilience. In some cultures, a consensus process is essential, aligning individuals to work cooperatively. This is particularly applicable in small communities.

Rather than a construct of specific future outcomes, scenario planning teaches a process, resulting in increased flexibility. Instead of concrete directions, pathways for intentions are opened. Give a recap back to the participating group to make certain that details recorded match the participant's intention. Collaborations become the foundation for new openings.

FOUNDATIONAL STEPS

Assessments of resources or assets, gaps in services, and innovative approaches are revealed by identifying the strengths, challenges, opportunities, and threats that change could bring. Community context is valuable for anticipating positive gains and potential negative impacts as a basis for future scenarios. The SCOT analysis (an alternative to the commonly known SWOT analysis[2]) assesses **S**trengths, **C**hallenges, **O**pportunities, and **T**hreats change could bring. Key issues are those facing a cultural organization that, when addressed, will establish a track to be more successful.[3] Some groups do not want to talk about "weaknesses," and it might be best to call them challenges.

- **S**trengths can be a foundation for moving ahead. Identifying strengths is a starting place for the community to become confident and inspired to move forward, both for preservation and new innovation.

- **C**hallenges are areas in need of improvement or in need of additional support. Strengthening the weaker links becomes a preparation priority for a shift to the re-envisioned museum.
- **O**pportunities are beneficial areas to identify in the planning process, in relation to potential shifts. Linking the community to resources forms the basis for program expansion in the optimal scenario—not always based on growth but rather on awareness and services. Community hope tends to open in this discussion.
- **T**hreats change might bring, addressed in the planning process, provide a basis for preventing negative impacts when used to identify different scenarios. In particular for traditional knowledge holders, resolving threats to cultural privacy is fundamental for respectful cultural sharing to unfold.

Assessing threats is particularly relevant for developing a nonlinear programmatic model. Frequently in mainstream planning sessions, those who express threats are seen as complainers and discouraged from expressing. Work with these participants by patiently asking questions, to turn statements of threats into potential positive actions. Empathy encourages creative ideas in a group context.

In relation to adaptive planning, analysis of threats is beneficial for "outside-the-box" thinking. Strategic planning plus periodic evaluation forms the basis for assessing shift opportunities.

EXPLORING KEY ISSUES

Key issues connect concerns considered to be the most important by the community as well as to the museum. These serve as a guide for the remaining planning steps. Addressing these concerns builds support within the community and helps prevent unwanted impacts.

In relation to the sharing of culture, key issues are often the pivotal points for moving ahead with re-envisioning a museum. Privacy and historical accuracy are likely to be important issues for both a museum and community constituents in a traditional cultural setting. Key issue discussions set in place for reimagining a museum are likely to follow.

PLANNING PROCESS

KEY ISSUE DISCUSSION

- How do the key issues of different groups overlap or express commonalities?
- How will the inclusive museum support the key issues of all involved ethnic groups and generational wisdom?
- What are the stories cultural groups want to tell?

- How will historical accuracy be furthered?
- How will cultural privacy be protected?
- How can cultural revitalization be encouraged?
- How will urban/rural linkages be enhanced?
- How will new technology be used to communicate central key issues?
- Does planning address diversifying sources of support to increase flexibility of the funding allocation process?

Key issues vary from community to community and require periodic re-examination from the standpoint of changing times. Exploring key concerns during public participation encourages ongoing involvement.

THE INCLUSIVE VISION

A vision guides actions into the future by drawing people together to create a common focus.[4] There will not necessarily be one vision, as several visions within a community or a region may be expressed. When differences emerge, the underlying process is to find aligning overlaps for shaping commonalities into a cohesive vision.

If a negative vision surfaces, the specifics are valuable for determining potential negative impacts. Listen deeply to those who see potential dangers inherent in a direction. Significant outcomes are likely: Potential negative impacts are addressed as challenges and as positive opportunities in the

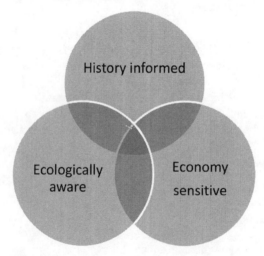

Figure 3.3.   Intersecting Perspectives

planning process. The persons who anticipate challenges feel acknowledged in the planning process, aligning as the topics move forward into programs. Document these.

One intention of multiple scenario planning is to create a flexible vision amenable to cultural, environmental, and economic shifts. The essence of community-integrated planning is to document different visions represented. Then, intersections of these visions are derived as a basis for cooperation. For some cultures, encouraging participants to close their eyes increases visual perception during this process.

A vision is essential to both the leadership and the people participating in museum programs. For this reason, the effective vision created supports a past-present-future continuum of local history, culture, and arts as the expression of tradition. Involving elders of the community is essential for wisdom guidance based on history.

PLANNING PROCESS

SUPPORT A CULTURAL VISION

See your community in the future.

- What are community members saying to each other about their culture?
- What activities are engaging them?
- Are they concerned that certain values or traditions will be lost?
- What is the community vision?
- How can the community vision be supported by the museum's vision?
- Is there a transformative process possible through the museum's activities?

A productive exercise is brainstorming vision phrases and ideas with participation. These statements are more easily grasped by community members when posted in public spaces or online. Artwork may be added to further local recognition and encourage audience engagement. Cultural styles of expressing vision are best captured by varying the process.

The following display style is an example that is visually easy to comprehend and translatable to the standard vision format. Using a word cloud format is another option. Explore participant suggestions with empathy, to "bring the community along."

Once a vision for the future is clear, participants may express their ideas for extending local hospitality through creating exhibits, protecting their ecosystems, and preserving traditions. In these rapidly changing times, a vision of the future must encompass conditions both internal and external to the museum.

Preservation * HISTORY * Cultural Understanding
EDUCATION * Cultural Learning * Youth
Art Appreciation * INTERGENERATIONAL CONNECTION
Referrals to Community Entrepreneurs
NATURE AWARENESS * Storytelling * LANGUAGE
Cooperation * Engagement
CREATIVE ECONOMY * Respect * Cultural Pride
AN EXPERIENCE

Figure 3.4. Display of Community Vision

Deep listening in forming a vision statement encourages long-term involvement for plan implementation. The more formal vision statement is useful for aligning partners and for use in documents such as funding proposals. The following example expresses community integration.

VISION

The vision of the Mountain Museum is to inspire the cultural expressions of local community and visitors.

The connection between forms of culturally appropriate development concerning the arts, culture, and visitation are then easier to consider in relation to technical assistance, training, promotion, and funding. A museum can create a poster with local values and this vision to remind community members in an inspiring way.

DEVELOPING A COMMUNITY-INTEGRATED MISSION

According to the American Alliance of Museums,[5] "a mission statement is the beating heart of a museum." It articulates the museum's educational focus and purpose, as well as a role and responsibility to the public and its collections. Vision and value statements underlie the concepts expressed in the mission statement.

These are different but related guiding documents for the museum: vision is future; mission is purpose; and values are beliefs. In many Indigenous cultures, the mission statement reflects process through being, doing, and becoming. Integrate culturally based expressions into the plan as well as the more formalized mission expected by funders.

PLANNING PROCESS

STATING A CLEAR MISSION

- What is the museum's purpose?
- Is there flexibility in this statement of purpose, to allow for changes in circumstances?
- Who will be served by the museum, and are different worldviews explored?
- Are community members linking to each other to teach?
- How are youth involved?
- Does the museum support all generations, particularly elders?
- Which programmatic areas could be expanded to meet changing community needs?
- How will the needs be met?
- What benefits are expected to be contributed locally?
- Why does the museum exist?

As a focused expression of purpose, a mission statement describes the long-term intention of the museum or cultural center. What does the mission hope to achieve? Who will be the primary recipients? A standard museum mission assumes collections and focuses on a specific structure.

> **STANDARD MISSION STATEMENT**
>
> The Mountain Museum's mission is to support the community through exhibitions, collections, research, and museum visitor education.

In contrast, the flexible, multiple-scenario mission expresses an experience and is community-integrated. This example presents a broadened intention.

> **COMMUNITY-FOCUSED MISSION**
>
> The mission of the Mountain Museum is to participate in a community-integrated network supportive of inclusive, culturally based education.

The Museum Trustee Association offers the following criteria[6] for evaluating a mission statement: Is this mission useful as a decision-making tool, inspirational, clear, and simple? Does the mission distinguish the museum from other similar institutions? Does it show a sense of connectedness to the museum's communities, the greater world, and the issues of our times?

When planning is carried out for specific projects, always relate projects back to the mission. This is one way of keeping the board of directors and museum partners in tandem with redirected intentions. A community-integrated mission builds collaborations while guiding perceptions of relevant contemporary topics.

INCREMENTAL STRATEGIES

A strategy is a central direction to attain a result, useful for resolving key issues. Defining a strategy creates a focus for development. In traditional cultures, strategy is not only a tool for survival but also for cultural flourishing. Study the traditional strategies in your community to gain insight as to ways the community can move forward in a cohesive and insightful way. Planning participants are more likely to engage in projects later when they have been part of the formation.

A clear strategy formed by the community is often a culturally relevant means of survival and preservation in traditional communities. Asking questions about traditional strategies can be an approach for gaining insight into ways of motivating within the community, as well as to carry out desired directions. In traditional cultures, strategies are sometimes imbedded in prophecies, stories, and philosophies, particularly in relation to cultural continuity. For example, in one Indigenous planning process, considering a prophecy "when the culture is dying out, the little people will bring it back" led to a museum emphasis on youth involvement and intergenerational teaching. Exploring these may lead to original concepts for museums.

In contemporary planning methods, strategy is usually developed after assessments, based on current strengths for moving forward. For example, "cultural expression through intergenerational education" is an underlying strategy drawing upon traditional values. Community members are more likely to participate in projects when the tie-in to traditional ways of being is perceived.

During the initial planning process of the Poeh Cultural Center and Museum,[7] a community-integrated museum planning effort at the Pueblo of Pojoaque, New Mexico, community and museum needs were prioritized. This analysis proved invaluable to phase construction of the complex and to gradually develop programs, as funds were raised over time. In relation to messages and needs, the process placed cultural arts learning as the highest priority, with the first phase being a series of classrooms built in the adobe tradition—one room added at a time. Initially, classes were taught in Pueblo homes and yards. The initial museum was located in a small, existing building while the first-phase classrooms were being built. Changing exhibits were featured in this temporary space, and the larger, permanent museum facility became a second phase of development.

A participant elder[8] called the process "planning from the inside out" a beautiful expression of community priorities. This is the reverse of the usual museum focus on collections and exhibit themes as primary. The process of placing a top priority on cultural teaching and activities first, then developing exhibits demonstrating progress on cultural revitalization, resulted in a unique approach to exhibits that became known as a national, Harvard-award-winning model. The point is to start and phase to secure resources in an incremental way.

Recording a range of strategies garners ideas for multiple scenarios. Examples of strategies developed with this approach might include the following.

- Fostering an intergenerational approach to participation and learning programs
- Nurturing nature connections
- Developing further interpretation for museum exhibits using multimedia technology
- Linking organizational partners for a strengthened cultural network
- Using new decision-making processes to further flexibility and cooperation in a community-wide network

By the end of a participation process defining foundational values, a vision, and a mission, clear paths will emerge. In contemporary times, the "multi" may include websites, blogs, apps, lecture presentations, podcasts, and use of social media. Multimodal options include text, images, or audio recording. These are invaluable for expanding committed participation, expressing culture, having meaningful interaction, and furthering desired priorities. There can be more than one strategy; however, a maximum of five is often the most effective for creating focus.

FLEXIBLE GOALS AND OBJECTIVES

Moving from determined needs to priorities focuses the formation of goals. These can be clustered into internal museum and external priorities, as well as intentions for public education. A positive museum impact is nurtured through expressed culturally based goals. Cultural goals are long-term desired outcomes of cultural expression, retention, cultural renewal, cultural change, or any other aspect of a group's lifeways and belief system. Considering history in relation to knowledge valuable for future actions produces strong goals.

Goals are long-term outcomes, effective for keeping a community group working together on a common track. Having goals creates motivation and unity in the community. Goals may be process-oriented, as well as outcome-oriented, depending on the culture or the intended uses. Goals are usually general; however, the more specific a goal, the easier it is to measure progress for that goal. Between three to five goals provide a starting place. Keep in mind goal statements allowing for flexibility over time.

Process-oriented goals, often called means-goals, tend to relate to capacity building and decision-making. These are important to include as guidelines for switching scenarios when conditions change. Frequently, goals are result-oriented, relating to end outcomes. Including both result-oriented goals and capacity-building goals supports an organization's ability to move forward.

Note: There may exist a "goal gap" between non-Western cultural orientations and those goals more relevant to mainstream cultures. Yet, funders tend to expect a certain format for goals more applicable to the mainstream, measurable form. In these communities, two sets of goals may be needed: an "internal" set reflecting nonlinear, process-oriented ways of being plus a translation to "external" goals suitable for funders, governments, and other entities steeped in a linear way of thinking.

PLANNING PROCESS

THE COMMUNITY-INTEGRATED MUSEUM

- What are the community's cultural goals?
- What are the community's economic goals?
- What are the local ecological concerns and current efforts to sustain the local environment?
- What are community members saying to each other about visitors coming to the area?
- What are the important uses of the museum collections and programs to connect to these goals?

Where goals fit in the planning process varies from culture to culture. Preliminary goals are sometimes discussed early, before assessments. This goal-setting point focuses the development, yet there is a caution to consider: Goals may create "tunnel thinking," narrowing options too quickly. Think creativity and innovation.

PLANNING PROCESS

OUTCOMES OF COLLABORATION

- Which local decision-making processes are strengths to draw upon?
- Which intentions support local participation?
- What improvements could be made to develop a collaborative style of decision-making?
- Which resources does the community have to support cultural efforts?
- How are cultural values central to museum visitation?

- How could museum visitation be encouraged with an emphasis on interaction and process?
- Which multimodal options for communication are appropriate to convey different topics?

Be open to revisiting the vision and goals with the community toward the end of the planning steps to see if other factors arise that would relate to alternative scenarios. Examples of community-integrated goals emphasizing an inclusive approach follow.

Goal 1: To reinterpret history with local participation reflecting inclusive, cumulative wisdom, fostering an appreciation of local cultures.

Goal 2: To support intergenerational participation in culturally based activities.

Goal 3: To further community accessibility to the Mountain Museum's collection for study through visual images, virtual interpretive tours, and on-site visitation when feasible.

Goal 4: To develop the Mountain Museum as a referral hub in a community-wide network of partners.

Goal 5: To foster a cohesive network of traditional economy through community partnerships, developing opportunities for artists and other cultural entrepreneurs.

Objectives are shorter-term steps that will be used to accomplish goals and "bring the community along." When objectives are stated in measurable terms, progress can be tracked and projects "re-tuned" as necessary. Specific objectives contain actions and targets, providing criteria for periodic evaluation (see chapter 11). The following example illustrates objectives for one community-integrated goal that may be new to some museums:

Goal 5: To foster a cohesive network of traditional economy through community partnerships, by developing opportunities for artists and other cultural entrepreneurs, through the following means:

Objective 1: Maintaining a database of cultural entrepreneurs to effectively offer training, referrals, and interpretation;

Objective 2: Identifying learning preferences plus arts at risk of becoming lost and working with partners to initiate learning programs;

Objective 3: Developing interpretation of the cultural arts, both for exhibits and to assist cultural entrepreneurs—including nature connections;

Objective 4: Selling cultural art items produced locally in the museum store, along with value-added interpretation; and

Objective 5: Working with partners to open cooperative opportunities for cultural entrepreneurs, thus encouraging continuation of time-honored traditions, as well as contemporary expression.

Planning as a process includes both result-oriented and capacity-building objectives to produce the best scale and capability-match. Continued participation and allocation of financial resources for museums usually only occurs if the community has clearly defined goals and proceeds to integrate these into specific projects. Effective goals and objectives address three to five years (short-term and long-term) at a minimum and are useful for prioritizing projects in tandem with capacity-building. In times of rapidly changing conditions, the three-year plan is practical.

Look for cultural goals in local planning documents. Strengthening the community interface keeps museum programs relevant while expanding opportunities for financial support. Put simply, a wide range of organizations present in a community improves access to a broad range of potential technical assistance and funding. Museum sustainability is increased through broadening interface and services.

The museum is in a position to serve as an advisor on historical and cultural inclusion—and be paid or included in grants for the service. As the museum meets its ethical responsibility in a multicultural world, community perception of museum value increases. This is the key to thriving beyond surviving.

COMPLETING PLAN STEPS

The action plan component of an adaptive plan maps out the specific steps needed to carry out the vision, mission, goals, and objectives. In this new era, flexibility is central. Specific, time-defined, and phased projects shape an idea into form, encouraging participation. By defining projects in the planning process:

- Actions mesh well with the museum's mission and goals;
- Project descriptions included in the museum plan design an agreed-upon path for moving forward;
- Funders and community members see how community participation formed the project idea;
- Partners are aligned into a well-defined sequence for each step;
- Funding options increase when projects include a broad range of benefits; and
- Project descriptions from the plan can form the basis of a funding proposal.

An important method for multi-scenario planning is the phasing of projects, such that decision points are integrated into the delivery of approaches or services. For example, in visitation-challenged times, training staff and community members in new technologies may become a necessary step for leadership. Addressing and bridging technology gaps will become ever more relevant in the future.

Ways of encouraging flexibility through adaptive planning are reflected in the following planning process. In this discussion, be careful to explore which uses of technology are culturally acceptable for sensitive topics. Boundaries may exist.

PLANNING PROCESS

ENCOURAGING FLEXIBILITY

- Does projected involvement beyond the planning process include inclusive perspectives?
- How are decision-making strengths emphasized culturally?
- How does inclusive programming encourage exploration and discovery?
- How will we use multimodal interpretation strategies and modern technology?
- How will our programs be interactive to include different communication styles and mediums, including online?
- Describe ways of broadening visitation, such as virtual exhibits on the museum's website or other uses of social media and the Internet.
- What are ways of furthering understanding of different worldviews by bridging cultures?
- How will diverse interpretations be valued as part of the story?
- How can we accommodate teaching for cultural continuance?

Scenario range expands when developed in a phased manner, for cumulative smaller-scale projects enable redirecting if conditions change to another scenario. When project designs respond to identified needs, alignment is created in the community. Then, in-depth partner contributions support a greater range of participation.

Once the project topic is defined, specific goals and objectives narrow the scope of the project, meshing with the museum's overall mission and goals. For many projects, a practical step is to distinguish between end goals and means goals. For example, the involvement or training of local people may be an important means goal of the project, leading to alignment. Including extra deliverables to increase positive community results is often but a small extra step. Partner alliances often provide solutions for sharing resources.

A "methodology," "work plan," or "approach" section of a project design describes the methods that will be used to carry out the project. For example, what are the central themes of an exhibit? Who will be involved to ensure inclusivity? What are their characteristics and interests? How many people will be reached? Which methods will be used to reach them?

In summary, project descriptions in the plan organize the work ahead, maximizing cooperative action among staff and partners. Steps provide a foundation for decision-making points and readiness for funding proposals.

Specific projections guide museum staff for an effective team approach and encourage continued local participation. A phased approach to steps needed for carrying projects forward allows for shifting directions or changing the pace of a project—either slowing down or proceeding faster, if conditions allow. A timetable for the completion of the project not only creates a tool for planning the steps of the project but also serves as a guide for staff training during the project—essential for a team effort. Phasing a project enables inclusion of decision-making points.

Which feature of the timeline creates a multi-scenario concept? Flow from one scenario to the next, or blended carryover of activities—rather than a whole new scenario start—brings both speed and ease. In Chart 3.5, a brief timeline illustrates a three-scenario approach to the database, entrepreneurial support, and museum store projects. Evaluation and decision-making points are incorporated to bring the flexibility needed for shifting.

One possible outcome of a community-integrated project carrying out the goal detailed in Chart 3.5 reflects a directory of cultural artists, with bios and possible video clips. The foundational step of creating a database is useful for contacting artists for demonstrations or classes, as well as interpretive assistance for exhibits and an interpretive guide. This is an example of deep collaboration when information is shared and the needs of several organizations may be met. Changing exhibits for artists' work show respect for the art, foster interest in learning of the traditional arts, and contribute to the overall continuation of the cultural arts.

The process of developing a cultural entrepreneur database is presented in chapter 7. Small projects, such as training, easy to derive from a database, may not be large enough to stand alone in a funding application. Inclusion in a larger project, such as development of a locally based museum store, brings a critically important opportunity for many cultural artists. The continuation of authentic, often nature-based and symbolic traditions results, while generating museum support.

Using a diversified approach to museum services, this inclusionary approach integrates steps for obtaining interpretive content for exhibits, teaching traditional arts, and developing authentic inventory for the community-integrated museum store. Why is this type of activity so vitally important to museums? Interpretation based on culturally biased history texts and museum store items sold as "out-of-cultural-context" objects do not lead to a decolonized perception of museum activities.

In the scenario planning approach, budget projections are calculated for changing conditions. These could include extra technology costs, web-based interpretive and educational programs, extra time in working with cultural entrepreneurs, or a shift in marketing approaches. Member donations are likely to be seen when costs are clearly defined, contingencies projected, and matches encouraged. Phased budgets lend more flexibility, depending on available resources.

TIMELINE FOR HERITAGE PROJECT

ACTION STEPS SCENARIO 1		QUARTER											
Heritage Programs **SUSTAINING THE CULTURAL ARTS**	RESPONSIBLE PARTY	2024				2025				2026			
		1	2	3	4	1	2	3	4	1	2	3	4
Create a cultural entrepreneur database from survey, to determine community interest, potential instructors, demonstrators, level of instruction, and topics/ update annually	Education Coord. Museum Director												
Complete decisions on classes to teach and priorities: 1) community interest 2) arts at risk of being lost 3) employment potential	Museum Director Board Partners												
Develop a curriculum integrating the arts, culture, traditional language, and entrepreneurial skills/ update	Education Coord. Museum Director												
Complete the store business plan focusing on priorities to address social justice (arts-at-risk) and economic justice	Museum Director Business Consultant												
Obtain commitment on venues to hold classes, instructors/ secure funding	Education Coordinator Partners												
Hold classes (online or in-person), student surveys for each class, evaluate progress	Education Coord. Instructors												
Obtain interpretive information on the cultural arts from instructors and students for use in exhibits and as "value-added" hang tags	Museum Director Evaluation Consultant												
Develop evaluation criteria based on cultural retention, student progress, sales/ redirect	Dir., Evaluator, Education Coord.												

ACTION STEPS SCENARIOS 2 & 3		QUARTER											
Heritage Programs **SUSTAINING THE CULTURAL ARTS**	Responsible Party	2024				2025				2026			
		1	2	3	4	1	2	3	4	1	2	3	4
Scenario 2: Minimal scenario: Revisions to business plan/online programs Develop online classes where appropriate	Business manager Education Coord.												
Fully develop online museum store, secure entrepreneurial funding, provide referrals for cultural entrepreneurs	Museum Director Board Partners												
Use interpretive material documented in Scenario 1 to create podcasts, lecture series, classes for members/ evaluate success of online expansion	Education Coord. Museum Director												
Scenario 3: Expansion scenario With phasing, further develop both online and physical stores, additional video podcasts	Museum Director Partners												
Create an arts and culture district and itineraries with other cultural orgs and amenities, link students with additional sales outlets	Education Coord. Museum Director												
Initiate exhibits concerning pressing cultural and ecological issues, strong community involvement/ link cultural continuity	Education Coord. Exhibit Designer												
Work closely with tourism entities to increase the museum draw and a cultural hub concept	Museum Director Tourism Entities												
Evaluate success in terms of both numerical targets and qualitative, process-oriented goals, redirect as conditions change	Director Evaluator Education Coord.												

Chart 3.5

FUNDING

The bridge from project idea to funders becomes more secure with a diverse approach to potential benefits. For example, interpretation of a cultural art for an exhibit educates the public on the materials used, symbolism, nature connections, time involved in art-making, and intergenerational cooperation. Such an inclusive approach to projects expands funding topics to include not only museum exhibits, but also art classes tied to exhibit themes, reinterpretation of history, youth programs, and assistance to cultural entrepreneurs represented in the museum store.

Since each funding source has internal goals and funding priorities, the most effective project descriptions include the key words most common for funding sources (e.g. museums, arts, entrepreneurial support, and environmental awareness). This approach is illustrated in chapter 10. As the range of benefits increases so, too, does the range of partners and funding sources expand. Consider this "creative framing," or "storing the seed corn." Rather than switching entirely, the flowing of activities from one scenario to the next is central to being prepared.

EVALUATION

Being clear on performance measures in the plan is fundamental to the effective evaluation process; the measuring of progress on need indicators enhances perception for when an adaptive shift will be necessary. All too often, evaluation is conducted at the end of a project as a funder requirement rather than as a means of accommodating a redirection process. By phasing projects and allowing for periodic evaluation, comparison is possible. Plus, being clear about decision-making processes, the decision-makers, and steps for redirecting transforms planning to an open path rather than one of debate. Evaluation ties heavily into the adaptive, ability-to-shift-direction process. Chapter 11 illustrates the evaluation process amenable to increased flexibility.

THRIVING IN SHIFTING TIMES

The stakes are high for cultural survival worldwide. Repeatedly, communities echo the same concern: Cultural traditions, including the cultural arts, are tied to all aspects of lifeways—food production, earned livelihood, good health practices, relationships in ecosystems, and spiritual beliefs. The physical museum design based on projected uses rather than architectural templates is possible when a thorough, inclusive planning process is completed. Community-linked projects are then supported.

Every contribution to the cumulative retention of knowledge and traditions begins with a local community. Expanding the museum's local and regional networks increases options and flexibility. Multiple scenarios, which are phased, allow for redirection or increasing community relevance as conditions change. The following chapters delineate planning processes for specific museum topics—leading to an inclusive, sustainable museum plan.

FURTHER READING

Fischer, Daryl, and Laura Roberts. *Strategic Thinking and Planning*. Museum Trustee Association. Lanham, MD: Rowman & Littlefield, 2018.
This guide to creating a strategic plan includes web-based templates to help boards consider options, identify priorities, and plan actions. One intention is to present tools for analyzing information and thinking about a museum's mission. A broader focus includes community values and impacts.

Kahane, Adam. *Transformative Scenario Planning*. San Francisco, CA: Berrett-Koehler Publishers, Inc., 2012.
Innovative approaches to finding a core diagnosis of turbulent situations in order to identify effective coping behavior are offered. Then, moving toward solutions, two additional components of scenario work detailed by Kahane are the following: 1) the need for the solutions to important issues becoming more central to peoples' personal identity and value systems, and 2) counteracting increasing turbulence with more focus on mobilizing resources and others' perception of what is happening, what could happen, discovering what can be done, and acting together to transform the system.

Lord, Gail Dexter, and Kate Markert. *The Manual of Strategic Planning for Cultural Organizations*. Lanham, MD: Rowman & Littlefield, 2017.
A "how-to" guide with concise case studies, this holistic approach to the creative world speaks to a broad range of cultural institutions. An emphasis on tools for operating in a time of great change brings applicability to museums and current conditions. Three key areas covered are leadership change, institutional change, and staff empowerment.

Ralston, Bill, and Ian Wilson. *The Scenario Planning Handbook: Developing Strategies in Uncertain Times*. Mason, OH: South-Western Educational Publishers, 2006.
Initially written for the business community, this classic text outlines a process for defining and making decisions in the face of uncertainty. Detailed descriptions of steps in the multi-scenario situation outline includes tips for strategic thinking, planning, mapping-out scenarios and moving forward with a team approach. The process outlined is relevant to museums.

NOTES

1. Isa, Nafisa. "Communities over Collections: Three Principles for Partnership." In *Change is Required: Preparing for the Post-Pandemic Museum*, Avi Decter, Marsha Semmel, and Ken Yellis (eds.), pp. 79–83. Lanham, MD: Rowman & Littlefield, 2022.
2. Guyette, Susan. *Planning for Balanced Development: A Guide for Rural and Native American Communities*. Santa Fe, NM: ClearLight Publishers, 1996.
3. Lord, Gail Dexter, and Kate Markert. *The Manual of Strategic Planning for Cultural Organizations*. Lanham, MD: Rowman & Littlefield, 2017.
4. Guyette, Susan. *Sustainable Cultural Tourism: Small-Scale Solutions*. Santa Fe, NM: BearPath Press, 2013.
5. Fischer, Daryl, and Laura Roberts. *Strategic Thinking and Planning*. Templates for Trustees series, Book 4. Museum Trustee Association. Lanham, MD: Rowman & Littlefield, 2018.
6. Ibid.
7. Guyette, *Planning for Balanced Development*.
8. Observation by Peter Garcia, planning participant from San Juan Pueblo in 1990.

4

Rethinking Collections

Access to collections is a contemporary issue relating to inclusivity. Collections are the material expression of culture; they reflect values, beliefs, and lifeways. In the museum world, collections are generally considered to be "works of art, specimens, or archival documents."[1] Yet, in recent years, the concept of a collection is expanding to include intangible expressions, such as stories, songs, dances, folkways, and other forms of cultural representation.

Exploration with an inclusive, participatory planning process focuses priorities at this pivotal reflection point in a rapidly changing economy. Simply returning to normal is not likely to be a winning proposition.[2] More likely, a museum model addressing collaborative and inclusive leadership is likely to be the successful approach. Now is the time for self-reflection through adaptive planning and reimagining museum purpose.

Why is the intangible particularly important in this new era? Seen through a collective lens, the potential contribution of museums to the global pool of knowledge is critical for solving contemporary issues—especially economic and environmental issues through cultural interpretation. Another reason to regroup concerns the stories linked to the materials in collections, often containing ecosystem interrelationship messages. These intangible, non-physical forms are critical to foster. Cultural continuity, often expressed through the creation of objects, is transmitted through meaning.

Cultural differences in the meaning of art are essential to understand. Art in American or Western culture tends to be valued for uniqueness and individualism expressed by the artist. In contrast, traditional cultures tend to consider art items as a continuity of generations, representing masterful art traditions continued by the stories of several generations through time. The practice of several generations working together on one art piece, as in the pottery traditions, is common. This orientation reflects collective representation more than individual innovation and requires mentoring programs to encourage specific art forms.

For example, in Indigenous communities, there are often cultural boundaries associated with intangible forms of cultural expression, and these are important to define. Intangible aspects of culture tie strongly to language retention—a very high cultural priority relating to expression. A recent document developed by the School for Advanced Research (SAR) discusses vitally important standards for museums with Native American collections.[3] Recommendations are addressed for the areas of 1) public trust and accountability, 2) collections stewardship, 3) education and interpretation, 4) mission and planning, 5) organizational structure, 6) financial stability, 7) facilities, and 8) risk management.

Differences in cultural interpretations of design ownership, an inclusivity factor for collections policies, need to be considered. There are cultural differences in perception expressing ownership. In American mainstream culture, individual ownership of design tends to be the common view, with "copying" a sensitive area. The originator should always be acknowledged, or the originator may restrict use.

In other cultures, designs belong to the group or tribe. For Indigenous groups, collective ownership involves symbolic designs passed down generationally, and may be limited to members of that culture. "Copying" is the key to cultural transmission, generation-to-generation. Who is allowed access and to see documentation, as well as the possible need for separate storage areas, are important decisions calling for community participation. Restrictions on sharing or reproduction must be documented and emphasized.

Expanding the community relevance of collections is one approach toward audience connection. Many museum administrators are rethinking the purpose of their collections and access issues in light of cultural considerations. For museums in traditional settings, the collection concept is often away from a purely object definition to the direction of continued cultural practice. For example, the collection is of a distinct significance in numerous cultures. Collections are comprised of "cultural treasures," those items carrying meaning with symbolism, interpretation, stories, environmental relationships, and intergenerational cooperation. Stories, songs, and dances express these connections.

Cultural memory is central in the past-present-future continuum. In some animate-worldview cultures, items are seen as alive,[4] and the separation of being located away from cultural home is hurtful. Returning items to their communities for proper cultural care is one ameliorating step. Sacred objects and pottery, or other items made from nature materials, are examples. Ceremonies and prayers held for these beings are other steps forward in the direction of culturally respectful treatment. These are topics to explore with participants.

Collections access, whether in-person or digital, increases community capacity for interpretation. Listening ability and developing trust relationships underlie the optimal community connection. These are responsibilities of the empathetic museum.

TO COLLECT OR NOT TO COLLECT

Often, museums begin with the assumption of a physical collection as central to the museum—or may even evolve around a donated collection. This is an object-oriented view, where assumptions may not hold true across all cultures. Collecting, curating, and storage of a larger collection may take resources away from other local priorities. Many small museums do not have collection storage areas or funding for curation. Diversifying funding is not just a wish-list item; curation needs are often vital for teaching, to ensure cultural continuity. Curation becomes a dire need, as these treasures are invaluable for study.

Community priorities are essential to consider in the past-present-future continuum. The future of museum collections may be one in which our collections are active, people-centered, and collaborative.[5] Such collections are capable of telling many stories.

Whether to collect or not to collect or what to collect in relation to the museum's mission is a sensitive issue. A planning process addressing collection needs, priorities, and realistic outcomes is needed to examine cultural goals and resources. When resources are limited, the decisions may not flow easily. To this end, exploring which collection items are needed for teaching is an essential part of the discussion.

At first glance, the donated collection might appear to be a cost-effective way to start, yet museums starting this way rarely factor in ahead of time the expense of maintaining a collection. Staff time plus expertise to document, catalog, and curate, as well as storage costs, insurance, and so on, need to be calculated.

"What is important to cultural sustainability?" becomes the central question when local representation is fully shaping the decisions. To focus a collection, the first basic question to ask community members in a planning process concerns the purpose of collecting. In many regions, there is an urgent need for curation and proper storage of historically important items owned by families. Yet, families may not want to donate these to a museum collection, as visitation privileges are essential.

Local groups may want to focus on storing these priority items, assuring ownership agreements are in place with families. Whether items are appropriate for general viewing would be determined with the families. Acquiring and making visible items representing artistic excellence in the cultural arts inspires learning by youth, an important objective for cultural continuance.

Not yet developed in many small museums, a collections catalog is essential for organizing and curating items, as well as for recording information relevant to interpretation. Making photographs taken for the collections catalog available, when culturally appropriate, to students in art classes is one way of encouraging the learning of traditional designs.

The decision of whether to acquire or expand a collection is one to be made carefully, because storing and maintaining a collection is expensive. For the last century and earlier, the Western museum concept assumed collections. In recent years, the practice of implementing a collections policy narrowed the range of items but often not far enough.

Today, many larger museums are returning items due to the cost of maintaining vast numbers of items. Also, in compliance with federal regulations, such as the Native American Graves Protection and Repatriation Act (NAGPRA) passed in 1990, repatriation and proper transfer is mandated of certain Native American human remains, funerary objects, sacred objects, and objects of cultural patrimony. Funerary items are considered to be those placed intentionally at the time of death or later, with or near human remains. Sacred objects are ceremonial objects considered necessary by traditional tribal leaders for the practice of traditional tribal religions in the present. Items with ongoing historical, traditional, or cultural importance central to a tribal group are "objects of cultural patrimony."[6]

By enacting NAGPRA,[7] Congress recognized that human remains of any ancestry "must at all times be treated with dignity and respect." These items are generally kept private and not to be viewed by the public. Note that the First Nations Ceremonial Objects Repatriation Act in Canada is a parallel effort.

The response to NAGPRA is varied. Some museums wait to be approached, while others understand their obligation to return collection items. The Smithsonian Institution's outstanding efforts to work with Indigenous groups on the return, both on NAGPRA criteria items and other culturally significant items, is a positive example.

To return culturally significant objects is often of immense value spiritually to the communities involved. The return of 100 Pueblo pots originating in six pueblos (Pojoaque, San Ildefonso, Ohkay Owingeh, Santa Clara, Tesuque, and Nambé) from the Smithsonian is a contemporary example. This pottery is considered to have life, and the return has benefitted the community in many ways. The resulting exhibit, "Di Wae Powa," at the Poeh Cultural Center and Museum has stimulated the internal community telling of stories about the pots and the makers while external visitors enjoy the story of the return in the exhibit.

One major barrier to return interaction occurs when a museum does not have all collection items catalogued. Even when there exists a willingness by larger museums to return items, funding for proper storage and curation may be lacking. To avoid small museums being overwhelmed on the receiving end, a phased approach to developing storage area(s) or storage at another regional museum, with access by origin community members, may be a solution.

A new museum awareness of collections and communities calls for caretaking to be proactive and collaborative. Establishing long-term relationships with communities is an essential step.[8] Inviting underrepresented people—often people of color—helps set the agenda for historical and collections research. Listening to voices on how to share stories enhances the interesting museum experience—a win-win outcome.

FOCUSING COLLECTION PURPOSE

Focusing a museum's collection is optimally attained when goals and a specific collection policy form the basis of action. Types of collections in a community-integrated approach relate to the local population, visitor, and research needs. Figure 4.1 includes an expansion of collection concepts.

Although teaching collections and storage of community-owned items are relatively new concepts, these considerations frequently tie to community relevance. In relation to teaching culture, several sub-collection types are important to consider for the future.

- Display collection
- Storage collection—fragile, not suitable for display
- Study collection
- Demonstration and storytelling collections
- Sacred, or culturally sensitive material with limited public access
- Teaching collections for use in classes
- Library and archival collections

When local participation in forming goals addresses a broad range of access and study needs, relevance and involvement in the broader range of museum programs increases. These needs include interpretation for historical understanding, study access for cultural retention, and the fostering of cultural pride. Diversifying a balance of historic preservation and access for current teaching carries local cultures into the future.

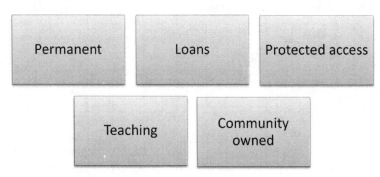

Figure 4.1. Collection Types

ACCESS OUTCOMES

In many cultures, a collection is supportive of cultural learning with an inclusive approach. Community members become inspired seeing the works of their families and the traditions of their ancestors. School children visiting the museum become enthusiastic about learning the arts, interwoven with other cultural traditions such as language, food gathering practices, storytelling, and the relationships between families. Collection items are studied in the museum's cultural art classes and are an essential resource for tradition continuance. Cultural pride flourishes.

Considering a museum's direction in relation to collecting is important, particularly when the collection is vital to cultural learning. Important questions to consider along the way include:

- What do we intend to collect, for whom, and for what purpose?
- How does knowledge of the past inform the present and create a foundation for the future?
- Do the objects have life or are they the reflections of spiritual guidance? Such aspects of collecting require special attention.

For these reasons, curation, or care of the collection, is a priority need of the museum. "How do collections connect to the cultural goals of the community?" is a central question to consider. Additional aspects to consider, as the museum develops further, include those in the following process.

PLANNING PROCESS

COLLECTION PURPOSE

- Is a collection useful or needed?
- What is the purpose of the collection?
- What do we intend to collect, for whom, and for what purpose?
- How does this purpose connect to the community's mission?
- How does the collection support the museum's mission?
- How does knowledge of the past inform the present and create a foundation for the future?
- Is a teaching collection possible?

Connecting collection purpose to the community-centered mission brings cohesiveness in a local network. The emphasis on a teaching collection—replicas or items appropriate for supervised observation or handling—is a new concept for many museums.

PLANNING PROCESS

COLLECTION FOCUS

- How important is preserving the past as a key objective?
- What categories of items are important to the story to be told in the museum?
- Is there an interpretive goal, such as correcting misinformation about an historical event?
- Is there a teaching goal for preserving the past, to bridge the transition between past, present, and future?
- Will beginning a collection support the community's cultural goals?
- Can a separate teaching collection be maintained?
- How will youth involvement be encouraged?
- What are effective bridges from the collection to interpretation?
- What size of collection can we afford to curate and maintain?

When facility space is limited, these questions become significant. A separate teaching collection of reproductions or contemporary art is useful for community access. By balancing preservation of the past and the present with the future, cultural arts can be supported through a focused, inclusive collection effort.

PLANNING PROCESS

STORAGE CONSIDERATIONS

- Is the collections storage area of adequate size?
- Is the collection away from direct sunlight?
- Is security adequately provided, on a twenty-four-hour basis?
- Are there seasonal limitations for viewing?
- Are there objects stored off-site and places that could better be utilized for learning purposes?
- Is there humidity and temperature control?
- Is a program to work with families for storage of their aging cultural items needed?
- Are museum staff members trained to curate items?
- Is preventive curation taking place for the collection?
- Are there fragile items stored on-site that would be better preserved in a facility off-site?

After the museum develops a collections storage area, potential sources of acquisitions to consider include: 1) collections at other museums (loan, digital images, purchase, or donations); 2) private collectors; and 3) local families. The integrated museum often addresses issues not as common in the mainstream world of museums, such as access for studying—essential for cultural interpretation. For this reason, a storage area visible through glass, yet safe from sunlight, might be developed. Such an area improves access to collections without the impacts of handling. A study area for supervised access of non-fragile items is essential in the design of a museum intending to support the cultures represented in the collection.

EXPANDING ACCESS

In *Museum Collection Ethics*,[9] Steven Miller makes the distinction between direct access and indirect access. Direct access generally means physical contact, which often poses risk from handling—especially with fragile collection items. Ways of carrying out indirect access usually involve posting and supplying digital photographs of items or the contemporary three-dimensional photographs showing all aspects of a design. These can be available either in the museum or online. To protect cultural privacy, some museums place material online for home and school study—with access by a password only, if restricted in access.

Cataloguing is a critical next step, often before collections care. Working with a cultural committee to define the parameters of the collections, as well as the cultural boundaries for sharing information, is an inclusive step in the museum's development. In particular, agreements with families guaranteeing visitation by family members may become a vital aspect of trust.

A balance between public programs, teaching activities, interpretation, and collections research (by community members or outside researchers) relates to community and museum missions. Policies best serve the community when revisited each year. A collection development strategy addresses priorities for collecting, uses for the collection, and projections of anticipated masters in the art as a source for collection items. The artist database formats presented in chapters 6 and 7 are fundamental to recognizing these treasured community members.

Evolving collection purpose and better serving community needs are priorities of interest to museum funders.

VIEWING OPTIONS

Who would be allowed or not allowed to view certain cultural information is important to define. For example, some Indigenous museums house two separate collection storage areas—one restricted to tribal member-only viewing and one for non-Native access. Collections storage, curation, and handling in culturally appropriate ways must be considered.

In some cultures, the viewing of objects is restricted to a specific group of people. This is particularly true in Indigenous cultures, where sacred objects may be restricted to people of cultural affiliation or to spiritual leaders. For example, the Mille Lacs Indian Museum of the Mille Lacs Band of Ojibwe in Minnesota contains two separate collection storage areas, one restricted to tribal members and another for non-Indian curators or members of other tribes. Collection policies detail viewing protocols. As another example, in Makah culture, a tribe in the Northwestern United States, certain gender restrictions apply to the handling of some items.[10]

To renew traditions, cultural material can be invaluable for study by cultural artists. Yet, there are curation concerns to making material available. The following comments reflect discussions on viewing and should be considered in designing a collections storage area:

- It is important that community access be a consideration behind policy. With few exceptions, community access should be considered an important part of conservation. Considerations include the need to schedule use of the space and essential security. Alternative forms of access, such as electronic photos, can be highly developed for community access.
- There are pros and cons of constant display: such as good access versus damage from light or movement, and so on. Middle ground is easy access by staff and periodic open houses with an arranged tour for study purposes.
- If the goal is the continuity of cultural traditions, the collections policy should have a section on "community deposits." Consider provisions for curation in a secure way, while also allowing the family depositing the material to access and check out non-fragile items for ceremonial and other cultural purposes. Authority needs to be established for each item, including who in the family can access and transfer rights.
- There are issues concerning ownership of images—intellectual property rights. In the museums of traditional cultures, a cultural committee or governing body may ask community members to go through access protocols. Designs may be distinct for families or tribes. The question that is important is, "Would access to collections create infringement problems?"
- Restrictions and stipulations regarding access to materials need to be made clear and documented.

Awareness of ownership issues, raised through recent legislation, relates to concerns about access and viewing, particularly important to underrepresented groups. This heightened awareness may stimulate the return of cultural items, presenting the opportunity for a community to acquire culturally important items. In considering access to collections, look at cultural restrictions, seasonal restrictions to viewing, and artistic study needs. A balance of adequate access and preservation measures is often essential to serve community needs.

ANALYZING THE COLLECTION

For the community-based museum, cultural factors are essential to consider during collection analysis. *Quantitative analysis* is helpful for facility and collections storage planning. Consider the following.

- Categories, based on uses, time period, or cultural boundaries for viewing
- Number of objects for categories
- Time periods represented
- Fragility and need for curation
- Item categories lacking in the collection, in relation to the museum's purpose
- Ownership (e.g. museum, other institutions, families)
- Collection storage needs
- Rate of growth of the collection

Qualitative analysis defines how the collection supports the mission of the museum and can include the intangible aspects important in the culturally diverse setting, such as:

- Description of the object, culturally based;
- Potential use of objects;
- Cultural significance;
- Importance for cultural teaching;
- Intergenerational or gender significance;
- Cultural limits on viewing or restrictions on touching;
- Relation to historical events;
- Usefulness in storytelling programs;
- Community needs for teaching; and
- Whether a teaching collection acquisition is needed to support the learning of the cultural arts.

Balancing the quantitative aspects of a collection with the qualitative, or intangible, brings the focus of collecting to respect for the cultures involved. Achieving a balance between quantitative and qualitative analysis ties the collection to local residents and keeps the purpose of the museum on track. In describing the collection, dividing the space by the number of items in a size category will allow for range of size.

This type of analysis sets the foundation for interpretation in exhibits, interpretive guides, storytelling, and other means of educating museum visitors about local culture. Understanding the relationship between collection purpose as stated in the collections policy and projected uses for the collection supports the development of, or adding to, an existing facility. For example, cataloging and proper storage of archival material is often important to local governments or for cultural survival teaching.

COLLECTIONS MANAGEMENT

Collections management, addressing both needs for security and access to materials, can be developed by the museum over time. In the inclusive view, staff training is a first priority, to increase understanding of the different cultural worldviews represented. All collection materials need to be cataloged, and there may be variable degrees of access to different categories of materials as long as there is accountability for the location of all materials. The comprehensive method guide, Inventorying *Cultural Heritage Collections*[11] by Sandra Vanderwarf and Bethany Romanowski emphasizes the importance of regular, sustainable, and ethical collections preservation and access.

The following factors increase accessibility:

- Integrating the collections management system to include all collections, including photography, library and archives.
- Availability of the collections management system on the network and the web, with restrictions based on user type.
- Compatibility of collection management needs with GIS system records search capability.
- Archaeological and ethnographic collections may tie into or reference a Historic Preservation Office records system.
- Separating storage spaces from the permanent collection.

At the time of this writing, many museums use the program PastPerfect to automate many of the time-consuming tasks associated with collections and contacts management. This software has the tools needed for consistent data entry including authority control and a built-in lexicon. Features include the ability to retrieve data with research functions and a report maker. If funds for software purchase are limited, consider Tap Forms, a relatively inexpensive software for small collections, yet limited in features.

THE TEACHING COLLECTION

If the museum becomes oriented toward linking the museum collection to cultural learning, a teaching collection is one solution for bridging access between community-defined needs and protected collection storage needs. A collections policy that links with the cultural learning process is vitally important for cultural continuance. Collecting with well-defined purposes and strategies is key.

PLANNING PROCESS

CULTURAL CONSIDERATIONS FOR COLLECTIONS

- Which material items and documentation support community priorities for cultural retention?
- How can collection items be protected and preserved yet visible to the community for study purposes?
- How can collections items be displayed with maximum learning visibility for the community?
- What are cultural protocols for collecting and for viewing collection items?

If the collection is expanded, creating a teaching collection of three-dimensional objects and photographs of non-culturally sensitive material—available for those learning the cultural arts—supports overall cultural learning efforts.

Teaching reproductions from experienced artists can either be new designs or reproductions of older, too-fragile-to-handle cultural items in the permanent collection. A teaching collection represents reasonably priced, contemporary-made cultural arts, valuable to use for study by students. Scheduled viewing in classes—as well as requiring gloves for handling in addition to established procedures—are still important to follow.

A storytelling and demonstration sub-collection is possible when adequate storage space is available, consisting of items used in a more public setting. Examples are the following: masks and headdresses; pottery, basket molds, basket-making, and carving tools; leatherwork tools; and traditional costumes or regalia. This type of collection is useful in interpretation to the public audience when viewing is culturally appropriate.

CURATION CONSIDERATIONS

Curation involves the caring of cultural items in a respectful way—specific to a culture. A preservation environment is one that encourages collections care rather than allows preventable damage to occur. To this end, protecting collections through care and climate-controlled storage is known as preventative conservation. Often, small museums lack adequate resources or training for preventative curation. Regional assistance from larger museums, universities, or more recent online trainings are financially reasonable solutions—combined with community guidance.

The most common threats to collections include the following: climate; light; pests (e.g. insects, rodents, etc.); mold; pollutants; contaminants; light and ultraviolet radiation; theft; human interaction; and disasters. Planning ahead for disasters is quickly becoming a global concern. In relation to the small community-based museum, preventing damage due to handling and environmental conditions are the urgent factors to address. Most collections preserve better in a stable climate, under cooler temperatures and dryer conditions.[12] Temperature and relative humidity (RH) are two major factors in controlling the rate at which chemical reactions occur and therefore, how fast collection items or artifacts deteriorate. Construction materials for storage are another consideration, as well as reducing off-gassing chemicals.[13]

RH is concerned with the amount of water vapor in the air compared with how much water vapor could be in the air, at a given temperature. High relative humidity can encourage mold growth and pest activity, while low relative humidity can lead to desiccation and embrittlement. This will vary slightly, depending upon the type of material being stored.

When the surrounding air is damp, the materials tend to absorb some of the moisture from the air: they may swell, warp, change shape, and/or lose strength. Dampness can also cause mold and fungal growth on organic materials. Collection items can also be damaged by changes or shifts in relative humidity.

A stable climate for collections storage involves keeping collection items being stored or on exhibit from temperature fluctuations 46°F to 72°F and RH of the space in which collections are stored or exhibited at 72 percent.[14] Visible daylight causes most of the damage to a museum collection.

When baskets are stored at low RH, they will tend to break, but at high RH, mold may form. Paintings stored at either low or high RH can warp or crack. Photographs stored at high RH will warp. The recommended environmental standard for paper-based collections is 35°F to 65°F and 30 to 50 percent RH.[15] Heating, ventilation, and air-conditioning systems are important factors in maintaining proper storage conditions.

Here are a few considerations.

- Control the overall light levels in the museum—taking light-level readings in the museum with a light meter or a UV meter is an interim strategy.
- Use shades and sheers to block daylight coming from windows.
- Move sensitive objects to areas with less light, potentially to the permanent exhibit area.
- Rotate light-sensitive objects in exhibits, to minimize light exposure.

Collection care may be a challenge in terms of funds for staffing or consultants to complete needed curation. Do not despair; there is a solution. Securing a collections management grant to support a collections management plan, staff time for curation, equipment, and training is an important step if staff trained in curation are not already part of the small museum.

Resources are available to assess and address museum assessment needs. In the United States, the Museum Assessment Program (MAP) is supported through a cooperative agreement between the Institute of Museum and Library

Services (IMLS) and the American Alliance of Museums (AAM; www.aam-us .org). Then, trained professionals must be hired and on-site training is continual to handle, clean, and preserve cultural materials.

Unfortunately, many collections are contaminated with pesticides and corrosive acids such as sulfur dioxide, nitrogen oxides, formaldehyde, and so on emitted by inappropriate storage or exhibit materials—posing health risks to persons who work with them. Constant exposure can cause multiple chemical sensitivities (MCS), a serious illness affecting the nervous system. While exposure to these toxic chemicals was widely accepted in the museum field until recently, employee safety is now coming to the forefront.

The most effective way to avoid damage from airborne pollutants is to use appropriate filters on heating, ventilation, and air-conditioning (HVAC) systems, ensuring that windows are not opened in collection areas, and using enclosures in storage and displays. Absorptive minerals, such as products with activated carbon, will help capture gaseous pollutants in enclosed spaces. Protecting people as well as objects is a respectful approach to curation.

Upgrading and implementing a security system is another important collection protection need for all museums. Thieves or vandals can negatively impact a collection, particularly a small collection.

THE ARCHIVAL RESOURCE

The focused archive reflects community memory for a cultural future. Frequently, small museums do not have a climate and water-protected storage space for storing historical documents. This is an urgent need possibly to be filled by a community-based museum, since often the protection of legal rights and historical interpretation—an ongoing process—depends upon preserving documents.

These items include:

- Photographs;
- Historical documents;
- Recordings of oral history, songs, and stories;
- Legal documents; and
- Historical maps.

Technical aspects of the collecting and storing of archival records are important to integrate into the formation of policies. Issues of access and developing a system to meet both the needs of community members and of local government are important. Determining cultural privacy needs is a step often missed yet critically important to establish openness for the sharing of valuable cultural, governmental, or personal documentation. Here are a few considerations.

- Archival assistance, professionally trained in this field, is needed.
- Policies are needed, with a checkout system, holding everyone accountable.
- Levels of access can be incorporated in an electronic system available throughout the museum and online.
- Technical reports must be kept confidential when they are used for legal purposes, if indicated by the participating parties.
- Community members benefit from access to certain aspects of the material (e.g. scanned images of photos can be made available on-site and online).

Cataloguing is an essential step, to make the information included in the archive more available to cultural teachers, researchers, local government, and to community members. Documents that are private to government use should be indicated. These may include information related to legal cases.

Whenever possible, older documents should be scanned, along with newer documents stored in electronic form. A link between important documents for community use and a private page on the museum website can be created, for easy access.

If the current museum facility does not have room for an archive, either additional space in the building would need to be dedicated, probably adjacent to collections storage, or this need would factor into the design if building a new facility.

LIBRARY CONNECTIONS

The museum library connects exhibits to interpretive programs and teaching efforts. In the small museum, space limitations may be the major constraint for developing or expanding a library. Digital copies are now improving the ability to expand acquisitions. The library is an important resource for artists to study designs, for students to learn about their history and complete school assignments, and for the museum to develop cultural interpretation for museum exhibits. Access can be improved with the following:

- A small library needs to be catalogued and the catalog made available to the community.
- Bar-coding capability in cataloguing software can be used for the library, as well as for artifacts.
- Researchers may connect to an Historic Preservation Officer (HPO) or a Tribal Historic Preservation Officer (THPO) for such information as site locations.
- In some instances, the community may indicate a preference to have location information protected.

- To address inclusivity, the reference library would evaluate whether information on history, arts, sciences, periodicals, and research is reliable.
- A practical focus relating to the collection, rather than on theory, tends to better serve the community.
- Census information is valuable for program development.
- Information on families of cultural artists and genealogy is important to collect.
- Original, rare books would be collected and handled carefully.[16]
- Access to scanned photographs and a library catalog on the museum website would ensure broadest access.
- Links to local universities and museums for research are essential.
- Levels for access are important to establish, to meet the needs of several groups.

If the museum cannot afford a part-time, trained librarian, a solution might be to hire a librarian consultant. Guidance and training on how to curate is worth the investment. Museum assistance is often available from local colleges, universities, and other museums—valuable for cataloging and developing documentation. Student interns are a possibility, with cultural advisor input on the handling of cultural items. An orientation to local values and concerns is the inclusivity step.

Training for community members by technical assistance providers improves continuity of a library project and annual updating of the catalog. Liaison with colleges and universities often assists the community in acquiring copies of historical documents and books that may be out of print.

A balance of protecting documents and developing access needs to be maintained. Creating a reference library, with researcher and community use at the museum, is one means of increasing inclusivity. Scanning documents or providing access to digital collections is the modern way of providing access without physical risk. Volunteer assistance may provide a solution for the small museum.

COLLECTIONS AND CULTURAL CONTINUANCE

Collections, if accessible to the community, can make the difference between cultural loss and cultural retention. These are the treasures from the past connecting to the future. A difficult situation is created for cultural continuance when these treasures are sequestered away. Access, either through supervised viewing or handling, reproductions, or digital images—now possible in 3D—is an important ethical role of the community-integrated museum. Reproductions of items in larger museums could be used to increase local community museum collections on display or to change out displays.

Access does not imply only direct reproduction of collection items, which can have the result of stereotyping a culture in time. Rather, communities studying collections tend to incorporate designs, embrace new methods, and constantly reflect culture evolving—in a constant state of change. The right to decide rests with the community.

Familiarity with cultural beliefs about handling items and protecting cultural privacy and appropriate levels of sharing information are essential qualifications of personnel. A collections management plan is needed to address these factors. Training for community members in collections care will be essential for keeping employment within the local area and knowledge of local traditions present in the curation process.

Access to cultural belongings and collaborations are central issues for moving toward inclusivity. The recent summary *Privileging Community Voices*, released by the Indian Arts Research Center at the School for Advanced Research[17] in Santa Fe, New Mexico, is also applicable to other cultures. Four strategies call for: 1) in-depth review of each collection item, 2) adding new, culturally appropriate information, 3) correcting inaccuracies, and 4) sharing the newly improved records with the community. Taking these collaborative steps is likely to build positive, long-term relationships with community members.

Organizing forums for discussion of cultural retention, acceptable change, access to materials, and authenticity is a role for the community-supportive museum. Cultural artists or groups have the right to provide input on the direction of change. These keepers of the traditions are likely to be less influenced by market pressures if they have access to their cultural treasures and a forum to discuss the past, present, and future interrelationships. Hint: This is a fundable project.

To this end, collection access greatly affects the past-present-future cultural continuum. The museum's role may include facilitating discussions, providing documentation, and becoming a comfortable source for knowledge continuance.

FURTHER READING

Catlin-Legutko, Cinnamon, and Stacy Klingler, eds. *Stewardship: Collections and Historic Preservation, Small-Museum Toolkit*, Vol 6. New York: AltaMira Press, 2012.

This practical text presents an overview of the importance of collections care while also offering specifics on collection care basics, collections management, and practices in collection stewardship. Practical advice for small museums on a limited budget is featured.

Cooper, Karen Coody, and Nicolasa Sandoval, eds. *Living Homes for Cultural Expression: North American Native Perspectives on Creating Community Museums.* Washington, DC: Smithsonian Institution, 2006. www.nmai.si.edu.

This development text from the Indigenous viewpoint addresses exhibition planning, teaching programs, public programming, and tribal collections—written from the direct experience of several Native museums and cultural centers.

Miller, Steven. *Museum Collection Ethics: Acquisition, Stewardship, and Interpretation.* Lanham, MD: Rowman & Littlefield, 2020.

Museums face issues regarding how they acquire, keep, and work with their collections. *Museum Collection Ethics* discusses the complexities inherent in preserving and interpreting the extraordinary range of culturally significant objects entrusted to museums. This text presents an encompassing look at aspects of the intellectual and stewardship duties museums assume by definition. The differences between ethics, laws, customs, and expectations are discussed. Ethics vary widely and are fluid.

Vanderwarf, Sandra, and Bethany Romanowski, eds. *Inventorying Cultural Heritage Collections: A Guide for Museums and Historical Societies.* Lanham, MD: Rowman & Littlefield, 2022.

Regular inventories are central to meaningful, sustainable, and ethical collections preservation and access. These authors argue that, in practice, inventories are uncommon: They tend to be evoked as a last resort when a museum has lost control of its collection. Part I offers a flexible project management framework that illustrates strategies for reining in control of collections now. Part II gives voice to practitioners around the world through case studies that affirm the vital role of inventories in regaining control of collections.

NOTES

1. Carrlee, Scott. "Caring for the Future: Collections Care Basics." In *Small Museum Toolkit*, Vol. 6, Cinnamon Catlin-Legutko (ed.), pp. 1–43. New York: AltaMira Press, 2012.
2. Vagone, Franklin. "Protect People, Not Things." In *Change is Required: Preparing for the Post-Pandemic Museum*, Avi Decter, Marsha Semmel, and Ken Yellis (eds.), pp. 153–56. Lanham, MD: Rowman & Littlefield, 2022.
3. Trimble, Stephen. *Talking With the Clay.* Santa Fe, NM: School for Advanced Research Press, 2007.
4. School for Advanced Research (SAR). "Standards for Museums with Native American Collections." Santa Fe, NM. www.sarweb.org/smnac, 2023.
5. Trimble, *Talking With the Clay*.
6. Berlanga-Shevchuk, Mariah. "The Collective Collection." In *Change is Required: Preparing for the Post-Pandemic Museum*, Avi Decter, Marsha Semmel, and Ken Yellis (eds.), pp. 117–21. Lanham, MD: Rowman & Littlefield, 2022.

Chapter 4

7. Watkins, Joe. *Indigenous Archaeology: American Indian Values and Scientific Practice.* Walnut Creek, CA: AltaMira Press, 2000.
8. The National Park Service, https://www.nps.gov/subjects/nagpra/index.htm.
9. Haakanson, Sven. "Caretakers of Our Histories." In *Change is Required: Preparing for the Post-Pandemic Museum*, Avi Decter, Marsha Semmel, and Ken Yellis (eds.), pp. 111–15. Lanham, MD: Rowman & Littlefield, 2022.
10. Miller, Steven. *Museum Collection Ethics: Acquisition, Stewardship, and Interpretation.* Lanham, MD: Rowman & Littlefield, 2020.
11. Mauger, Jeffrey, and Janine Bowechop. "Tribal Collections Management at the Makah Cultural and Research Center." In *Living Homes for Cultural Expression: North American Native Perspectives on Creating Community Museums*, Karen Coody Cooper and Nicolasa Sandoval (eds.), pp. 57–64. Washington, DC: Smithsonian Institution, 2006. www.nmai.si.ed.
12. Vanderwarf, Sandra, and Bethany Romanowski. *Inventorying Cultural Heritage Collections: A Guide for Museums and Historical Societies.* Lanham, MD: Rowman & Littlefield, 2022.
13. Carrlee, "Caring for the Future."
14. King, Brad. "Understanding Collections." In *Museum Planning*, Barry Lord, Gail Dexter Lord, and Lindsay Martin (eds.), pp. 189–211. Lanham, MD: AltaMira Press, 2012. https://siarchives.si.edu.
15. Craddock, Ann Brooke. "Construction Materials for Storage and Exhibition Conservation Concerns." In *Conservation Concerns: A Guide for Collectors and Curators*, Konstanze Bachman (ed.), pp. 93–128. Washington, DC: Smithsonian Institution, 1992.
16. Community consultation is a fundamental step, for some books may be considered inaccurate by the cultures involved.
17. School for Advanced Research. *Privileging Community Voices.* Santa Fe, NM: SAR, 2021. https://guidelinesforcollaboration.

5

Exhibits with Life

The hopeful prospect of new ways to connect people, concepts, and objects through further integration expands the cultural context of exhibits. In an age where environmental crises or contagious diseases may limit physical visitation, ever-expanding twenty-first-century technologies present a myriad of opportunities. Contributing to solutions with widespread community involvement, representing different worldviews through storytelling and interpretation, brings exhibits to contemporary relevance.

How does cultural bias slip into interpretation? History is subject to several interpretations of events. Historically, the story tended to be told by the conqueror rather than by the conquered. One ethnic group may tell the story and fail to consult with other groups in the event. Or reliance on the written word stops short of being inclusive, biasing toward literate cultures and ignoring the richness of oral history.

Increased access tends to encourage storytelling involvement. In non-Western cultures, storytelling is often the means of interpreting the past in the present, and these stories continue into the future as a means of transmitting history and culture—or "storying our children." Objects are often not viewed as just a physical representation but rather as part of a symbolic or spiritual meaning in the culture.

Including these representations is culturally important for being "respectful" to the object. Generally, some aspects of spiritual meaning are considered as culturally private; therefore, cultural boundaries must be explored and respected. For example, in many Indigenous cultures, several aspects of ceremony are not to be shared outside of the culture and stories are only told in certain seasons.

PARTICIPATIVE PATHS

With the expansion of new options, the museum experience no longer begins upon physically entering a building. The physical space is but one site in a continuum of visitation options.[1] Virtual exhibits, augmented reality, websites, and mobile devices prepare the visitor before the on-site visit, providing a museum experience for those not able to make the trip. And the follow-up is yet another option to keep visitors interested.

This chapter is not intended to present the nuts and bolts of exhibit design but rather to encourage exploration into exhibits that are participative and encourage the incorporation of different presentation styles. Varying the style increases effectiveness for taking in comprehension for both individuals and diverse cultures. Several resources for detailed exhibit planning are in the "Further Reading" section at the end of this chapter.

Nina Simon, in *The Participatory Museum*, raised awareness of engaging the viewer in a discovery and learning process.[2] Exhibits planned in this way hold the potential to promote cultural understanding among and between groups. Additionally, excitement generated encourages repeat visitation and future engagement.

Museums that plan to support cultural continuance attract the general public. A community-centered museum shows not only history but also the learning programs in the present, plus an anticipated cultural future for the community.[3] This information need not be detailed with culturally private information but rather reflect the concept of tradition continuity. Changing exhibits showing student work and interactive exhibits are two features appreciated by the public. In turn, when the public becomes involved, then support for the museum is likely to follow.

Thoughtfully planned exhibits, deep with participative processes, support a community focus through the following aspects of well-being.

- Stimulating cultural learning
- Networking participants
- Furthering community participation and cohesion
- Bringing together community organizations for collaborative action
- Raising the self-esteem of children
- Stemming out-migration of youth who leave because of lack of historical connection and jobs

Designing exhibitions with participative processes, combined with efforts to make collection images more accessible to the community, adds life to exhibits. As access to collections leads to widened cultural context, interpretation forms the bridge from collections to exhibits. Multidimensional exhibits through community participation are exciting to the museum participant.

Inviting exhibits can be:[4]

- Multimodal (e.g. verbal descriptions, touch tours, and sensory experiences);
- Engaging of the different senses—sight, sound, and touch;

- Nonlinear, with visitors choosing their own path;
- Temporal experiences, linking different aspects of an important message or story over time;
- Three-dimensional, using objects and other three-dimensional components; and
- Context-engaging, for small video alcoves with seating provide an interpretive opportunity, as well as a chance for the visitor to rest.

Simon emphasizes multiuser exhibits[5] that feature personalized interactions. These may involve network content displayed back to the individuals participating. Such exhibits teach reciprocal relationships and can be valuable for teaching group cooperation as well as communicative skills. Some cultures are more modest in their expression. Information need not be detailed with culturally private information, but rather reflect the concept of cultural continuity. Inclusivity with depth is a process.

Newer concepts encouraging participation use modern technology to allow for flexibility, interactive exploration, and dynamic representations of culture. This emphasis allows for the adding or changing of material easily, encouraging repeat visitation. There is a difference between "drawing attention of" and "engaging" the museum visitor. In this new era, museums supporting cultural continuance are attractive to the general public—particularly featuring healthy foodways and environmental stewardship in this era of health and environmental crises. Awareness is now evolving quickly.

FROM VISITOR TO PARTICIPANT

Recognizing differences in learning styles is valuable for reaching the visitor on a deeper level, as a participant. Success for reaching deeply with a broad audience lies in innovating several new elements that link to the participant's prior ideas, feelings, and other value-based experience. Taking the time in planning to allow the interpretive process to flow leads to improving exhibit effectiveness.

Differences in learning styles vary culturally and with the individual. Incorporating diverse styles will engage the broadest range of museum visitors. Multimodal exhibits appeal to different learning styles. Both cultural understanding and cultural learning will be served well with this approach.

Ways of engaging learning styles in relation to a museum exhibit[6] varies:

- The cognitive style of learning is more educational or intellectual, focusing on information.
- The affective or emotional style of learning responds to being aligned, moved, or empowered to action.
- The experiential style focuses on the behavioral or physical aspects of presentation.

As emphasized by Polly McKenna-Cress and Janet Kamien in *Creating Exhibitions*,[7] visitors "make their own meaning," linking their prior experiences, ideas, and feelings to new information and materials. In other words, facts and questions are perceived differently among individuals and cultures.

PLANNING PROCESS

FROM VISITOR TO PARTICIPANT

- What are the differences in interests between local residents and tourists?
- What are the similarities in interests among local residents and tourists?
- Which key messages are desired to convey to each group and to both?
- How are background and context best presented?
- Are there activities encouraging participation that can be linked to the exhibit?
- How can a sense of discovery be fostered?

The traditional or rural community view of exhibit purpose may differ markedly from an urban or mainstream American museum. Rather than a focus on objects and interpretation of objects or history, a community-determined exhibit is likely to focus on cultural learning, meaning, and the relevance of objects to cultural continuity. This is the link from tangible to intangible culture.

Features for the successful transition from tangible to intangible culture[8] are characterized by the ability to draw in the viewer, use interpretive techniques, and have representation of different points of view. A thought-stimulating exhibit is experiential in this way. Inclusivity follows when encouraged by an exploratory approach and representation of different worldviews.

RETHINKING INTERPRETATION

Interpretation is the communication bridge from collections to exhibits. A glimpse into a worldview, exhibits give an introduction to the message through objects or visual representations. An experiential interpretation broadens the impact. Audiences retain only 20 percent of what they are told yet retain 80 percent of an experiential visit. Museum visitors become excited about the prospect of continuing their inquiry, and a broader sense of interpretation guides them to this point of satisfaction with the exhibit.

PLANNING PROCESS

BRIDGING HISTORIC MEANING AND CULTURAL CONTINUANCE

- How will cultural worldviews in your community be represented?
- Are there organizations for interpretive collaborations?

- Which collaborative styles exist now in your community?
- What are the intentions of the exhibit?
- How will exhibit themes connect past, present, and future in relation to interpretation?
- How does the exhibit connect to all other museum programs?
- How does interpretation promote an understanding of events according to multiple views?
- Which collection items or community intentions support cultural revitalization?
- How will cultural retention success be recognized and celebrated by the museum?
- How does the exhibit connect to resources in the community?

Interpretation imparts meaning to an object. Explaining objects from multiple perspectives to museum visitors may convey the significance of different worldviews. There is not just one view of history, as is often implied in an exhibit. But first, a discussion about objects is necessary to place interpretation in cross-cultural perspective.

Stereotyping is a basic concern of traditional groups and emerges as a caution for interpretation. Traditional people tend to see themselves in a range of different time periods, such as historical traditional, contemporary traditional, or modern. How people want to represent themselves is an important discussion—both internally and then communicated externally to the public—through museum guides, publications, websites, and other forms of media. One solution for avoiding the cultural stereotype is to present "re-slices of time" to show the change in traditions. The current culture is the cumulative result of all these time periods.[9]

REINTERPRETING HISTORY

History is culturally sensitive, for often more than one cultural group is involved in an event. Cultural bias in the written record is common, depending on the perspective of the person recording the event or telling the story. What hasn't been recorded in one account may be as important as the documented interpretation. Presenting multiple viewpoints not only enriches the narrative but also improves accuracy. These are important aspects of museum inclusivity.

Representing multiple worldviews is not always an easy task. The following techniques are useful.

- Utilizing several written sources to discover differences in interpretation of an event
- Using oral histories to complement the written record

- Tapping the advice of advisory board members representative of cultures and age groups
- Using different interpretations throughout the exhibit, with the differences in interpretation readily visible
- Planning adjacent exhibits, each telling one cultural perspective
- Implementing oral interpretation, using several audio cones to keep noise levels down

Some stories are awkward to tell yet are vitally important to optimal interpretation. Fear of offending frequently is a barrier to outreach. As we enter an era of demographic shifts, telling multiple perspectives will become increasingly important for inclusivity.

Specialized museums arise to tell a perspective not told in other mainstream museums. Sometimes these are needed, and other times the alternative interpretation might be integrated into the exhibit.

PLANNING PROCESS

IMPROVING INTERPRETATION

- Is the museum representative of all cultural groups in the community or region?
- How can multiple interpretations be communicated?
- Do exhibit messages convey hierarchical bias terms, such as "developing," "civilized," "progress," "primitive," or "myth"?
- In what ways does the museum's interpretation tend to justify colonization or conquest?
- From what point of view is the story told?
- Which messages illustrate a diverse interpretation of exhibit themes?

How to breathe life into your museum? Cultural expression, interpretation, and community connections make exhibits come alive. Balancing the needs for community participation and activities complementing exhibits while keeping building costs and maintenance low requires creative use of space.

Examples of steps for infusing life into an exhibit include the following.

- Ensuring representative community participation
- Determining the purpose of the exhibit, as connected to community
- Focusing the topic to be culturally relevant and useful in everyday life
- Creating the main message[10] to be inclusive of multiple cultural viewpoints
- Developing community-integrated themes
- Determining the best technology for communicating the message and themes, often multimodal

- Preparing content
- Advisory review of community-relevant and historically correct content

People wanting to be understood forms the basis for engaged interpretation. By presenting several interpretations of the same event, cross-cultural bridges are created. Participants begin to perceive that different worldviews coexist and cultural tolerance is expanded, overcoming ethnocentricity—or seeing from one point of view only. As a result, community collaborations are apt to increase.

Correcting misinterpretations or one-sided views of history through an exhibit is a common goal of decolonization. Avoiding the objectifying of a people lends empathy to interpretation, increasing the understanding of multiple points of view. As an example, Plimoth Plantation (Massachusetts) includes an interpretive exhibit with responses to a set of questions from both the Native American and colonist points of view, illustrating cultural contrasts and differing interpretations of history. Audio cones are used to give the visitor options for listening to each point of view.

The Historic Patuxet Homesite, a recreated seventeenth-century Native American village, offers an experiential visit, with the opportunity for the visitor to sit by a fire in a wigwam and listen to storytelling, in addition to viewing a canoe-making demonstration. (www.plimoth.org). Discovery comes from direct experience with voices and messages.

GIVING VOICE TO CULTURE

Local interpretation of history is a topic of appeal to visitors. A *written historical record* is often documented from the viewpoint of another culture. In traditional cultures, history is frequently passed down *orally*, rather than through written texts. New era stories include survival, hope, elder wisdom, plant knowledge, wild medicines, adaptation, cultural foods, family networks, and communities connecting. Respecting different points of view in telling stories brings cultural groups together.

Contemporary interest in ancient prophecies is vitally relevant to current planetary crises. The points of the story may be allegory, not a literal interpretation—often a misrepresentation leading to the label of a "myth." Assess the comfort level of the sharing participant. How the question is asked is apt to influence the response. For example, "Could you tell me about your tribal prophecies?" is not as likely to elicit a response as "Are there prophecies you could talk about that are appropriate to share?" or "Are there stories you can share with restricted access to the information?" Thinking through sensitive questions in terms of cultural appropriateness is part of the inclusive process.

An excellent expression of Indigenous methodology relevant to the dilemma of reducing global warming—while emphasizing the importance of solutions from within cultural frameworks—is presented by Bagele Chilisa, an African educator. "How do we capture and interpret a reality that takes into account our 'being' relations with the earth, the living, and the nonliving; and how can Indigenous knowledge shed light on this reality?"[11] is the pertinent question posed by Chilisa.

In Indigenous cultures, practices and procedures are communicated orally and stored in songs, dances, artistry, cultural taboos, and other traditions. The response to reviving culture lies in an interactive way of viewing the aliveness of the entire universe and the traditional ways of passing on the wisdom and teachings, such as ceremonies and talking circles.

Stories of cultures in conflict, whether contemporary or historical, are often delicate but possible to tell. Such stories intrigue visitors and lend authenticity to the visitation experience. In brief, almost any story can be told while keeping the following in mind.

- Decide a viewpoint or multiple viewpoints for telling significant stories through community participation.
- Avoid anger in telling the story by staying with the historical facts and describing the impacts on culture.
- Present more than one interpretation; two or three versions of a story tell different cultural perspectives. A unifying understanding between cultures may result.
- Balance the positive outcomes with the difficult impacts, showing the persistence of culture over time.
- Include information about traditional arts and foods to enhance the cultural experience and make the link to other community offerings.

Messages, exhibit content, learning programs, and even the design details of the building communicate culture. Discussions internal to the community determine information appropriate to share, as well as information intended for private, internal use within the community.

PLANNING PROCESS

DISCUSSING CULTURE

- How will past, present, and future of ongoing cultures be represented?
- How will important cultural values be communicated?
- How will the museum support messages the community wants to communicate?
- What are unique lifeways or customs that could be told?
- Which are still practiced today?
- How does our interpretation of history differ from published accounts?

- What are our important stories, appropriate to share, and how will we tell them?
- Are there seasonal or cultural restrictions to telling stories?
- How will we document stories or viewpoints as told by community members and use technology to share these?

One powerful example for addressing stereotypes is the National Museum of the American Indian's "Native Knowledge 360° Education Initiative," at https://americanindian.si.edu/nk360. Several Native lecturers explain stereotypes and strategies for correcting misperceptions. In the online program "Selecting Indigenous Images for Your Classroom," teachers examine why commonly used imagery and language about Native peoples are detrimental to student understanding of Native histories and cultures. As part of the webinars, teachers explore how to use several award-winning artists' NK360° imagery as well as their graphic novel and comic book art in the classroom.

STORY FROM WITHIN

Exhibits can be inexpensive yet powerful. For example, photographic exhibits with interpretive guides tell a moving and educational story from an internal point of view. Decisions concerning how to tell the several facets of a story connect to internal community and culture and communication. The effort is well worth the time for discussion and consensus on presentation. Community involvement is central for defining stories relating to a center's mission, as well as defining details to be kept culturally private. Good interpretation contributes to the uniqueness of the authentic experience offered by the community.

PLANNING PROCESS

TELLING A COMMUNITY STORY

- How does the style of telling the story reflect local worldviews?
- Are there seasonal restrictions for telling the story?
- Which story elements illustrate the exhibit theme?
- How does the story engage the listener?
- What is the potential for conveying community-relevant messages?
- What are the unique opportunities for interaction and response?

Reinterpretation of history is powerful when expressed from different cultural viewpoints. Cultural relevance is essential, for community and visitors like a story well-told.

PRESENTING CULTURAL FOODS EXAMPLE

Information on traditional cultural foods, those made from whole, fresh ingredients with a history tied to the region, is intriguing to museum visitors—both local and tourists. Taking visitors back to the time before processed and fast foods became mainstream is a treat to the imaginative palate. Culinary tourists travel to find interesting and flavorful foods, while cultural tourists like to taste the foods plus learn about the connection to culture. Making the link from exhibits on foods to serving foods is stimulating to visitors and can inspire a community return to a healthy, traditional whole foods diet.

Emphasizing the health benefits of traditional foods on placemats or tent cards on tables intrigues the visitor to eat locally. For example, chili in the Southwest United States or in Central and South America is rich in vitamin C and reduces inflammation. Salmon, a traditional food in the Northwest United States, and other seafoods are high in beneficial omega-3 fatty acids. Visitor education can either be continued in a museum's restaurant or through collaboration with local restaurants. See chapter 7 for more connections leading to employment, such as a museum café.

PLANNING PROCESS

EMPHASIZING TRADITIONAL OR LOCAL FOODS

Interesting stories told around the following topics draw visitors:

- How are foods grown?
- Are there special historical aspects to the foods?
- Which heirloom or ancient varieties are being grown?
- What are the nutritional and health benefits of these foods?
- Are there current efforts locally to preserve seeds and growing practices?
- How are different traditional varieties used to adapt to shifting climate conditions?
- Are these foods being grown in the community?
- How are they harvested, stored, and cooked?

Ties to local ecosystems, ways in which traditional food varieties are being revived, and the need for protecting traditional varieties are of particular interest to those visitors seeking alternatives in the face of climate change—when this information is considered appropriate to share.

EXAMPLE: THE IROQUOIS LEGEND OF THE THREE SISTERS

A story told in different ways facilitates an understanding of different world-views, in addition to content. The museum participant "experiences," particularly if songs and stories accompany, rather than only written information. Traditional version:

The term "Three Sisters" emerged from the Iroquois creation story. It was said that the earth began when "Sky Woman" who lived in the upper world peered through a hole in the sky and fell through to an endless sea. The animals saw her coming, so they took the soil from the bottom of the sea and spread it onto the back of a giant turtle to provide a safe place for her to land. This "Turtle Island" is now what we call North America.

Sky woman had become pregnant before she fell. When she landed, she gave birth to a daughter. When the daughter grew into a young woman, she also became pregnant (by the West wind). She died while giving birth to twin boys. Sky Woman buried her daughter in the "new earth." From her grave grew three sacred plants—corn, beans, and squash. These plants provided food for her sons and, later, for all of humanity. These special gifts ensured the survival of the Iroquois people.

Contemporary Interpretation:

In traditional wisdom, inter-planting the three sisters—corn, beans, and squash—is a sustainable system providing long-term soil fertility and a healthy diet, for the plants complement each other nutritionally. Stories and planting rituals surround the three sisters, foods planted together, eaten together, and celebrated as the basic foods of sustenance. The corn plant becomes a natural pole for bean vines to climb, while the bean vine stabilizes the corn plants from the wind. Beans provide nitrogen in their roots to the soil, utilized by the other plants. Squash leaves, spreading along the ground, block sunlight, thus helping to prevent the emerging weeds and become a living mulch, retaining moisture in the soil. Spiny squash plants help protect the corn and beans from predators.

The three sisters, eaten together, provide complementary protein, since corn lacks both lysine and tryptophan, with amino acids contained in the beans. Stews made with beans, squash, and corn provide healthy sustenance for people, while maintaining the health of the earth.

Presenting both traditional and contemporary interpretation is an interesting way to frame interpretation. In reference to this story, it is important to note that the concept of the three sisters is widespread throughout the Indigenous people of North and Central Americas, with several interpretations of the story.

If appropriate, give a recipe to exhibit visitors. Travelers interested in other cultures tend to be intrigued with food tasting, a creative link to the museum café. Visitor surveys conducted in traditional communities generally show a strong visitor interest in traditional and healthy foods. Fried foods are difficult for many travelers to digest; therefore, your menu should have variety. If traditional foods are spicy, serve the spiced sauce on the side.

Interest by visitors sometimes sparks community interest in eating more of the traditional, healthier foods. Community benefits of bringing back food traditions, away from fast foods, are heightened when prices are kept reasonable and local residents eat at culturally themed restaurants. The link between tourism and museum fosters the market, developing a resource for the community.

STORYTELLING AND CULTURAL CONTINUITY

Storytelling is an experiential method of interpretation, the way of teaching in a broad range of cultures, and is an art declining in practice. Much of Indigenous cultural knowledge is nature-based, transmitted through stories about animals and plants, as well as their relationships to humans and the environment—all reflected in the cultural arts. We are all related, sharing Mother Earth, interconnected by bonds in the intricate web of life—species to species. One depends upon the other, and in the Earth-focused view, these complexities are reflected in everyday life. Restoring healthy and balanced relationships in our ecosystem is vitally important to the future of our species. Museums and cultural centers are uniquely able to communicate the cultural aspects of these connections.

Inclusive storytelling addresses cultural experiences from another time period.[12] Feedback from the community is the essential ingredient for achieving this intention. An example is the recently opened Museum of the Southern Jewish Experience in New Orleans, with the mission of encouraging new understanding and appreciation, diversity, and acceptance.[13] Choosing to present "experience" over "history," the emphasis on themes rather than chronology encourages visitors to see interconnections across eras while exposing trauma and intolerance.

Stories of cultural history and revitalization set the context for visitation in many communities. In relation to Hispanic cultures, illustrating with *dichos*, or the wise sayings, reinforces use of these daily reminders. Likewise, *cuentos*, or stories that teach us how to live, enrich an exhibit with centuries-old tradition.

As a traditional way of passing down an interpretation of history, storytelling is possible through audio clips on a virtual museum, if this is acceptable to the community. Merging traditional sources of learning with digital sources enhances youth participation in cultural activities, as well as language learning. Traditional youth may not fully understand the accounts of history from different viewpoints, and such a resource is valuable to realizing local cultural identity. In contemporary traditional cultures with Internet access, this is an additional way of recovering the kinship worldview.

Learning how to be the human animal in our own ecosystems can be a central message of a storytelling program. This sustainable view is vitally important to communicate to the public for the twenty-first century. A storytelling project is an opportunity to educate the public on cultural arts, upcoming community activities such as art shows, and to make referral links from museum visitor to artists for culturally sustainable employment.

EXAMPLE STORYLINE

The following example illustrates relationships in an ecosystem. A concise message is described in one sentence.

Exhibit Title: Indigenous Lifestyles
Main Message: We are still here.
Goals of the exhibit are:

1. To teach visitors about the difficult, yet rich history of the region;
2. To further understanding of cultural values;
3. To communicate cultural differences in worldview, between Indigenous peoples and the American mainstream;
4. To educate the public about the Indigenous language;
5. To communicate contemporary cultural goals; and
6. To foster cultural pride and encourage youth to learn the culture and language.

DETAILED MESSAGES

We are but one species connected to dozens of others in our ecosystems. Full attention is needed to keep from driving those species away or, even more importantly, to drive them into extinction for lack of habitat. We must collaborate and work together to preserve natural ecosystems. We live in harmony, kinship, and respect in our habitat, learning from animals and retaining the knowledge for what it takes to live—by teaching the importance of observations in our ecosystem. We form a network where we cooperate together. Green and environmental concerns are a priority for maintaining this knowledge.

The exhibit example in Figure 5.1 includes historical context, present-day activities, and intentions for the future. Exhibit themes for this exhibit preplanning include the following: history; traditional lifestyles (life by the seasons, dwellings, subsistence activities, leadership structure); cultural arts; language; stories; foodways (growing, tending, hunting, eating); contemporary services and enterprises; and we are still here—our culture is thriving.

One way of connecting interpretation to the local ecosystem is to feature animal stories, including totems and the skills learned from observing these animals. Teaching through storytelling is an important way of multigenerational learning in many cultures. "Storying our children" in Indigenous cultures refers

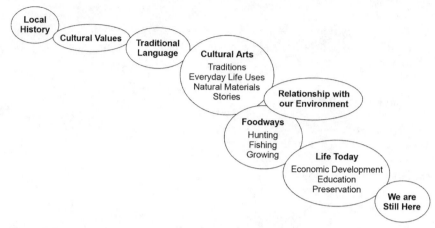

Figure 5.1. Indigenous Lifestyles, Preliminary Storyline

to the prevalent means of teaching values, traditions, and bonds to plants and animals in the environment. Examples from a nature-based culture may be highlighted in the storytelling program, such as:

- Cleverness of the fox
- Strength of the bear
- Quickness of the deer
- Accuracy of the hawk
- Bravery of the eagle

Filming storytelling events and making these available in the museum's video kiosk area is another aspect of a project important to visitor education as well as to community members. As an archival project, taping traditional storytelling can make stories available for school children and as well as adults into the future, for cultural teaching purposes.

The following example illustrates active ways to communicate a cyclical worldview.

- Seasonal times for telling stories are important to observe.
- Storytelling connects to other aspects of culture—there should be a stage area with props.
- The best setting in a children's area could be a circular area where the children can sit, reflecting cultural symbolism of connections in the story.
- Culturally related items such as a canoe in the children's area could be a place to sit and listen to stories.
- Cultural connection is key.

Storytelling tailored to animal stories or history for youth may develop into a more detailed level of history for adults. Adding a storytelling component to local celebrations may be an added draw to raise funds for the museum's operations and local storytellers, while raising environmental awareness with large numbers of people as well.

The storytelling program may also become a means of recording oral history, or time-honored traditions important for teaching in future years. While a high-resolution video is preferable, video-recording software such as Zoom or smart phone recordings may be an option. If this technology is not available to the community, consider audio. Documenting now is an opportunity to further serve the long-term, as well as to broaden sources of funding. Starting now is the point, for oral history is a vitally important means for recording and preserving traditions. The following guidelines are suggested.

- Use fluctuating lighting (LED) and control heat for comfort. (Careful, some types of lighting such as fluorescent may cause a headache.)
- A restroom nearby is important for senior/elder access.
- When recording long distance, use a telephone with an on/off switch or silence incoming calls to reduce interruptions.
- For visual assistance, use a wall with enough surface for a local reference map.
- Using a small electronic recorder is a nonintrusive way to document.
- Consider digital recording and extracting audio; this will allow more options for exhibit, education, and website integration when appropriate.
- Use lapel microphones, which will give good sound quality while being nonintrusive or intimidating; room microphones produce poorer quality sound and are harder to control.
- Use a separate room for recording/editing equipment, and use a room as buffer to the recording area to minimize interruptions.
- Use comfortable chairs for elders and refreshments—such as frequent snacks and tea.
- Soundproofing for the room and good acoustics for recording are very important—no noisy vents. This might be developed for a future facility.
- Spaces are needed for storage of items—cabinets that lock, with a glass front to show fragile items to seniors as prompts.

In summary, storytelling is a vital tool for interpretive programs, particularly when diverse local cultures are represented. Youth are encouraged to learn local or traditional stories when direct interaction is possible. Consider the storytelling program as a possible way to use multiple sources of funding (e.g. documentation, teaching the cultural arts, or youth programs). Youth interviews with seniors engage the continuing generation in learning traditions.

Posting recordings in the personal narrative, using video kiosks or videos in the museum building or on websites, stimulates in an experiential way.

SMALL SPACE EXHIBITS

Small spaces hold significant potential for setting a message apart. The amount of information or experience-creating can be enhanced with the use of modern technology. Use of multimodal technologies is an exceptional way to incorporate use of the difference senses in a small space. The electronic screen affords options with different levels of complexity. At a basic level, one narrative or story can be heard from the pressing of a button. At a second level, several buttons offer choice in which topic or interpretation of a topic the participant chooses. At a yet more complex level, interactive programming engages the visitor as a participant in sequential learning. A similar concept with online exhibits is achievable with branching.

Advantages of the electronic-screen kiosk include: 1) the ability to communicate an in-depth message with additional content; 2) changing the exhibit without expensive approaches requiring construction and a high level of exhibit development expertise; 3) incentive to complete documentation projects with multiple community uses; and 4) ability to use images of collection items in other museums, thus reducing need for an expansive collection.

The two examples that follow effectively united communities through both low-tech and high-tech approaches. Example 1 is appropriate for a small community museum starting with limited resources. Example 2 requires a higher budget and degree of technological expertise.

EXAMPLE 1: LOW-TECH GENEALOGY AT THE POEH CULTURAL CENTER AND MUSEUM

A basic yet extremely effective exhibit idea furthering the local goal of understanding community relatedness occurred in the initial stages of the Poeh Cultural Center and Museum at the Pueblo of Pojoaque, during the development period of the 1990s. This small tribal community consisted of five families in the re-settlement period during the 1920s.

The Pojoaque Pueblo Genealogy Exhibit involved taping a stream of paper to the museum wall and providing pencils to participants. The surnames of the original families were posted at the top of the sheet, allowing space for the descendants to fill in the names of their relatives. Interaction between participants stimulated community pride, sharing, and cohesiveness as relationships between people were discovered. At the ending period of the exhibit, funding enabled the printing of a book on the community genealogy. The basic strategy of this exhibit demonstrates the power of personal interaction and the effectiveness of low tech.

EXAMPLE 2: HIGH-TECH GENEALOGY AT THE TULALIP MUSEUM

The Hibulb Cultural Center at the Tulalip Reservation in Marysville, Washington, utilizes technology and few collection items. The richness of local stories is told mainly with electronic-screen kiosks, the foundation of exhibit development. These document historic events, traditions, and cultural stories, as well as current issues and events.

In one alcove of the museum, a private genealogy electronic exhibit is available to tribal members, with the use of a password. Genealogy and other private uses are made available to youth for learning the interconnectedness of the community. In this electronically based way, both public and private uses of the one-room museum space are used to the fullest—allowing for changing narratives by uploading new content.

An evolving exhibit, with the topic changing in complexity and content, is one way of presenting an ongoing story through time. An example is the genealogy exhibit, with the community actively engaged in developing the exhibit, learning about the families and the connections between families.

CHANGING OR TEMPORARY EXHIBITS

Central to the concept of a community-centered museum are the connections to cultures and continuity. Sometimes referred to as a temporary exhibit, the changing exhibit space can feature topics sequentially. A rotation of low-cost exhibits may connect with resonance to community.

Changing exhibits hold the potential for dynamic interaction with community priorities, reflecting community connections. For example, a community-centered museum sponsoring cultural art classes has the potential to tell an exciting story around cultural revitalization efforts. Reflecting community efforts to address contemporary issues through the collection is one way of creating an experiential visit.

One example of the changing format is to exhibit children's work. This inclusion raises cultural pride and self-esteem, giving incentive to learn language, cultural arts, oral traditions, and local interpretation through storytelling. Cultural transmission modalities are retained while visitors are fascinated. Exhibits showing adult or children's student work and interactive exhibits are a feature appreciated by the public. In turn, when the public becomes involved, then local support for the museum is likely to follow.

Posting interpretive videos on Internet sites with links on the museum website provides the thread for a continued interpretive narrative through time. Blogs with visitor comments not only lend additional participant information to the interpretation but also give the museum feedback as to whether messages were adequately communicated. Consider feedback as part of the planning process for future changing exhibits.

New levels of public interest in preserving ecosystems and slowing climate change are of keen interest to the public in this era. Through appealing to those visitors seeking solutions, museums can foster respect for natural material culture and information on ways of healing through a lower ecological-imprint lifestyle. Exhibits showing interrelatedness and ways of connecting will contribute to the sought-after, new means of addressing issues in the twenty-first century.

VIRTUAL MUSEUM APPLICATIONS

Presenting a virtual interpretive museum concept in the museum as an exhibit complement, or on the Internet, is an opportune avenue for furthering cultural understanding, interpreting historical events, and explaining the cultural arts—particularly in times of reduced travel. The virtual museum on a website may be a starting place in the sequential development of a museum or cultural center and may serve the community well on its own.

To be community-focused, the first intent of a virtual museum is the creation of a cultural information base for the community. Positive benefits of a virtual cultural center include the following: increasing cultural pride within the community, making information readily available, enhancing the traditional economy, and stimulating language learning. Including history, historic photos, and photographs of those collection items curated in other museums widens the impact. Travelling exhibits are another resource for presenting content and worldview. This direction is supportive for improving traditional community members' access to their own cultural resources for learning purposes.

As Lois Carlisle points out in "Museums in Your Pocket: Digital Storytelling Strategies in Cultural Institutions,"[14] museums hold a unique opportunity to create trusted digital spaces, particularly when tapping into the power of first-person storytelling. Inspiring empathy by presentation positions the museum as a source of accessible, invaluable knowledge.

There are ample advantages of thinking in the virtual direction. Restrictions on visitation during times of communicable diseases or natural disasters illustrate the importance of moving on this path. Visitor education through a virtual museum minimizes environmental and privacy impacts of widespread visitation—instructing the visitor on history, arts, events, and visitation protocols before the physical visit. This increases respect for community and culture in advance of the visit.

Virtual museums are an economical way to provide both visitor education and interactive activities. Rural locations can utilize the virtual museum as a means of creating a tourism draw. Although common for a community to consider developing a museum or cultural center with a building, costs of maintaining and staffing a center may be prohibitive. For this reason, the first phase of a cultural center may be a virtual information center, serving multiple purposes.

When building space is limited, one technique for involving the public is the virtual exhibit. Use the same planning process to include themes, messages, and interpretation combined with photos of collection items—yours or from another museum. Condensing the story to between ten and thirty minutes further expands the audience. Uploading the exhibit on YouTube or a similar site, with a link on the museum website, is easiest to manage.

Effective visitor education orients pre-visit tourists coming to communities for a culturally-based vacation. A virtual museum site is useful for 1) visitor education at the pre-visit stage, 2) on-site visitor education with access at museums or cultural centers, 3) virtual exhibits, 4) use at visitor centers and locations of tourism partners—both on websites and physical locations, 5) an exit survey to assess visitor comprehension, and 6) collecting suggestions for improvement. The virtual cultural center or museum exhibit or interpretive narrative provides an orientation to visitors that understaffed centers do not have the capacity to fulfill.

Virtual exhibit tours build a storytelling presence on the Internet. Bringing a museum into the digital world can be accomplished at a basic level or the complex. For small museums, starting with photos and interpretation requires few resources. A tribal virtual museum website example, the House of Seven Generations at the Jamestown S'Klallam site, features history, photographs, and artifacts (see www.tribalmuseum.jamestowntribe.org).

TimeLooper, a digital tour assistance organization, recommends a stepped approach[15] for the basic virtual tour.

1. Create a 360-degree panorama of the setting (e.g., an exhibit room or an historic site) by merging a photo series.
2. Add photos of objects, people, or historic sites, layered on the physical setting, to highlight interpretive points.
3. Add the audio narrative, enlarging the photos as the speaker explains, enhances interpretation.

A more advanced approach starts with a video for a walk through. The following uses are representative.

- Recreation of an event, historical or contemporary
- Designing a narrative from existing interpretive guides
- Creating a sense of adventure through an enticing narrative
- Creating a floor plan to guide visitors on a walk through

A third level possible is interactive. With specialized programming, visitors can branch into more detail or physical locations for a topic, based upon choices. Designing this type of tour would require a consultant who specializes in interactive programming.

Exhibits with Life

If the content reaches across cultures and communicates to a range of ages, stories of cultural history and revitalization set the context for visitation. Storytelling, a traditional way of passing down an interpretation of history, is possible through audio clips on a virtual museum application. Apps are commonly created for virtual tours or for museum programs. Since mobile phones are now the most common type of technology available, a virtual tour is accessible to potentially millions of virtual participants—using social media as a draw.

Merging traditional sources of learning with digital sources enhances youth participation in cultural activities, as well as language learning. Traditional youth may not fully understand the accounts of history from different viewpoints, and such a resource is valuable to realizing local cultural identity. In contemporary traditional cultures with Internet access, this is an additional way of supporting cultural retention.

Not all traditional cultures approve of storytelling on the Internet. This may have limited applicability, both in content and depth of the story. A short message may be allowed, rather than the entire story. Also, culturally private information can be protected with a password.

Cultural artists are encouraged to engage in cultural art-making when authenticity is widely understood through digital cultural exhibits and video interviews with artists. When community members practice and earn a living through the cultural arts, they may not leave rural or tribal lands as young adults but instead stay to earn a living and teach other community members. This factor is basic to cultural continuance.

Additionally, researchers and scholars gain ready access to materials difficult to locate by other means. Travel expenses are reduced, as well as repeated permission needed for access. Collections at urban locations are frequently without interpretation from the culture of origin. By including photographs and interpretive statements from cultural artists, cultural history and material culture become better understood.

Assessing materials readily available for a virtual cultural museum is a foundational step. Community input into preliminary planning holds the potential to indicate the messages to convey. In summary, recommendations[16] for topics to be addressed on a virtual museum website may include the following.

• Traditional welcoming
• Traditional history
• Interpretive podcasts
• Storytelling videos, if appropriate
• Photographic collections
• Artifact and cultural collections
• Documentation and interpretation for collections
• Virtual exhibits

- Event listings
- Video interviews with artists
- Local efforts to further cultural knowledge retention
- Directory of artists
- Connections between regional communities and offerings
- Membership information
- E-newsletter (with member password)
- Donor names (to honor)
- Links to other websites, organizations, and other museums with culturally related collections

Cross links to the websites of other museums and organizations interest potential visitors to explore for greater participation while expanding cultural understanding.

INTERACTIVE EXHIBITS

Interactive exhibits encourage learning through involvement. Multimodal presentations using recordings or live music as a complement to labels bring the exhibit to life. People-focused exhibit design brings learning experiences to a range of local audiences, fostering a sense of discovery.

Augmented reality is quickly becoming a path for expanding museum interpretation. Phone apps allow for content detail, personal stories, and additional illustration with collection items. Placing video kiosks in the museum facilitates visitor access to a broad range of interpretive topics, enhancing cultural understanding tools at on-site locations. Storytelling should be continuously explored with the community to determine which stories are appropriate to share and which should be kept private. This may have limited applicability, both in content and depth of the story. A short message may be allowed rather than the entire story.

One of the most effective ways of initiating interaction is through a multimedia tour[17] consisting of designing a guide to a museum's permanent exhibit, collection, temporary exhibits, and interpretive program. Storytelling as interpretation holds the potential to combine a variety of media, to include audio, text, photographic images, videos, and interactive programs.

Once limited to handheld devices, technological options now include cell phones and tablets, with apps as a format for downloadable tours. Images and audio combine to enhance the visitor's learning process by utilizing several different types of sensory information at the same time. Both virtual reality technology and nature experience may be the popular upcoming trends. Consider the storytelling potential as a fundable project, both for archival and teaching functions.

Interactive maps on a mobile device (e.g., mobile phone or tablet) can highlight objects and convey content automatically, based on location. Mobile phones allow visitors to bookmark and record ideas by sending text messages to themselves or recording memos. The affordable option of virtual tours is particularly useful for the small museum. As new technologies evolve, exciting options for technology-assisted or augmented reality interpretation will increase. Sharon Vatsky points out in *Interactive Museum Tours*[18] the value of multimodal activities such as writing activities, virtual teaching on Zoom, collaborative poetry, drawing activities, multisensory aids (sound, touch, movement), and interesting touch objects generate engagement and discovery.

Appealing to the interests and learning modalities of youth will be an ongoing challenge. Interpretive programs developed by museums hold potential for distance learning in the classroom. This new direction will be particularly valuable in times of restricted travel and visitation.

MOVING TOWARD THE SHIFT

The community-centered museum tends to depart from the past emphasis on permanent exhibits, dioramas, and objects on display. Less emphasis on physical spaces in a new era of social distancing and health concerns indicates new applications for interactive virtual museum applications, augmented reality (AR), and social media for interpretation. An understanding of potential audience demographics and interests takes into account inclusive variables—age range, gender, ethnic identification, income level, household size, and educational level—helpful for designing museum programs.

Keeping current with changing visitor interests is also central for improving relevance. While a characteristic of baby boomers is a focus on material culture, millennials and Gen X are interested less in things. They are seeking experiences plus information to stay healthy. Subsequent generations will express new interest; therefore, a periodic review of museum and tourism studies plus conducting your own survey will form the foundation of an updated museum strategy.

In summary, storytelling is an experiential way to represent multiple viewpoints. To draw on the storytelling expertise of multiple cultures, using contrast when different interpretations of history exist, is useful. Adaptable to augmented reality approaches, storytelling enriches breadth of the museum experience. Consider the vitality of messages conveyed: exhibits may well become the catalyst for community-wide benefits. Creating an arts and culture district (chapter 8) is one way of fostering authenticity, connecting, and generating community integration.

FURTHER READING

Hansen, Beth. *Great Exhibits! An Exhibit Planning and Construction Handbook for Small Museums*. Lanham, MD: Rowman & Littlefield, 2017.

The nuts and bolts of exhibit planning and installation is covered in this basic text for the museum on a small budget. Practical assistance through worksheets, photos, drawings, and instructions are suitable for both staff and volunteers. Topics covered include the following: Who will create the exhibition? What will the exhibit be about? What will be the content? How will interpretation be carried out? Which construction and hanging systems will we use, to include interactive and hands-on? How will we evaluate success?

Langer, Adina, ed. *Storytelling in Museums*. Lanham, MD: Rowman & Littlefield, 2022.

Contributors across the museum field and worldwide explore the efficacy and ethics of museum storytelling. The book shows how museums use personal, local, and specific stories to make visitors feel welcome while inspiring them to engage with new ideas and unfamiliar situations. Pandemic examples are included.

Piacente, Maria. *Manual of Museum Exhibitions*. Lanham, MD: Rowman & Littlefield, 2022.

As museums move from a transmission to a visitor-centered model, exhibitions are more experience driven, participatory, and interactive—built around multiple perspectives and powerful storytelling. The exhibition development process is more complex than ever as audiences demand more dynamic, diverse, and inclusive experiences. This edition includes expanded chapters on evaluation, virtual exhibitions, multimedia, travelling exhibitions, curiosity and motivation, and diversity, equity, accessibility and inclusion (DEAI)—while retaining the essential content related to interpretive planning, roles and responsibility, and content development.

Slack, Steve. *Interpreting Heritage: A Guide to Planning and Practice*. New York: Routledge, 2021.

This practical guide to planning and interpretation presents a question-based interpretive framework, giving examples for inspiration. Interpretation planning, interpretive outcomes, the interpretive catalogue, managing interpretation, and evaluating interpretation are key topics covered.

Vatsky, Sharon. *Interactive Museum Tours: A Guide to In-Person and Virtual Experiences*. Lanham, MD: Rowman & Littlefield, 2023.

The author covers the entire tour experience including planning, facilitation, and reflection. By providing a flexible tour-planning template, this book articulates strategies that encourage participants to think together and think deeply. Museum educators share how they adjust the tour-planning template to accommodate the attributes and strengths of visitors to include family learning, school tours, virtual tours, promote social and emotional learning, and work effectively with students with autism, adults with low vision and blindness, and adults with Alzheimer's disease and other dementias.

Vermeeren, Arnold, Licia Calvi, and Amalia Sabiescu. *Museum Experience Design: Crowds, Ecosystems and Novel Technologies*. Switzerland: Springer International Publishing, 2018.

This book explores how museums are developing dialogical relationships with their audiences, reaching out beyond their local communities to involve more diverse and broader audiences. With these applications, crowds reach beyond passive audiences, to become active users, co-designers and co-creators. The potential for a museum, particularly the small museum, to become part of a connected museum system, increases the reach of the interpretive story.

NOTES

1. Sanis, Peter. "The Exploded Museum." In *Digital Technologies and the Museum Experience*, Kevin Walker and Loïc Tallon (eds.), pp. 3–18. New York: AltaMira Press, 2008.
2. Simon, Nina. *The Participatory Museum*. Santa Cruz, CA: Museum 2.0, 2010.
3. This statement is applicable only in communities where anticipating the future is appropriate.
4. Dillenburg, Eugene and Janice Klein. Creating Exhibits. *Small Museum Toolkit*, edited by Cinnamon Catlin-Legutko and Stacy Klingler, Vol. 5. Lanham, MD: Rowman & Littlefield, 2012, pp. 71–99.
5. Simon, *The Participatory Museum*.
6. McKenna-Cress, Polly, and Janet A. Kamien. *Creating Exhibitions: Collaboration in the Planning, Development, and Design of Innovative Experiences*. Hoboken, NJ: John Wiley & Sons, Inc., 2013.
7. Ibid.
8. Tilden, Freeman. *Interpreting our Heritage*. Chapel Hill, NC: The University of North Carolina Press, 2008.
9. Personal communication with David M. White, 2004.
10. Dillenburg, Eugene, and Janice Klein. "Creating Exhibits: From Planning to Building." In *Small Museum Toolkit*, Cinnamon Catlin-Legutko and Stacy Klingler (eds.), Vol. 5, pp. 71–99. Lanham, MD: Rowman & Littlefield, 2013.
11. Chilisa, Bagele. *Indigenous Research Methodologies*. Thousand Oaks, CA: Sage Publications, 2019.
12. Grohe, Michelle. "Transformative Inclusion in Exhibition Planning." In *Storytelling in Museums*, Adina Langer (ed.), pp. 217–34. Lanham, MD: Rowman & Littlefield, 2023.

13. Tucker, Aura. "Building A New Museum on the Personal Stories Paradigm." In *Storytelling in Museums*, Adina Langer (ed.), pp. 33-52. Lanham, MD: Rowman & Littlefield, 2023.
14. Carlisle, Lois. "Museums in Your Pocket: Digital Storytelling Strategies in Cultural Institutions." In *Storytelling in Museums*, Adina Langer (ed.), pp. 119-32. Lanham, MD: Rowman & Littlefield, 2023.
15. TimeLooper. "Starting Up Virtual Tours Quickly." www.timelooper.com.
16. Knell, Simon J., Suzanne MacLeod, and Sheila Watson, editors. *Museum Revolutions: How museums change and are changed.* New York: Routledge, 2007.
17. Fantani, Fillipinx, and Jonathan Bowen. "Mobile Multi-Media: Reflections from Ten Years of Practice." In *Digital Technologies and the Museum Experience*, Loïc Tallon and Kevin Walker (eds), pp. 79-96. Lanham, MD: AltaMira Press, 2008.
18. Vatsky, Sharon. *Interactive Museum Tours: A Guide to In-Person and Virtual Experiences.* Lanham, MD: Rowman & Littlefield, 2023.

6

Inclusive Learning Programs

As homes for cultural expression, community-integrated museums expand their supportive role beyond the conventional definition of a museum education program. Seen through an expanded cultural lens, learning programs address community-focused teaching as well as museum capacity-building topics. The good news, given the recent diversification of online platforms for sharing history and traditional knowledge, is that participation potential is increasing rapidly.

What is a museum's ethical role in the past-present-future continuum? Inclusion is about creating a different future, one based on deep service and shared leadership.[1] Access to collections becomes pivotal in considering a museum location for classes. When local resources are being used for museum support, this question becomes even more relevant. Decolonizing involves integrating local values as an essential step for addressing specific aspects of collection, expression, interpretation, and outreach. That is, the community bond is increased when cultural access and relevance evolve in tandem.

Learning programs for cultural entrepreneurs foster participation in creating a locally authentic museum store inventory. Inclusivity is enhanced, and the museum store tends to benefit with interpretive tools, as described in later chapters. In-reach from the community to a museum supports cultural relevance while boosting the local economy.

Incorporating cultural considerations from a broad range of ethnic groups in the community is central to decolonization. Keepers of the traditions, often the instructors in learning programs, are also the treasured link to interpretation.[2] There are several options to explore with a range of cultures, as well as programs internal and external to the community. Educational programs extending into the local public with symbolism and earth connections enable the museum to keep up with changing contemporary interests. Earlier chapters address the significance of a museum's potential for preserving parts of the cumulative global knowledge of how to live in a caring balance on Mother Earth. Truly, a nature-based cultural future is at stake.

Architectural design of the museum or cultural center is foundational to the building's capacity for housing learning programs.[3] For example, a carpeted conference room is not conducive to teaching pottery, whereas a cement floor with drains and a water source are essential. Teaching carving requires a floor easy to clean and a wood storage area, preferably outside. Or a circular seated area may be traditional for storytelling. For this reason, a museum planning process tailored to local needs meshes with architectural design. Another option is an energy efficient addition to the museum, or a retrofit of the building.

Potential projects at a museum or cultural center cover a broad range of community-connection possibilities to include:

- Lectures and demonstrations;
- Workshops and activities complementing exhibit themes;
- Online programs such as lectures and courses;
- Strengthening the museum store inventory to include locally sourced and online options;
- Easier access for school groups;
- In-depth classes, or a series of classes to teach a skill; and
- Staff training in museum-related skills.

Learning programs for artists and cultural entrepreneurs at the museum or cultural center are an effective way to encourage cultural retention. When cultural entrepreneurs are able to earn a livelihood through their arts, cultural practice and the transfer of knowledge to the next generations is "jump-started." Revitalizing an art is a topic to explore in the planning process, when generations are skipped in the learning process. Art integration inspires creativity as well, an essential for flexibility during this era. The potential for a uniquely local museum store concept is high when locally sourced entrepreneurial services and products are tapped.

In times of pandemics or environmental crises, online programs increase new-era options. Creating a portal with a password on the museum's website is a good technique for restricting views of culturally private information. When learning programs are designed to reflect cultural learning styles represented in the community, overall participation in museum programs is likely to increase—an important benefit.

THE COLLECTIONS ACCESS LINK

To review, collections represent a tremendous resource for studying symbolic designs, historic techniques, materials, and contemporary trends. Making collections visible is central to the learning connection. The range of options for policy, regarding collections in the study context, represents a broad opportunity. In certain museums, some items may be handled in a teaching setting—with training and gloves—according to set museum policies.

Some items may be too fragile and are best viewed from a distance. Storage designed with visible areas created through glass and shelving are another option for making collection objects available to learners. Photographs of collection items are an alternative means of making objects available to artists and entrepreneurs, with contemporary 3D-scanning technology facilitating a multidimensional view for study.

A computer dedicated to a study area at the museum expands the potential learning value of the collection while protecting objects from the potential impacts of handling. Online images posted on the museum website are another means of making the collection accessible for learning purposes.

When local priorities determined during the museum planning process are derived from an open exploration of museum functions, the potential for continued involvement expands. Consider the broader benefits—teachers and students often represent pools of cultural wisdom for interpretation. The following process is useful for answering central questions.

PLANNING PROCESS

INCLUSIVITY AND LEARNING PROGRAMS

- How will local history be told inclusive of different perspectives?
- Who will be involved?
- What are traditional styles of learning in the community (e.g., oral history, written, participatory)?
- Are there cultural arts community members want to learn?
- Does the community have teachers with matching skills who are willing to participate?
- Are there limits to the sharing of information in local cultures (i.e., restricted to specific groups or individuals)?
- How will families become involved, furthering intergenerational learning?
- Which groups or organizations are potential partners?
- Which methods will be used for community member involvement?
- How can museum activities tell an important story and serve pressing local needs as well?
- Does the museum provide entrepreneurial opportunities for instructors and students, inspiring learning?

Facilitating the museum's capacity as a gathering place expands connection to the interests of local groups. By serving as an interface between museum programs and other community-focused activities—such as language teaching, youth programs, tourism participation, and local events—the museum furthers resources and gains access to programmatic funding through grants or donor support. Donors and museum members are often inspired when a broad definition of museum services includes cultural continuance programs.

CULTURE, ARTS, AND WORLDVIEW

Traditional cultural art continuity is closely intertwined with cultural vitality. Culture, language, and the arts are meaningful approaches for addressing multiple concerns—such as community-building, land stewardship, tradition-based means of earned livelihood, youth involvement, and intergenerational interaction. Decolonization effectiveness depends upon broadening an understanding of different worldviews and respecting contributions to the richness of the global pool of knowledge.

Patience, respecting nature, stewardship in nature, connecting, appreciating people, and honoring traditions are skills taught through gathering materials in the natural environment—as well as the art-making processes. An example is the basket-making process in Diné (Navajo) culture, recognized culturally as a process for teaching patience and leadership skills.

PLANNING PROCESS

PREPARING FOR CULTURAL ARTS TEACHING

- Which cultural setting is the most appropriate for local arts to be taught?
- Are facility renovations needed to accommodate the arts to be taught?
- Where are the cultural boundaries for learning each art (e.g., internal community only or visitors)?
- How can individual expression be encouraged while observing traditional boundaries on form and meaning?
- How will traditional learning styles be incorporated?
- How will all generations be involved in the learning process, to transfer knowledge?
- How will both in-person and online programs be addressed?
- Which materials are identified as authentic for each art?
- What protections will be implemented to safeguard natural resources from depletion?
- How are local and cultural arts changing or evolving?
- Which contemporary arts are emerging forms, incorporating elements of tradition?

The community's cumulative cultural inventory—in terms of both objects and knowledge—is important to future collections. A framework for conducting the museum's cultural inventory provides essential information relevant to a starting level, or a sequence to levels taught. Several levels of training are beneficial—beginner, intermediate, or advanced. Assessing the level of business skills and matching the training to the right level are essential steps.

Community members practicing local traditions sometimes become discouraged if the training content is not culturally relevant or if the level is not a good match. Training offered for small enterprises at small business development centers is often designed for a larger scale and the profit motive than the scale needed to benefit the cultural micro-entrepreneur. Consider the good cultural fit.

ADDRESSING AUTHENTICITY

How is the definition of authenticity changing? Cultural arts evolve over time, and certainly traditional designs and materials become incorporated into contemporary art. For some cultures, authenticity factors include:

• Who made the object;
• Cultural affiliation;
• Materials used;
• Location; and
• Historical continuity.

In past decades, some academic views of the folk arts opposed the selling of traditional arts due to the possible influences of market pressures. This is a valid concern and one that can be addressed by local art groups or in forums organized by a museum to determine cultural boundaries. In this view, communities, rather than external critics, determine their own cultural future—a vital aspect of decolonization.

The upside of training artists in entrepreneurial skills is increasing the incentive to learn. Also, in many cultures, intergenerational participation in learning, plus making and selling art together, provides a meaningful activity for youth—an essential process for cultural continuity. Funding for job creation and substance abuse prevention are excellent resources.

Business training for artists benefits from increased awareness of potential market pressures. Consequently, such questions as the following may arise. Is the traditional method of producing items changing, and is change negatively affecting the meaning of the cultural art? What measures will be taken to protect traditional items and cultural meanings? To determine answers to these questions, the museum may decide to hold periodic meetings or symposia to discuss the relationship between business and culture. This is a fundable topic.

Pairing experienced entrepreneurs through mentoring with those beginning to learn skills is an excellent way to provide practical experience. Although sharing information within a particular culture may be the traditional way of learning, participation in a cash economy sometimes skews ways of learning, particularly if competition for sales is sensed. Or the experienced entrepreneur may not be willing to commit the time required to be a mentor. Perks for teaching or mentoring, such as bios featured on the museum website or income from demonstrations, increase incentive for the time invested.

A range of training options expanding community connection are fundable through grants and contracts and are appealing to donors as well. These include training in the arts, entrepreneurial skills, interpretive skills, and museum administrative skills.

COMPLETING AN ARTIST DATABASE

Completing cultural inventories to examine the status of traditions is the most valuable way to organize for the involvement of keepers of the traditions. Understanding the extent of knowledge retention is basic to preventing further cultural loss. Inclusivity opportunities for retention of traditional culture, as well as income generation for both local artists and the museum store, are increased through assessments.

By compiling the data from a cultural inventory, the resulting database is useful for finding the traditions that are strong and the traditions at risk of being lost—as well as the number of people with knowledge of particular traditions. Chart 6.1 illustrates a database sample designed to identify potential students, level of expertise in the art, and teachers. One outcome of the cultural inventory is the determination of priorities for teaching and identifying traditions at risk of being lost.

Variables for teaching include the following.

- Name and/or contact information
- Age grouping
- Specific art known
- Arts want to learn
- Willingness to teach
- Willingness to demonstrate

Keep in mind possible benefits to the museum. Potential teachers are also ideal for demonstrations, interpretation, documentation, and for future sales in the museum store. Plus, the database produces a contact list for notifying the community of museum programs, increasing inclusivity.

The database concept is continued in chapter 7, addressing the criteria needed for marketing the arts. Cultural inventories can be viewed as a needs assessment for cultural continuance. Building a two-way benefit between community and museum builds trust while multiplying benefits to both. Cultural privacy is important to maintain, according to local preferences.

Date: _____

Community: _____

Person completing: _____

Age Codes:
1= 1-19 years
2= 20-29 years
3= 30-39 years
4= 40-59 years
5= 60 or over

Name /Address/ Phone/E-mail	Art(s) know	Age Group	Demonstrate (yes/no)	Teach? (yes/no)	Arts want to learn
Artisan A (contact info)	Pottery	2	yes	yes	Basketry
Artisan B (contact info)	Dolls	2	yes	no	Embroidery
Artisan C (contact info)	Beadwork, earrings	2	no	no	Jam-making
Artisan D (contact info)	Carvings	3	yes	yes	Sewing
Artisan E (contact info)	Basketry	4	yes	yes	none
Artisan F (contact info)	Miniature pottery	3	yes	yes	Sculpture
Artisan G (contact info)	Silver jewelry	3	no	no	Beadwork
Artisan H (contact info)	Candle-making	2	no	no	Pottery
Artisan I (contact info)	Carving	4	yes	yes	Basketry
Artisan J (contact info)	Silver jewelry	2	no	no	Basketry
Artisan K (contact info)	Basketry	5	yes	yes	Carving
Artisan L (contact info)	Beadwork	2	no	no	Carving
Artisan M (contact info)	Beadwork	3	no	no	Basketry

Figure 6.1. Cultural Arts Teaching Assessment

Assessing the age range of the keepers of the traditions and whether or not they are willing to teach identifies the status of each cultural art and the risk of these cultural arts becoming lost. When these inventories then are given back to the community, the priorities for cultural teaching become readily apparent. For example, when only one elder has knowledge of a particular tradition, the teaching of this tradition may quickly become a priority to stem cultural loss.

In analysis, the brief sample database reveals priorities. Two participants indicate ability to teach basketry and are in the upper age ranges—indicating urgency to teach. Having more than one potential teacher lends a backup for initiating a class. A number of younger participants indicate wanting to learn basketry, showing potential for cultural continuity. Carving interest signals a similar pattern—older generation ability to teach and younger people wanting to learn. Retirees often have the time to learn and then may teach.

In relation to trust, underrepresented groups tend to show hesitation about data collection due to past participation experiences with researchers or planners when no concrete benefit or community feedback was perceived. Being clear about how the data will be used to benefit community efforts is a critical part of the process. Thinking through potential benefits with a concrete plan of action will make an enormous difference to data-gathering efforts.

A note on trust: There may be a reluctance to participate in such a project unless the intention of the data gathering is clarified. Stating that a class held at the museum or jointly with another community organization is the intended purpose of the database will increase responses. The database questions may be included on the overall museum-planning questionnaire, with a perk for survey completion. Keep the database basic, regarding questions and software used, for flexibility in later use with communities.

CULTURAL ARTIST AND ENTREPRENEURIAL TRAINING

What is the relationship between cultural entrepreneurs and the museum? The tie to cultural continuance is central. And the museum benefits as well, with a pool of entrepreneurs supplying the museum store. Including the needs of these stakeholders in the planning process is vital to determining needs for both cultural expression and participation.

Planning must take learning styles into account. The curriculum of a teaching program shapes learning opportunities and sets boundaries for the sharing of information. In traditional communities, limitations on persons appropriate to include give delineation to learning the traditional arts. Symbolism connected to these arts may be private information. Other limits to learning and selling are central to identify.

Assist participants to consider whether certain arts are for ceremonial purposes only and are not appropriate to sell. Concerns about market pressure stemming from visitor interest are significant to explore. The design of teaching programs in a cultural center or museum context effectively addresses these special cultural considerations.

Training tailored to a specific cultural and environmental setting is frequently difficult for community members to find when available sources use standardized textbooks and approaches. Local needs and learner level are essential starting places. The quality of the training relies heavily on an interface between the community (i.e., value-based), the training topic, and the correct learning level (i.e., beginner, intermediate, or advanced). A train-the-trainers approach is valuable, combining new skills with traditional techniques and ensuring program continuity.

Internet skills are essential for the entrepreneur, yet the starting level for some communities may be basic computer skills. An Internet-skills assessment of potential students is well worth setting the starting level—beginner, inter-mediate, or advanced—at the correct point. Working collaboratively with other organizations—such as business incubators—to pace entrepreneurs through a skill set is an integrated-community approach.

Tailoring training to a specific community or culture—not a pre-prepared "canned" approach—is a factor in cultural continuance. Collaboration with a college or a small business development center is possible, if space is not available at the museum. Consider an interactive process tailored to local cultures. The museum's role, as a center for cultural expression, is providing the liaison for local content—as well as access to collection information that enriches the learning process.

The museum store presents an opportunity for continued interpretation as value-added, a factor often overlooked. Museum visitor interest is peaked with information on current efforts toward cultural preservation through teaching, documentation, and educational efforts. Connection to local, regional, national, and international audiences is stimulated as cultural pride expands.

COMMUNITY-FOCUSED TRAINING

In-reach increases participation in several ways. Offering community-focused training transitions the museum to the center of a cultural-hub concept. In this way, the museum develops in-depth relationships involving museum partners. As other organizations begin to understand a possible interface, new dimensions of training regarding culture, economy, and ecosystem connections become possible through collaborative design and cooperative delivery.

For example, art organizations see the value of developing study tours of the museum collection. Or the local small-business incubator might develop a special program for cultural artists. If there are local ethnic groups with distinct cultural styles of doing business or entrepreneurship, the museum might assist the business incubator with the development of a culturally based curriculum. Depending on which organization has the classroom space, the museum might take the lead and secure the majority funding.

The learning program to exhibit connection strengthens exhibits in many ways. For example, designing a changing exhibit at the end of each class honors those who took the time to learn an art. Encouraging students to invite family and friends builds the museum connection to community.

Forming an advisory committee contributes to the development of content, particularly balancing expertise in cultural knowledge, entrepreneurial skills, and product development. Consider the following training topics as a way of presenting the concept and content. Often, opportunities are launched forward with funding, on the basis of a brief outline.

1. THE CULTURAL ARTS

Traditional cultural arts are the medium for cultural expression. Worldview, relationships with nature, and language are learned through the cultural arts. Relevant to the history of local cultures, a wide range of cultural arts, both utilitarian and decorative, may be integrated with the story of everyday life-ways. The arts may also be important to the traditional trade custom, when relationships with other groups resulted in an increased food, materials, tools, and arts supply.

Relevant to attendance success is the good match between student skill level and content of the course. Topics relevant for carrying on traditions include:

- Historical context of the art;
- Current practice;
- Connection to cultural traditions;
- Restrictions on persons allowed to learn, if any;
- Art-making processes;
- Cultural and environmental protection aspects of the art-making materials;
- Intergenerational cooperation in the art-making process, if applicable;
- Online resources; and
- Contemporary expression.

Differentiated skills complement each other, and stories convey the meaning of the art. Intergenerational approaches to teaching can restore family interaction and reinforce traditional ways of learning in addition to language. Having a place for gatherings and classes is another important factor for reviving traditional practice. Apprenticeships sponsored by the museum further the transfer of knowledge and are fundable. These are factors essential for cultural continuance.

2. ARTIST ENTREPRENEURIAL SKILLS

Cultural survival is often interwoven with building a local economy. Flexibility for community members to stay in the traditional geographic location, with access to traditional plants, animals, sacred sites, and sense of place, is often essential for cultural traditions to continue.

For this reason, sustaining a cultural future based on tradition may depend upon generating cash flow to supplement subsistence activities or when multiple income streams are necessary. Use of the Internet opens place-based opportunities. Local needs may include employment options that offer freedom of schedule to participate in the annual cycle of cultural activities. Recommended topics include the following.

- Cultural values and business
- Interface between tourism and local art markets—the regional profile
- Product development
- Focusing the business idea
- Assessing the market and marketing strategies
- Restrictions on selling cultural items or designs
- Developing a style or "brand"
- Completing the mini-business plan
- Creating the bio-card with artist information
- Selling online
- Financial record-keeping
- Artist websites
- Use of online vending platforms
- Social media
- Taxes; vending, art shows
- Evaluating success and redirecting efforts

Intentions for being in business in the traditional community setting often differ from the mainstream. Exploring cultural considerations connects to local worldviews. Museum symposia are a valuable service for understanding these differences.

3. FOOD-SERVICE TRAINING

Providing food service is a basic amenity for helping museum visitors to stay longer and engaged in programs. Many cultures consider the availability of food as a part of respectful visitation. When the length of stay is extended, more visitors will come to the museum, take tours, and purchase from the museum café or entrepreneurs, which, in turn, benefits the entire community.

If space is limited, a kitchen is lacking, or there is a concern about bugs in the museum, then basic food, such as sandwiches, local stews, and culturally specific cuisine, may be provided by entrepreneurs. Outdoor vending and picnic tables are an option. Topics include:

- General food-preparation guidelines;
- Cultural food preparation and interpretation;

- Nutritional benefits of eating locally grown foods;
- Food handling and storage;
- The work environment;
- Safety practices (e.g., lifting and carrying);
- Welcoming customers;
- Taking orders at tables;
- Appropriate clothing for the cultural setting; and
- Opening/closing; cash register procedures and operation.

Foods representing local culture engage visitors, and when menus connect to exhibit themes, the engaging museum experience is created.

4. PRODUCT DEVELOPMENT

Learning to design new products from existing skills using traditional forms, designs, and authentic materials—where culturally appropriate—taps into an innovative opportunity. Gaining input from a committee representative of tradition keepers provides a foundation for advising on cultural appropriateness. There may be a fine line between cultural exploitation and appropriateness, which is important to explore.

Community involvement in educational programs, coupled with customer surveys in the museum store or online, keep balance in the inventory. Potential museum store inventory is expanded, while opening a link to entrepreneurial employment. Effective topics include:

- Market niches for new products;
- Assessing museum visitor preferences;
- Transferring existing skills to new product designs;
- Cultural restrictions on sharing designs, if any;
- Acquiring new skills;
- Accessing resources;
- Assessing quantities to match the market;
- Creating the client database for sales;
- Quality control;
- Filling orders;
- The entrepreneur website;
- Record-keeping;
- Taxes; and
- Evaluating customer satisfaction.

An overview of niches created through an understanding of marketing trends—as well as care to assess natural resource use and protection—guides entrepreneurs in their design and marketing of new products. In particular, the souvenir line holds potential. Cultural considerations as to whether traditional designs may or may not be altered might be of concern. Careful exploration of cultural boundaries at the launching of a learning program is a critical step and one to inspire community confidence in the museum.

MUSEUM CAPACITY-BUILDING TOPICS

Inclusivity in the twenty-first-century museum will depend upon developing a highly qualified staff and resource base to implement desired community-based strategies. Learning programs are essential to expand local expertise needed for delivering an authentic experience based at the museum. For example, respecting cultural traditions in museum management leads to increased community involvement, when sensitive issues regarding cultural privacy are present. See chapter 4 on collections for more detail.

In terms of internal museum programs, developing training based upon local values, history, and culture leads to a unique museum concept. The visitor is drawn to the museum, and repeat visitation is increased by an evolving, rather than a static, concept.

Often a disconnect between the museum and community is substantial, particularly if museum staff are hired from outside of the local area. Building regional expertise and rapport with local cultures requires not superimposing the trainer's values. Web-based training and virtual conferences are valuable for instructing staff members, docents, and interns.

The chapters in this book provide culturally flexible content. Make certain to orient potential trainers and consultants to the community-integrated approach. Often, training available is oriented to the history museum approach or does not address local cultural values. If the museum is making a successful linkage to the community, then a critical opening is created for entrepreneurs, particularly in relation to visitor education, the museum store, the museum café, or the online store.

The training topics presented in the following sections integrate cultural considerations into the outline. Three to four trainings a year are recommended for most sites, to keep expanding expertise. It is important to note that all trainings need to have a cultural value-based orientation for community inclusivity over the long-term. Information on basic skills, with cultural integration considerations added, include the following topics.

1. MUSEUM PLANNING AND DEVELOPMENT

As a museum plan is completed and programs expand, the plan will need updating to reflect current needs. Investing in continuous planning will be valuable for sustained community participation, as well as producing an evolving document for training staff, showing funders long-range development intentions and encouraging donors. Useful inclusivity topics include the following.

- Overview of cultures in the community
- Community needs assessment options
- Inclusivity factor identification
- Cultural values as a core starting place
- Museum mission and goals in relation to community goals
- Possible scenarios
- Annual workplans
- Timelines and action plans
- Resources for the collections assessment
- The diversified museum-funding strategy

Making a bridge between the long-range vision and an annual workplan brings staff and volunteers along as a team. The ability to shift as new conditions and visitation restrictions arise is strengthened with planning.

2. MUSEUM MANAGEMENT

Training is necessary both to develop internal skills from within the local population and to orient museum staff or technical-assistance providers as to the special considerations of working with local cultures. Relevant topics include:

- Museum plan implementation;
- Addressing diversity, equity, accessibility, and inclusion (DEAI) factors;
- Awareness of local cultural calendars and employee participation needs;
- Connecting museum content to local cultural activities;
- Community liaison;
- New technologies related to collections and exhibits;
- Audience development (i.e., attracting visitors);
- Staff scheduling;
- Staff development maps;
- Financial planning;
- The museum website as an evolving educational resource for dialogue;
- The museum newsletter as an exciting way to keep community and visitors involved;
- The museum app;
- Targeted use of social media;
- Fundraising skills;
- Security systems; and
- Developing evaluation measures to assess progress and redirect.

When management addresses culture, economy, and local ecology, museum sustainability is likely to follow. Adapting to new technologies enhances audience reach and generates interest.

3. POLICY DEVELOPMENT

Policies are needed for general operating procedures and collections. Staff training in museum skills is essential for ongoing policy development. Since some cultural items may be subject to privacy restrictions, culturally based policies shape the respectful museum. Topics to consider include:

- Connecting to local cultural values;
- Implementing DEAI factors;
- Messages to communicate effectively;
- Online topic appropriateness;
- Criteria for access to information where culturally appropriate;
- Cultural boundaries for viewing and touching;
- Policies in relation to the museum mission and goals;
- Acquisitions;
- Accessioning;
- De-accessioning;
- Loans; and
- Policy revisions.

Adapting standard museum policies to existing community and cultural needs creates local relevance.

4. EXHIBIT DEVELOPMENT

Current exhibits may need updating and further interpretation to enhance public understanding of local cultures. Topics for new exhibits or changing exhibit space are content to identify in the museum planning process. Contemporary exhibit practices emphasize interactive techniques using modern technology, such as video-screen kiosks and recordings. Topics to address include:

- Researching community and tourist interests;
- Urgency in relation to community cultural revitalization efforts;
- Exhibit themes;
- Historical context;
- Telling a story;
- Cultural accuracy;
- Researching content;
- Online exhibits;

- Selecting objects to express the theme;
- Exhibit labels;
- Online interpretive presentations;
- Three-dimensional scanning techniques;
- Curator seminars;
- Multimedia presentation; and
- Interpretive guides.

Updating exhibit interpretation encourages repeat visitation and membership. One option to keep audiences engaged is adding new content with video kiosks or online programming.

5. COLLECTIONS DEVELOPMENT AND MANAGEMENT

Encouraging an ongoing internal community discussion to guide the collection may include: 1) items for educating the public, 2) historical cultural items, 3) less valuable items to use as a teaching collection in cultural art classes, 4) private, religious, and returned items, and 5) purchasing from local artists. Consider the following topics.

- Which items are culturally ethical to collect
- Responsibilities of the registrar
- Relating acquisitions to local needs for study (cultural continuity)
- Tying acquisitions to museum mission and goals
- Determining priorities for collection acquisition
- Culturally appropriate storage and handling
- Cultural restrictions on viewing and handling
- Cataloguing
- Storage options and requirements
- Digital-image accessibility
- Budgeting for collections storage
- Software available for management
- Teaching collections
- Community-owned collections

Collections management with a collections catalogue and local input for access furthers participation in museum programs.

6. CURATION

Curation, or care for collection items, may involve culturally private collection items—an important inclusivity factor. As visitor education concerning cultural items on display in a museum heightens awareness of value, security needs become increasingly important to avoid theft.[4] Climate-control needs are urgent to observe and address, to prevent disintegration. Valuable educational topics include the following.

- Cultural protocols and considerations
- Determining collection storage needs
- Curation procedures
- Handling
- Physical considerations
- Temperature
- Light
- Non-toxic pest control
- Protection from pollution
- Cleaning collection items
- Digital backup copies of collection images
- Protecting the fragile
- Protection from disasters

Initially, a staffing-needs section of the plan reflects the topics needed to develop knowledge and skills on technical topics integrated with cultural considerations. Training programs based on a thorough assessment of current skills, staff interests, and needs within the museum lead to a dynamic approach to staff training.

7. STAFF DEVELOPMENT AND SUPERVISION

As the museum expands in both programming and resources, additional staff members are needed. Training should emphasize ways of training community members (such as a trainer-of-trainer approach) and culturally appropriate supervision. How to work with culturally sensitive issues is vital to address for inclusivity. Topics include the following.

- Museum positions and responsibilities
- Inclusion of cultural knowledge keepers
- Values important to cultural groups involved
- Evaluating staff skills and capabilities
- Ethnic balance considerations and restrictions on sharing
- The staff development plan
- Recognizing signals for needed scenario shifts
- On-site training opportunities
- Encouraging use of traditional language
- Online training availability
- Off-site training possibilities

- Museum supervision
- Museum conferences, gatherings, and other community learning options

If non-local staff members are hired, they most often need training in community and cultural issues from a local cultural perspective. A staff development plan should be created for the inclusive ongoing training outcomes desired by community members. In other words, training should occur in both directions. Encouraging fresh approaches to staff training and giving innovative examples stimulates staff capacity for out-of-the-box thinking.

8. BUSINESS MANAGEMENT

Future development or redirecting at a museum will depend upon generating resources for sustainable support. Successful business operations increase financial sustainability, usually while increasing both primary (museum) and secondary (vendor) employment. For example, managing and promoting income-generating activities and holding cultural events supplement admissions, memberships, grants, and support from tax revenues. Consider the following topics.

- Managing the museum as a business
- Differences in cultural business styles
- The web-based museum store
- Income generators for museum support
- Enterprise business plans (e.g., store, café)
- Online product tours
- The interface between exhibits, programs, and enterprises
- An integrated approach to marketing the museum and businesses
- Business management
- Serving community needs by purchasing locally made items
- Personnel skills for business success
- Cultural responsibilities for giving back to community
- Evaluation of income-generating success and redirecting as needed

Potential for museum income exists through tours, a museum café, a museum store, and online sales—yet management skills must be in place for these to succeed.

9. GENERATING FUNDING IN THE MUSEUM SETTING

Diversifying museum activities opens the door to a broad range of funders, as detailed in a later chapter. A community approach to funding is value-based and inclusive—often emphasizing local economic benefits, extended family cooperation, being in relationship, integrated cultural retention efforts, entrepreneurial employment, nature connections, and sustainability. Adequate resources facilitate implementation. Interactive programs are ideal for engaging donor enthusiasm. Recommended topics include the following:

- Securing participation for desired directions
- Addressing inclusivity factors
- Matching scenarios with funding options
- The good funding and community values fit
- Diversifying sources of funding
- Creating the annual funding strategy
- Matching new strategies through diversification of museum program
- Donation structures
- Online auctions
- The museum-membership program
- Developing communications with the funder
- Conveying cultural benefits
- Understanding guidelines
- Writing the proposal
- Developing partnerships for a project
- Sustainable evaluation criteria
- Follow-up to express gratitude

To sustain the desired level of staffing and programming funds, proposals need to be submitted on a continual basis. Training staff members to write proposal sections invites creative and inclusive approaches. Proposals require specific skills related to funders as well as to reach the general public with innovative topics. An updated museum website, use of social media, and an electronic newsletter are essential tools for generating new outreach.

10. PUBLIC PROGRAMS

There are two publics to consider: the community, and the general public or tourists. Presenting local culture to the general public is important because educating a museum audience on local history promotes cultural understanding, encourages museum admissions, and stimulates the purchase of locally made products. Inclusive topics include the following:

- Audience development with both local and tourist strategies
- Receptions as exhibit introduction, online and on-site
- Interface with local events
- Involving diverse cultural groups
- Virtual tours

- Learning programs for the community
- Linking interpretive programs to outdoor spaces
- Heightening connections in nature—historic places, natural materials
- Outreach programs for youth activities
- Community education on the museum website

Programs available to the public are important for cultural learning, language retention, and self-esteem building.

11. TOURISM DEVELOPMENT AND MANAGING TOURS

Drawing an audience for museum programs involves reaching local residents as well as visitors to the region. Tourism development involves learning to identify and target markets, ways of linking with the tourism industry, and promotion.[5] Effective topics include the following.

- Assessing local resources (e.g., history, people, buildings, ecosystems)
- Developing the culturally appropriate visitor etiquette
- Defining cultural landscapes
- Connecting the museum to tourism networks—local, regional, and national
- Planning a tour
- Developing a script
- Virtual tour introductions
- Marketing a tour
- Maintaining consistency in delivery
- Tour management and scheduling
- Communication skills
- Storytelling
- Tour evaluation and redirection, as needed

If tours are identified in the planning process as beneficial for both support of the museum and as a way to create a draw for community-based entrepreneurial sales, tour development and management skills are essential.

12. TOUR-GUIDE SKILLS

Two types of tours enhance the museum visitation experience. Museum tours further interpretation of exhibits and museum programs. Extending tour options to the cultural landscape, including historic sites, gardens of culturally relevant plants, and local events linked to exhibit themes, are ways of enhancing the visitor learning experience while generating museum income.[6] Topics include the following:

- Presenting local histories
- Natural history and cultural landscapes of the region
- Connections *in* nature
- Considerations for cultural privacy
- Preventing environmental impacts
- Storytelling skills
- Code of ethics for guides and travelers based on traditional values and visitor etiquette
- Customer service
- Leadership and conflict resolution skills
- Equipment operation
- Safety and survival techniques
- First aid
- Evaluation of success and redirecting
- Business skills for tour managers

Adding formal training on tour-guide topics builds local entrepreneurial skills. Local visitation policies, particularly involving cultural privacy and fragile ecosystems, are important to respect. Evaluation expands resources by improving efficiency and evolving content as audience interests change.

13. PROGRAM EVALUATION

Measures of success within a cultural framework are essential to address from an inclusive perspective. Meeting readiness within a local network is relevant to community integration success. Training in program evaluation must focus on museum programs plus community perceptions of progress. A definition of progress should include both museum targets and community-related topics, such as job creation and contribution to the local economy. Potential topics include the following.

- Defining a culturally sensitive evaluation framework
- Values represented and cultural ways of asking questions
- DEAI targets met
- Measuring both qualitative and quantitative outcomes
- Setting goals and objectives
- Using meetings or online platforms for survey feedback
- Assessing baseline data on current conditions
- Cultural relevance in measures
- Museum measures of progress
- Comparing goals to progress
- Achieving attendance targets, both in-person and online
- Evaluating income-generating success

- Relating evaluation results to needs for scenario shifts
- Writing the evaluation report
- Suggestions for redirecting programs as necessary
- Using evaluation results to generate new funding

Trainings may be provided by the partners identified in the museum plan; however, they will need to be well-oriented to the goals of your museum and to local values and cultures. If evaluation measures developed in the museum plan (see chapter 11) are given to future trainers of museum staff, then the training is likely to be more community-relevant and effective.

LINKING PAST AND PRESENT TO THE FUTURE

People, culture, economy, and ecology shape a community. The museum's role as a hub in a larger network expands through both education and opportunity. Careful consideration of needs identified through participation in other local planning efforts brings meaningful connection to outreach in museum programs. Shaping exhibits and programming to meet evolving needs is an ongoing process.

Examine local assessments or planning meetings as valuable data for both determining needs and redirecting as necessary to the integrated approach. Community-integration is key for not seeing the museum's needs in isolation. Other community or regional organizations provide valuable collaborations benefitting the museum. Participation is integration.

Video kiosks in exhibits, art demonstrations, and lecture series, as well as classes, are effective ways of complementing different learning styles. As community learning connects to exhibits, both contributing to learning and reflecting progress in learning, visitor interest increases. This is particularly true for the traveler interested in cultures.

How a museum evolves reflects uniqueness, lending inclusivity and an authentic experience to the museum visit. Connections from museum to community open a process of endless discoveries for the museum visitor.

FURTHER READING

Porter, Jason. *Museum Education for Today's Audiences: Meeting Expectations with New Models*. Lanham, MD: Rowman & Littlefield, 2022.

In response to the physical distance the pandemic placed between museums and their visitors, museum educators are tackling urgent social issues, addressing historic inequalities, innovating for accessibility, and leveraging technology for new in-person and virtual learning experiences, as well as cultivating partnerships with schools, businesses, elders, scientists, and other social services to build relationships and be of service to their communities.

This book and its accompanying online resource share lessons from innovators in the field to support ongoing professional development efforts with essays about current issues.

Colwell, Ken. *Starting a Business Quickstart Guide*. Albany, NY: ClydeBank Media, 2019.
This guide for beginning entrepreneurs, a training tool useful for the makers of local arts, covers the bridge from an idea to an opportunity, pricing, competition, customer identification, marketing, and distribution. Steps are explained for writing a business plan, which include financial projections with templates.

Catlin-Legutko, Cinnamon, and Stacy Klingler, eds. *Reaching and Responding to the Audience, Small Museum Toolkit,* Vol 4. New York: AltaMira Press, 2012.
This text emphasizes the new roles small museums take on to engage with and advocate for their audiences. Practical advice from experienced museum managers emphasizes accessibility for everyone. Programming to meet their needs and interests is part of this process.

Luna, Pi, and Ed Worden. *Life Savings: Navigate the Financial Course*. Santa Fe, NM: Engage Press, 2015.
This is a practical guide, suitable for training entrepreneurs, that focuses on making informed decisions in managing finances to support goals. Basic business math skills are emphasized, as well as steps for writing business plans. Skills addressed include how to open a small business and learning to use spreadsheet programs for management of the small enterprise.

NOTES

1. Murawski, Mike. *Museums as Agents of Change: A Guide to Becoming a Changemaker*. Lanham, MD: Rowman & Littlefield, 2021.
2. Hague, Stephen G., and Laura C. Keim. "Preparing an Outstanding Concert: How to Plan and Implement Interpretation." In *Interpretation: Education, Programs, and Exhibits*. Small Museum Toolkit, Vol. 5, Cinnamon Catlin-Legutko and Stacy Klingler (eds.), pp. 1–25. New York: AltaMira Press, 2012.
3. Guyette, Susan. *Planning for Balanced Development*. Santa Fe, NM: Clearlight Publishers, 1996.
4. Lord, Barry, Gail Dexter Lord, and Lindsay Martin (eds). *Manual of Museum Planning: Sustainable Space, Facilities, and Operations, Third Edition*. New York: AltaMira Press, 2012.
5. Ibid.
6. Guyette, Susan. *Sustainable Cultural Tourism: Small-Scale Solutions*. Santa Fe: Bear-Path Press, 2013.

7

Cultural Entrepreneurs and Employment

Economy is a part of culture, an exchange concept—until the relatively recent emphasis on the accumulation of money. Integrating the museum into all aspects of life brings multiple benefits, an ethical responsibility. In addition to contributing to the collective well-being of society, incorporating local employment as a museum strategy opens opportunities for the larger grants that sustain a museum's operating budget. Including cultural entrepreneurs and contemporary artists benefits the museum, as well as local economy.

Depth in the cultural entrepreneur relationship is commonly an overlooked resource. Artists and entrepreneurs directly involved in museum programs become a ready resource for stories enriching interpretive programs. With a few extra steps, a museum gains a much larger community connection and impact, as well as the expanded cultural experience. Selling opportunities through the museum encourage local audiences to learn and retain traditions. By linking interpretation to current traditions, the past-present-future continuum supports cultural continuance and the experiential visit.

To the greatest extent that museums interface with economy, support for museums is likely to follow from funders. Earned income is an invaluable grant-matching source. As another plus, funders are recognizing the value-added of the arts for retaining cultural knowledge in a worldwide pool necessary for global survival and thriving. Creativity and resourcefulness are fostered by the arts—a factor worthy of mentioning when approaching funding sources.

The call for museums "empowering communities"[1] can extend to widespread local economy benefits. This community-integrated view of museum and cultural center purpose considers all aspects of cultural practice. Beyond immediate employment possible through staffing and internships[2] are the added benefits of cultural continuity and reduced out-migration of community members in search of employment. Out-migration reduces the cultural knowledge base and opportunities to learn in cultural place.

Why is extended museum impact important? The creative economy is potentially more sustainable than other forms of economic development, particularly in relation to family cohesion and reduced environmental impacts. Small-scale entrepreneurial businesses, when linked in a network, tend to withstand fluctuations in the economy with more stability than do larger enterprises. Businesses with "pre-existing conditions," such as lack of management skills, absence of a business plan, and poor financial monitoring, led to business failures during the COVID-19 pandemic.

Given the high level of economic uncertainty nationally, assisting cultural entrepreneurs, especially micro-entrepreneurs, to grow in skills and providing opportunities for marketing their culturally based inventory is a growing museum niche. Plus, linking entrepreneurs into a network adds economic flexibility to a community. Consider organizational partners as possibilities for learning programs if space is not available at the museum. Linking to other local resources such as employment programs and small business incubators enables a museum to achieve a broader impact as part of a network.

STRATEGIES FOR INCREASING EMPLOYMENT

Linked networks of small enterprises hold the potential for resilience in changing economic scenarios. Creating jobs by increasing both primary and secondary employment not only expands the numbers of jobs but also creates the environment that increases economic multipliers—necessary for boosting a local economy. *Primary employment* is defined as full-time or part-time jobs provided through businesses, museums, or local organizations—usually with a set income and employee benefits. *Secondary employment* includes entrepreneurs providing services or products to local businesses, organizations, or to businesses outside of the region. Sometimes these concepts are called "direct" and "indirect" forms of employment.

Addressing high unemployment in an area usually implies creating *many* jobs. Pointing out to local government the role of creative industries in boosting tourism, plus increasing the number of job-creation results, is a successful strategy for museums. Offering support for services to provide secondary employment is a critical way of addressing these employment needs. Embracing cooperative values rather than a mainly competitive outlook at business leads to a community-oriented outlook and builds a culturally interesting draw to visitors as well. A strategy for obtaining an accurate way of counting actual impacts on earned livelihood is to calculate primary employment plus secondary employment to document the widespread, actual economic benefits of a museum.

INVOLVING CULTURAL ENTREPRENEURS

Cultural entrepreneurs provide services involving the arts, storytelling, demonstrations, tours, local foods, and interpretations of history.[3] When interfacing with cultural entrepreneurs, the museum supports cooperative and extended family-based cultural values, enriching the tie between community and interpretive connection. The interface between a museum and cultural entrepreneurs is felt strongly in small and rural communities striving for cultural continuance. Several opportunities for assisting cultural entrepreneurs include:

- Sales within the museum store or cultural center;
- Launching an online store;
- Organizing artist booths outside the museum facility;
- Hosting demonstrations;
- Changing exhibits;
- Sponsoring art shows, at the museum or in other public spaces;
- Organizing special events such as festivals;
- Holding opening receptions; and
- Facilitating auctions.

How to support these activities? These are projects suitable for grant sources or sponsors. Donors then tend to become more involved when interactive events are hosted by the museum or cultural center.

Respect for the art is conveyed when programs interpret the cultural meaning of the arts. Interpretive materials accompanying the selling of arts foster greater respect for the art-making processes. In-depth interviews with artists and other cultural entrepreneurs, as part of a larger project, yield information applicable for use later—for interpretation, biographical cards to accompany artwork, and online data.

To make the best tie between store, website, exhibits, and community, the adaptive planning process is valuable for identifying items appropriate for sale, as well as those arts in need of further internal discussion. When support for the teaching and continuation of cultural arts comes through a museum or cultural center, both positive and negative influences from market interest must be considered.

Positive results coming from museum visitor attention include reviving arts through increased teaching of those arts at risk of becoming lost. Cultural continuity is then enhanced. Examples of cultural revitalization include quilt-making in the Southern United States and the Native American pottery revival in the Southwest. One of the dangers of exposure to commercial market demands is an imbalance—focusing on certain arts of appeal to visitors. Care taken to teach a range of cultural arts maintains a balance between earned livelihood and internal, cultural use.

PLANNING PROCESS

HONORING THE CULTURAL ARTS

- Which locally made arts match well with museum visitor interests?
- Are there arts that should not be sold outside of the community (internal market)?
- What are the opportunities for exhibiting local arts?
- How will information on the arts be communicated to the public to further an understanding of history and the handmade, authentic process?
- How will information about the artists be communicated, to honor the tradition?
- How can a tie-in be created between art items, agricultural products, or other locally made items, and exhibit themes to support local livelihood while educating on topics now coming to global awareness?

Museums frequently purchase souvenir lines and art items sourced from outside of the community for reasons of ordering convenience. Although working with local entrepreneurs individually requires more time and effort than ordering in bulk, organizing to work with the local population for sales facilitates a strong community connection. Available economic development grants are useful for supporting the extra staff time.

Understanding cultural perception toward artmaking and marketing is important for cooperative efforts. In some traditional communities, the concept of a "product" tends to be a culturally sensitive issue. There are many cultural boundaries concerning both items and information about the use of these items. Ultimately, the community must make its own decisions based on tradition, values, and the need for livelihood. Organizing a forum to discuss market appropriateness is a fundable topic.

Cultural entrepreneurs may not perceive themselves as being "in business."[4] By not planning income and expenses, marketing, or managing finances, the entrepreneur loses possible sales. Personal financial management training called "financial literacy" may be training already available in the community; however, the content may not be a good cultural fit. Enter the museum opportunity.

The importance of putting extended family first in many culturally diverse settings is as important as the process of generating and managing resources. In cultures with a family orientation, the freedom to work from home is precious. Participation in spiritual activities, a part of culture, is often linked to self-employment. Learning how to balance family obligations and the balance sheet are challenging aspects of business.

Business trainings available frequently assume a retail approach. When the training is not tailored to a specific level, the instructor will find that participants are at different levels. Then, the trainer has to adjust to a medium level, therefore not providing the depth of information essential for the experienced entrepreneur—oftentimes losing comprehension by the non-experienced entrepreneur.

For these reasons, courses need to be carefully designed and the appropriate level of entrepreneur attracted to them. Promotion for a course needs to be clear about the topics and about the level. Here lies the museum opportunity for collaboration. The role of the museum may be to explain cultural perceptions to trainers, tailoring applicable context.

A potential museum tie-in to tourism requires entrepreneurial services and products—comprising 80 percent (in the United States) of all tourism enterprises—as detailed in the next chapter. Yet not everyone is well-suited to being an entrepreneur. Essential traits for this type of business are vision, initiative, creativity, persistence, tolerance for risk, and the ability to grow from mistakes and failures.

Assisting entrepreneurs to see their abilities in terms of these skills—plus needed additional skills—combines for good training. In many rural and tribal communities, several extended family members make the arts together, and another family member markets them. A cooperative entrepreneurial system draws upon local values, extended family cooperation, and reinforces learning within the family.

An opportunity for the museum opens by coordinating trainings relating to cultural arts and tourism, as well as assisting with the integration of cultural values into those trainings. Two types of job training needs are important to distinguish: the storefront enterprise and the small entrepreneur enterprise or cottage industry. Training for entrepreneurs and cottage industries may be developed from collaborations with partners, if guidance is given about incorporating cultural factors. Combining the skills of knowledgeable business managers with those of successful local entrepreneurs gives a tailored cultural perspective. The venues of partners may be the training sites.

Gaining a true count of employment in an informal economy, or where an industrial economy of "eight-to-five" jobs is not prevalent, creates baseline data for measuring progress. Funders often use definitions of employment that do not fit in rural areas where *multiple income streams* are the norm. Defining measures of employment and educating funders is a way of representing the community successfully and increasing accuracy in documenting need. Additionally, secondary employment generated by entrepreneurs provides the local "supplier" end to tourism, thus enhancing a unique tourism concept.

Small business development loans, business training, online platform learning, and Internet promotion is indicated as a priority for supporting the expansion of secondary employment, thereby reducing the unemployment rate. Developing a curriculum for small-business skills tailored to cultural values increases entrepreneurial involvement—as described in chapter 6.

CULTURE AND BUSINESS STYLE

What does the cultural connection bring to entrepreneurial success? Many ethnic groups have a distinct style of conducting business, different from the American mainstream. Often, available technical assistance and training is taught from a mainstream profit-motive perspective rather than from traditional cultural viewpoints. Put simply, businesses succeeding over the long-term often depend upon incorporating local values and cultural norms, such as hiring and managing family member employees. Barter also remains important to rural communities and is often undervalued in economic analyses. These older forms of business management offer resilience and may see a return in the new economy.

Traditional peoples tend to see the mainstream way of developing business as high risk and may want to pursue a slower, gradual way of developing business. These communities are correct in their caution about the amount of risk in the mainstream style of developing business. In the United States, over 60 percent of small businesses fail—usually due to capital-intensive start-ups, poor customer service, and lack of marketing, plus lack of monitoring profit and expenses.

As alternatives to the larger scale, businesses can be small, family-owned, and operated from the home. In places where retaining traditional culture at a high level is an important goal, extended family-owned businesses link family members together in a cooperative system meeting some of their needs. Cultural artists and entrepreneurs often operate on this level of business. Cash tends to be supplemental income when several income streams are pieced together for a livelihood, reinforcing family and community inter-dependence. To this end, participation in the creative economy, coupled with season extending through online sales of items, provides substantial income supplementation.

In summary, the museum or cultural center is in an ideal position to be a catalyst for the creative economy by offering classes to cultural entrepreneurs. Museums stand to benefit by encouraging cultural involvement and increasing inventory expansion in the museum store. Collaborations with other local organizations—with the museum as host—bring new opportunities to cultural entrepreneurs. Often, achieving sustainable results requires restructuring the forms of technical assistance offered. A "trainer-of-trainers" approach is often the most productive when an introductory training is adaptable to local needs and cultural ways of conducting business. Drawing upon the substantial pool of experienced business owners for mentoring is an approach with potential.

RESILIENCE IN CHALLENGING TIMES

Thriving in an economic crisis calls for flexibility. When a community-wide effort encourages participation in a network of cultural programs and small locally owned businesses, relative stability is created in times of economic fluctuations. The potential as a resource for the creative arts opens new avenues for participation. The museum or cultural center as a hub shows promise for this approach. Examining entrepreneurial trends in two times of crisis—the COVID-19 pandemic rising in 2020 and the US economic downturn precipitated in 2007—is useful for identifying resilience factors.

Entrepreneurship as an adaptive strategy lends insights into the resilience needed to absorb impacts.[5] Crises are economic and social stresses that cause change to occur. As seen during the COVID-19 pandemic, a resilient attitude is fostered by creativity in problem-solving, a positive attribute of artists. In times of epidemic, economic downturn, and natural disaster, the trend of protecting established businesses lends economic stability.

Cultural entrepreneurship refers to the wise use of cultural resources for business opportunities.[6] Business planning, frugality, emotional support, and increasing online competence[7] are keys to success in epidemic times. The ability to work at home or in studios increases adaptability in times of isolating policies. Use of symbols and stories enhances authenticity, increases value-added appeal, and attracts customers. Creative shifts, such as the development of a mask industry, is an example of recent innovation during the pandemic.

Over the past decade, the creative industries grew to become a major sector of the global economy.[8] According to the United Nations Educational, Scientific, and Cultural Organization (UNESCO) in 2017,[9] the creative industries generate US$2,250 billion of revenues annually, with a projection of 10 percent of global GDP in future years. Cultural entrepreneurs create revenue from cultural industries. Challenges for these entrepreneurs include the cancellation of cultural events, exhibitions, concerts, performances, and festivals combined with restrictions on social distancing and fewer face-to-face interactions.

Significant limitations on economic activities created a negative effect on cultural workers and the self-employed.[10] In response, cultural organizations were forced to reorganize their interactions with customers in a more dynamic way to survive and, in the best of instances, to thrive. The information technology industry experienced a surge in demand for innovative products and services.[11] Digitization and online platforms were quickly adopted to improve accessibility.

Creativity used to improve adaptive capacity expanded viewer and participant outreach by museums and other cultural organizations. Developing digital capabilities quickly became a successful tool for involving the public. The impact of the digital divide and digital safety nets also rapidly became apparent.

Key adaptive strategies used during the COVID-19 pandemic[12] include:

- Increasing understanding of the variety of entrepreneurship activities, plus closely targeting markets served;

- Perceiving the contributions of cultural entrepreneurs in mitigating community impacts during an epidemic, financial, or climate crisis;
- Gaining an understanding of the ways in which audiences engage with digital services provided by the creative industries;
- Adopting digital tools and learning skills to adapt to new market conditions, retain a customer base, and navigate through fluctuations in income;
- Use of online platforms and digital technologies to support museums and libraries in sustaining their income and increase the number of online visitors;
- Organizations integrating skills required by social media and other digital technologies; and
- Understanding the role of livestreaming and digital presence for transitioning to new business models.

Managing a business with income and expenses increases the ability to adapt in changing scenarios. Financial advisors recommend the following steps.[13]

- Continually evaluate the impacts of an uncertain environment
- Assess the financial health of the business
- Increase tracking of business success using digital tools
- Analyze different funding options, revenue streams, and other potential pivots for business resilience
- Use financial tools and metrics to discover new opportunities and a "new normal"

In summary, responses to the challenges created by the impact of the COVID-19 pandemic on the creative industries are positive, considering adaptive value. Which leadership roles are possible for museums and cultural centers? Cultivating an entrepreneurial ecosystem that focuses on a nonprofit or societal gain[14] fosters positive forms of innovation and is a natural step for cultural organizations. Above all, lessons from the COVID-19 pandemic show how non-decisions lead to worsened conditions.[15]

Pre-pandemic studies examining economic crises indicated resilience of creative industries. A study analyzing the effects of economic crisis on workers from three categories[16] concluded that a large presence of creative workers in a region lessened the impact of the recession. The comparison of three worker classes—the Creative, Service and Working Class—looked at the causes of the economic slowdown of 2009, with one of the main causes being the housing crisis and the decline of employment conditions in construction occupations.

The housing boom led to a "false economy" with expanding retail and food service-related employment. An additional factor was the structural change of investments in computer technologies as "substitutes" for workers who perform tasks according to a set plan—whereas computers are "complements" to those involved in problem-solving and complex communications.

> Finally, as the economic crisis was, indeed, a major worldwide slowdown in economic activity, jobs that rely heavily on export-driven growth were likely hit harder than occupations that are capable of generating locally-originating growth.[17]

Of the three classes of employees, Creative Class occupations, had substantially lower unemployment rates than the Service and Working Class occupations, with Working Class occupations showing an unemployment rate of 15 percent, or over three times greater than the unemployment rate for Creative Class occupations, followed by Service Class occupations with an unemployment rate of 8.7 percent near the end of the recession.

The importance of locally generated employment is emphasized by Ann Markusen[18] in a consumption-based theory of development—where investments in arts and culture can increase local spending and growth due to less reliance on a region's ability to export goods to other regions. Richard Florida[19] suggests that the productive and innovative capacities of the emergent knowledge-based creative economies are running "smack up against the outmoded institutions, economic and social structures and geographic forms of the old industrial age." For these reasons, an innovative twenty-first-century concept is essential for museums to participate in small-scale economic development.

A creative industries study conducted in Massachusetts[20] explored the factors most relevant to business success. Ten recommendations from this study include the following.

1. Networking and business development
2. Access to capital
3. Marketing
4. Industry visibility, such as a "Buy Creative Local"
5. Talent and workforce development
6. Mentorship
7. Training
8. Communicating value of their goods and services when speaking to potential clients
9. Using a business model, with creative industries to be more "entrepreneurial" and working to evolve with the marketplace
10. Space for both an incubator and a focal point for the creative industry

Collaborations between cultural organizations and cultural institutions are valuable for filling in the gaps as a support network for cultural entrepreneurs.

Knowing success factors is valuable for designing training programs and delivering support services, such as marketing assistance, and is applicable for museum participation.

Remembering the planning principles of form, scale, and timing outlined in chapters 2 and 3 will increase organizational patience. Phasing-in projects on a smaller scale not only lightens the staff workload but also gives time to raise extra funds for projects while increasing the ability to shift when a new scenario is needed.

THE ENTREPRENEURIAL DATABASE

Organizing information for marketing purposes is essential for effective inclusion of cultural entrepreneurs. Identifying cultural artists is a strategy communities use successfully to begin cultural center or museum planning. Conducting such assessments requires caution to protect cultural symbolism and meanings that are for the eyes and ears of community members only. These restrictions vary from culture to culture; understanding the cultural boundaries is essential for inclusivity to occur.

The basic cultural inventory presented in chapter 6 generates community participation for learning the arts, organizing teaching, and serves as a reminder of steps ahead to meet cultural retention needs—while organizing for community needs. Expand the database to include the following variables for maximum usefulness in both teaching and marketing projects.

- Name, contact information
- Age grouping
- Specific art known
- Arts want to learn
- Willing to teach
- Willing to demonstrate
- Whether interested in business skills training
- Interest in marketing at the museum or cultural center
- Number of items could market per year
- Price range of items

The process of completing a database of cultural entrepreneurs encourages community participation and momentum. Chart 7.1 illustrates a database format useful for both documentation and organizing.

The arts inventory is also useful documentation for demonstrating needs to a funding agency or organization for a marketing program or a museum store. Although additional staff time is needed to work with local entrepreneurs rather than placing a large order with a corporation, keep in mind the financial benefits of potential grant support for entrepreneurial training, marketing, and job

Date: _____
Date: _____
Community: _____
Person completing: _____

Age Codes:
1= 1-19 years
2= 20-29 years
3= 30-39 years
4= 40-59 years
5= 60 or over

Name /Address/ Phone/E-mail	Art(s) know	Age Group	Demo? (yes/no)	Teach? (yes/no)	Arts want to learn	Want business skills training? (yes/no)	Want to market at Museum (yes/no)	Number of items could market per year (yes/no)	Price range (retail) items want to market (yes/no)
Artisan A (contact info)	Pottery	2	yes	yes	Basketry	yes	yes	10	$50-$100
Artisan B (contact info)	Dolls	2	yes	no	Embroidery	yes	yes	25	$25-$50
Artisan C (contact info)	Beadwork, earrings	4	no	no	Jam-making	no	yes	30	$25- $40
Artisan D (contact info)	Carvings	3	yes	yes	Sewing	no	no	12	$50-$100
Artisan E (contact info)	Basketry	4	yes	yes	none	yes	yes	10	$50-$100
Artisan F (contact info)	Miniature pottery	3	yes	yes	Sculpture	no	no	30	$25-$35
Artisan G (contact info)	Silver jewelry	3	no	no	Beadwork	yes	yes	20	$50-$75

Chart 7.1. Cultural Arts Teaching and Marketing Assessment

creation. Guiding the benefit to community entrepreneurial activity produces the local gain, both economically and culturally.

Maintaining a mix of products and representing a range in pricing attracts visitors. The souvenir line generates the majority of sales in the museum store or gift shop. The mid-price and upper-end relate primarily to the cultural arts and depend upon the local region and culture.

THE MUSEUM STORE OR CULTURAL CENTER STORE

When designed in alignment with community-based priorities and in coordination with exhibit themes, the museum store becomes an inclusive opportunity for a continued interpretive experience. Moving away from the "gift shop" concept featuring commercial souvenirs toward locally made art creates a museum store or an art gallery image. The online store featuring bestsellers is a valuable addition, providing a flexible scenario for closure times.

Several methods for complementing exhibit themes include the following.

- Hang tags (physical and online)
- Biographical cards (physical and online)
- Informational flyers, explaining cultural arts, foods, and so on
- Video kiosk screen displays, featuring artists speaking about their arts or interpretive stories about the arts
- Demonstrations in the museum
- Books sold on the featured arts or other items
- Dishes for cooking and serving local cuisine

Expanding the store with a local focus is likely to involve product development. The concept of a "product" may carry cultural considerations, for the word "product" tends to imply an object to be sold. In traditional communities, there are many cultural boundaries concerning both items and information about the use of these items. For example, certain items, such as the sacred, may carry limitations on an appropriate owner.

Sensitive museum planning in traditional cultures involves identifying the cultural boundaries associated with locally made items, in addition to limitations on conveying cultural information. Each community must make its own decisions based on a balance of tradition, values, and the need for livelihood. With local group participation, consider the range of positive benefits and ways of translating these benefits into museum income.

The well-structured museum plan will direct benefits to local groups rather than to an inventory comprised of items sold by large corporations, often imported. The Museum Store Association publishes valuable guides for the basic "nuts and bolts" of store management. The following list shows souvenir line products that sell well in the museum setting.

Finding the match between local skills and market interest is the innovative aspect of a process resulting in maximized community benefits. Consider ways

• Historical reproductions	• Pottery
• Posters	• Coffee mugs with local designs
• Photographs	• Tablecloths and napkins with
• Dolls	local designs
• Books	• Candles
– Cookbooks	• Local Foods
– History, with interpretation	– Honey
– Novels set in the region	– Jams
– Children's books	– Dried stew mix
• Tote bags	– Dried jerky
• Key chains	– Dried fruit
• Hand-made cards	– Trail mix
• Value-added agricultural products,	• Clothing
such as dried foods sealed in	– T-shirts and sweat shirts
packages	– Scarves with local traditional
• DVDs/ CDs of local genre music	designs
• Children's toys	– Purses or bags with regional
• Culturally-linked games	symbolism
• Jewelry	– Caps and other hats

Chart 7.2. Product Lines with High Museum Store Potential

Chapter 7

of creating innovative combinations of locally made items. This strategy works best with tourists if shipping services are provided for large or difficult-to-carry items.

Refining effective business practices increases sales. Listening to customer feedback is essential for fine-tuning product lines. For example, repeat orders from long distance are an additional source of income for both the museum store and entrepreneurs. To further repeat orders, include contact information through a business card or a bio-card at the time of the sale. Setting an artist bio-card in a piece of pottery or a coffee cup, or attaching the card to an item, increases the likelihood of the information staying with the piece.

An explanation of authenticity adds value to an item in the museum store. A biographical card produced for each artist represented in the museum store, with ethnic affiliation, a sentence about the art, a photo of the artist, and a photo of sample art increases the collector value of the art piece. In addition to showing respect for the artist, the tradition, and the piece, the selling price benefits. Artist bios on the website are another means of increasing visitor-purchaser education.

Educational efforts tied to inventory include flyers describing the art-making techniques or the cultural revitalization efforts taking place through community learning programs. These enhance the buyer's understanding of the time and materials taken to produce an authentic cultural art item. Educating the buyer on the value beyond an object as part of history will increase the willingness to pay a fair price in exchange for the privilege of owning an authentic piece. Boundaries around revealing sacred or traditional meanings are essential to respect.

A kiosk in the store with a video of the art-making process contributes to visitor education on the value of the authentic, locally made piece. Emphasizing authentic materials, cultural uses of the item appropriate to share, the average time length involved in making an item, seasonal considerations, the tie-in to local economy and lifeways, and use of traditional languages in the art-making process are all potential topics. Videos on several arts can be rotated to generate public interest. Grant funding is available to make such videos, if framed as documentation of the art and an educational complement. Keep in mind the value of a video for extracting clips to be posted on YouTube and the museum website as a means of audience development.

Cultural tourists spend more on local products and souvenirs than any other category of tourists. Bringing the item home extends the experience beyond the visit. For example, selling cookbooks on regional cuisine and providing a list of restaurants serving local cuisine connects an exhibit, linking local foods to everyday experience. Looking for unique opportunities to link cultural education with museum programs extends the museum experience. The placemat, tent card, and music are examples of education through unification.

THE MUSEUM CAFÉ

Cuisine is a part of culture. Continuing the interpretive experience through the museum café is an opportunity to engage all of the senses—smell, taste, sight, and hearing. These are several means of accomplishing visitor engagement. For a small museum, a menu of limited choices, cooked simply and offered with education about the foods, can become an adventure.

Visitors seeking unique and quality food experiences are called culinary tourists. Potential for the interface with cultural tourism is strong. Baby boomers, comprising a large segment of the cultural tourism market, tend to be family-oriented and interested in an educational experience for grandchildren. Learning about healthy foods and nutritiously dense foods are also a keen interest.

Food service focusing on regional specialties ranks high in visitor appeal. Visitor surveys conducted in regional and state settings indicate that cultural tourists have a high interest in trying local and traditional foods. Additionally, recreational tourists are interested in "food to go," such as trail mix and boxed lunches to pack.

Ethnic foods are generally made with whole unprocessed foods, offering more nutrient gain than processed foods. A museum café holds the potential for a healthy alternative as a local eatery, plus it encourages a link for continued local audience participation in museum programs. No space in the museum? Consider an addition or a food truck outside with local cuisine and staffing.

MENU CREATIVITY

When a connection is made between menus and exhibit themes, food choices continue the interpretive experience. The museum café, designed educationally, becomes a valuable resource to the local economy when farm-to-table principles are applied. The story accompanying the food is key.

PLANNING PROCESS

FROM EXHIBIT TO TABLE

- What local dishes are communicating cultural and regional uniqueness?
- What is the history of these foods in relation to community and culture?
- How can locally grown ingredients be incorporated into the menu?
- How can farm-to-table connections be presented?
- Are local heirloom varieties represented on the menu?
- What are the food requests of museum visitors?

Visitor education is easily provided at the table. This is an opportune time to present interpretation in a fun yet educational way since the museum attendee is at a pause, sitting and relaxing. Providing material to read at the table or ahead of the visit via the website inspires the palate. Information on the menu can include: the food history of local cultures; nutritional benefits of featured foods; use of heirloom varieties; and stories about local farms.

Foods to take along the trip or for home, continuing the memorable experience, may include locally made products such as the following examples.

- Snack foods or trail mix
- Dried stew or soup mixes
- Popcorn with unique, locally inspired seasonings
- Packages of dried fruit or nuts
- Packaged baked goods connected to local cuisines

An understanding of visitor preferences may be gained through the museum attendee survey. A video clip on the museum website, with content based on the survey, might illustrate how to cook a local dish. Other ways of presenting visual information include paintings of local foods and local plants in the café.

The International Museum of Folk Art in Santa Fe, New Mexico, in coordination with the adjacent Museum Café, produced an innovative exhibit-to-table concept. An exploration of the dawn of world cuisine as we know and consume today, the *New World Cuisine* exhibit explored how foods around the world developed from mixing the old and the new and how many of the tastiest dishes and desserts came to be associated with New Mexico. The exhibition (2012–2014) was complemented with interactive gallery activities including a scent station, magnetic world map, and a special selection of chocolate and cuisine in the museum shop. Furthering the experience, the Museum Café, located on museum hill in Santa Fe, collaborated to serve delicious dark chocolate dishes, extending the exhibit experience.

THE PLACEMAT

Another effective project for museums is to create placemats for use in local restaurants—featuring history, locator maps for shops, and a calendar of events. A placemat is a win-win project since visitors have an activity of learning the basics about local culture while waiting for food. Printed versions can offer the following.

- Local or regional history
- Local cuisine recipes
- Stories to complement exhibit themes
- Games reflecting local cultures
- Maps

Featuring local recipes and hiring a local chef or cook encourages cultural retention, or knowledge of traditional foods. As a complement, providing additional placemats for visitors to take home is an inexpensive form of promotion and encourages repeat visitation. Providing information and changing content annually evolves a new aspect of learning. Repeat visitation is linked to the sense of a new experience.

TENT CARD POTENTIAL

A tent card is a display of information or an advertisement, usually placed on the tables in a restaurant. Often, tent cards are used in restaurants to advertise the specials or a new wine or liquor available. The tent card is printed and folded to be readable on either side of the fold and placed on a table top, counter, or other flat surface. Information for a possible display includes the following.

- Listing of local foods on the menu
- Nutritional benefits of an outstanding local food (e.g. anthocyanin, a powerful antioxidant in blue corn)
- Information on books on local or cultural foods for sale by the cash register

The "exhibit-to-table" tent card connects to the menu, furthering experiential potential.

MUSIC

Providing music, either live or downloadable, furthers the experiential concept. Songs featuring local stories extend the depth of the visit. Local bands expressing cultural themes through a variety of instruments and languages add to a deep sense of history and contemporary presence. Linking with musicians expands another means of employment locally.

MARKET NICHES FOR CULTURAL ENTREPRENEURS

In the small-scale sense, there is a concept of product significant in a culturally connected way—such as selling cultural items with respect so as to not objectify cultural meaning. Art items, handmade clothing, souvenirs, and packaged local foods are all opportunity niches. Market niches of high potential for cultural entrepreneurs include.

- Higher-end cultural arts, such as baskets, paintings, and quilts. This niche can be expanded by developing bio-cards for the artists and educational material distributed at the museum, as well as providing space for artists on the museum website. Information on the art-making processes and authentic materials also assists sales.

- A mid-line in smaller paintings, prints, jewelry, handmade clothing, and pottery appeal to potential collectors on smaller travel budgets.
- A souvenir line, priced at $30 and under, increases employment through sales—not only through the museum store but also for sale at art shows. Successful souvenir lines frequently tie to local culture or to exhibits.
- Tours, such as of the museum, local historic trails, cultural districts, or cultural ecology, may be developed either through the museum or by furthering referrals to local guides. Policies on where, how many, and allowable seasons are needed to manage visitors according to community requirements.
- Food service not only benefits food vendors but also keeps visitors longer in the community, thus encouraging more sales for entrepreneurs.
- Demonstrations further show appreciation for cultural processes, generating visitor interest and assisting local artists with sales.
- Storytelling events enrich interpretive efforts.

Broaden the options, present the authentic, and the "experience" is created. Museum visitors enjoy learning about the significance of cultural items, particularly through direct contact with cultural entrepreneurs. Demonstrations tied to exhibit themes and local arts stimulate learning, as well as local sales.

CREATING A LOCAL INVENTORY

The museum's role in community economy can facilitate a flexible network of local entrepreneurial services and activities, with the addition of support services in marketing and business training. Serving as a hub, the museum might coordinate entrepreneurial activity, conduct marketing, and provide book tours as a service. Directing the benefit to community entrepreneurial activity produces the local gain from museum services.

PLANNING PROCESS

THE LOCAL INVENTORY

- In analyzing the artist and product database, where do clusters of potential inventory exist?
- Where are unique items represented?
- How do these items connect to exhibit themes?
- Which items tie to local history and context?
- How does contemporary art reflect a past-present-future continuum?

- Where does the analysis show a need for increased cultural continuance efforts?
- How can a story be woven relating to tradition?

Frequently, defined needs to further develop artwork and souvenir sales include the following types of assistance.

- Promotion and marketing through business cards and bio-cards
- Assistance with product development to ensure diversity of products and high quality
- Visitor education on local culture
- A trademark for locally made
- Museum website links and brochures to create awareness of products offered
- Sharing of the artist database with other museums and organizations
- Bridging the producer/sales gap with entrepreneur access to information
- Assistance to artists that do not have resources to purchase marketing
- Establishing criteria for authentication

A focused effort for training entrepreneurs in product development benefits both the museum store and community. Product development is more likely to match local offerings with visitor preferences through training by a consultant familiar with the preferences of the market and sensitive to inclusivity considerations mentioned in the last chapter.

PRODUCT DEVELOPMENT STRATEGIES

In summary, management of the museum enterprise or café is enhanced with the following strategies:

Strategy 1: Stay informed about potential product niches by analyzing visitor statistics on an ongoing basis, furthering inventory success by learning of changing market niches for cultural arts and other products. Keeping in touch with local gift shops in a collaborative network assists management in tracking product inquiries from visitors and updating inventory according to trends.

Strategy 2: Train community members in artistic and business skills, providing community service while ensuring a dependable inventory. Developing and maintaining artist and entrepreneurial databases enables the museum store to contact artists for training and marketing opportunities. Teaching workshops in the cultural arts, as well as new skills identified for product development, contributes to local cultural retention efforts as well as an evolving inventory for the museum store.

Working with artists to produce bio-cards, emphasizing authenticity, local materials, and artist statements about their work adds an additional educational benefit to museum visitation. Developing a series of entrepreneurial and small arts business workshops furthers entrepreneurial skills, in addition to expanding options for the museum or cultural center's financial support.

Strategy 3: Educate the public on local arts, expanding the store's market. By including information on local arts in interpretive guides, the general public becomes educated about the arts, history, and art-making processes.

If possible, develop a changing exhibit at the museum, featuring local artists, to assist with art sales and efforts regarding cultural retention. Networking with regional and local art shows and notifying museum attendees, as well as local artists for participation, increases experiential opportunities.

Strategy 4: Open new market avenues for local artists and entrepreneurs. Providing liaison with regional and museum stores increases sales for local entrepreneurs. Sponsoring art shows at the museum increases selling opportunities. Booths set up outside the museum or in a foyer provide an interesting visitor experience, with the opportunity to interact directly with entrepreneurs.

Strategy 5: Provide opportunities for cultural entrepreneurs to link and market collaboratively using social media—increasing the market draw to the museum or cultural center. By designating a website page for local artists and entrepreneurs, promotional opportunities are increased for those who take the time to learn traditions.

EXTEND THE EXPERIENCE

Often overlooked by museums, sales beyond the actual visit are a way of continuing income after the initial visit. By maintaining linkages to tourism organizations and submitting notices of museum events in calendars, marketing of the museum is furthered through inclusion of exhibits, local art shows, and products—in visitor guides and on websites.

Museum visitors are encouraged to purchase from the museum store when provided information on the museum's role in cultural retention, continuity, and community connections. As visitor interest in community and environmental sustainability increases with current trends, providing information on entrepreneurs, items, and materials translates to "value-added" in the museum experience.

Visitor education is central to the experiential museum visit. Repeat orders from long distances are an additional source of income for the museum store. Setting a bio-card in a piece of pottery or a basket, or attaching the card to an item, better ensures that the information will stay with the piece. When visitors jot notes, whether on paper or on their mobile devices, these often become lost by the end of the trip.

Additionally, procedures for shipping and ensuring a steady supply of shipping materials are a part of an effective museum store policy. Reliable delivery of orders maintains the integrity of the community network. A marketing card or online link with upcoming events expands the impact of the sale.

Cultural arts evolve over time. Some evolve more slowly than others due to symbolism connected with those arts. If the art form is used for cultural reasons, the form and materials tend toward cultural significance. Commercialization of an art may affect the art form.

Demand through the market holds the potential to impact traditional arts by depleting natural resources needed for traditional uses when natural materials are found locally. Protecting these resources is vital to cultural survival. Museum sponsorship of symposia, talking circles, and involvement of a cultural committee provides a community forum for discussion of these issues vital to cultural continuance—all fundable projects.

FURTHER READING

McKibben, Bill. *Deep Economy: The Wealth of Communities and the Durable Future*. New York: Holt Paperbacks, 2008.
This classic discussion of economies advocates moving beyond a growth motivation, which produced more inequality than prosperity. Shifting to a more local direction, with communities producing more of their own goods and food, is highlighted. This people-focused concept of economy illustrates the valuable role possible for museums.

Museum Store Association. *Museum Store: The Manager's Guide*, 4th edition. New York: Routledge, 2016.
A practical guide covering visual merchandising, measuring performance, and managing volunteers. Supporting worksheets illustrate the topics of basic store management. The fourth edition also covers info on social media and mobile shopping.

Romhardt, Kai. *We Are the Economy*. Berkeley, CA: Parallax Press, 2020.
As a valuable questioning of people-centered economy, the author illustrates steps to creating a more human, small-scale approach to reconfiguring our core economic relationships and work, consumption, and money. The author recommends searching within ourselves for ethical frameworks to relate in society rather than seeing the economy as outside of us—leading to increased satisfaction in life.

NOTES

1. Decter, Avi, Marsha Semmel, and Ken Yellis, eds. *Change is Required: Preparing for the Post-Pandemic Museum.* Lanham, MD: Rowman & Littlefield, 2022.
2. Moore, Porchia, Rose Paquet, and Aletheia Wittman. *Transforming Inclusion in Museums: The Power of Collaborative Inquiry.* Lanham, MD: Rowman & Littlefield, 2022.
3. Guyette, Susan. *Sustainable Cultural Tourism: Small-Scale Solutions.* Santa Fe, NM: BearPath Press, 2013.
4. Luna, Pi, and Ed Worden. *Life Savings: Navigate the Financial Course.* Santa Fe, NM: Engage Press, 2015.
5. Ratten, Vanessa. "Coronavirus (Covid-19) and Entrepreneurship: Cultural, Lifestyle and Societal Changes." www.emerald.com/insight/2053-4604.htm.
6. Gehman, Joel, and Jean-François Soublière. "Cultural Entrepreneurship from Making Culture to Cultural Making." *Innovation* Vol. 19, No. 1 (2017).
7. Giones, Ferran, Alexander Brem, Jeffrey M. Pollack, Timothy L. Michaelis, Kim Klyver, and Jan Brinckmann. "Revising Entrepreneurial Action in Response to Exogenous Shocks: Considering the Covid-19 Pandemic." *Journal of Business Venturing Insights* Vol. 14 (2020).
8. Khlystova, Olena, Yelena Kalyuzhnova, and Maksim Belitski. "The Impact of the COVID-19 Pandemic on the Creative Industries: A Literature Review and Future Research Agenda." *Journal of Business Research* Vol. 139 (February 2022): 1192–1210. https://www.ncbi.nlm.nih.gov/pmc/articles/PMC8490124.
9. United Nations Educational, Scientific, and Cultural Organization (UNESCO). 2017.
10. Joffe, Avril. "Covid-19 and the African Cultural Economy: An Opportunity to Reimagine and Reinvigorate?" *Cultural Trends* Vol. 30, No. 1 (2021): pp. 28–39.
11. Bartik, Alexander W., Zoe B. Cullen, Edward L. Glaeser, Michael Luca, and Christopher T. Stanton. "What Jobs are Being Done at Home During the COVID-19 Crisis: Evidence from Firm-Level Surveys." *National Bureau of Economic Research.* 2020. doi:10.3386/w27422.
12. Khlystova, Kalyuzhnova, and Belitski. "The Impact of the COVID-19 Pandemic on the Creative Industries."
13. "Goldman Sachs 10,000 Small Businesses: Business Strategy and Financials in Uncertain Times." Webinar. March 29, 2022.
14. Ratten. "Coronavirus (Covid-19) and Entrepreneurship."
15. Milstein, Brian. "Thinking Politically About Crisis: a Pragmatist Perspective." *European Journal of Political Theory* Vol. 14, No. 2 (2015): pp. 141–60.
16. Gabe, Todd, Richard Florida, and Charlotta Mellander. 2011. "The Creative Class and the Crisis." Working Paper Series: Martin Prosperity Research, Martin Prosperity Institute: University of Toronto.
17. Ibid.
18. Markusen, Ann. "A Consumption Base Theory of Development: An Application to the Rural Cultural Economy." *Agricultural and Resource Economics Review* Vol. 36, Issue 1 (2016): pp. 9–23.
19. Florida, Richard. *The Great Reset.* New York: HarperCollins Publishers, 2010.
20. CreativeNEXT. "Supporting the Creative Industries of Massachusetts: Listening Tour Summary Report." 2012. www.mass.gov.

8

Cultural Districts and Welcoming

Cultural understanding, fundamental to inclusivity, grows through relationships. How is such connection created? Sense of place connoting cultural identity, belonging, and homeland—as a cultural way of life and a physical landscape—is reflected in museum programs. Making the past-present-future connection is central to creating sense of place: the museum has potential to play a vital, unifying role as a hub connecting to other cultural venues. With this intention, community connection deepens the museum narrative.

Culture is more than an ideal but rather a belief system and a lifestyle. With a value-based approach, a unified effort is likely to emerge. Adding community relevance to visitation by creating a place-making theme and welcoming are first steps toward a cohesive experience. Such a unified concept encourages art, history, storytelling, and cultural learning by the local population while supporting employment through the creative economy.

Museum visitors are more likely to become engaged in cultural learning as local cultural issues are acknowledged and addressed. How to strengthen engagement? A cultural district is a community location where cultural history, the arts, job creation, and community pride are enjoyed. And a cultural welcoming signals entry into a unique space.

ENVISIONING CULTURAL LANDSCAPES

Cultural landscapes are treasures to a community, reflecting relationship with place. Local landscapes in which people feel they belong represent a cultural sense of place, history, and cultural identity. With shared local knowledge and experience reflected in symbolism, these places become meaningful and socially important.[1]

Rather than seeing land as a commodity to use up, as in the American mainstream, the community-integrated viewpoint sees land as the memory and future of the culture—past, present, and future. To this end, land use decisions regarding visitors must incorporate past history, and needs of the present as well as a balance of future economic and cultural needs. In this regard, interpretive programs connected to cultural landscapes are central to furthering understanding.

Maintaining and enhancing quality of life is at the very heart of the community-integrated museum. Access to historically significant places, and the maintenance of cultural landscapes—land and sea—are significant to cultural pride. Museums serve a unifying purpose by:

- Enhancing a sense of place by communicating a rich cultural heritage;
- Increasing visitor awareness of local history;
- Managing the flow of visitors, particularly through tours; and
- Inspiring cultural pride and involvement in cultural activities, such as learning the cultural arts and language.

Maintaining and enhancing cultural landscapes are essential in bringing forth the strengths inherent in diverse cultural wisdom. Benefits of connecting the interrelated elements of place include fostering respect for diversity and local environmental stewardship. Museum programs can foster sense of place and inclusion with the following aspects.

Sustainable development supports and advances quality of life to provide jobs, opportunities for citizen creativity, cultural enrichment, and recreation as well. All of these aspects of quality of life are crucial to sense of place, culturally-based employment, and a cultural future. Put simply, the interconnected whole provides a greater educational experience than the individual amenities.

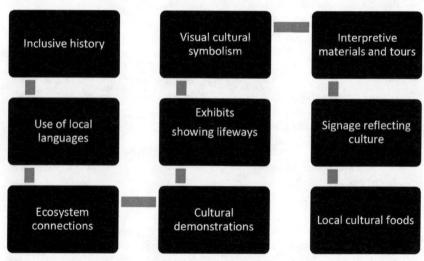

Chart 8.1. Cultural Landscape Linkages

Chapter 8

Wayfinding is more than following a series of signs. Museums may participate in enhancing place-making through providing a welcoming, offering interpretation, distributing a visitor etiquette, and guiding visitors with signage that reflects cultural symbolism—four ways of realizing and communicating sense of place.

LINKING IN A CULTURAL DISTRICT

A new movement internationally holds great promise for integrating museums with their cultural landscapes. Cultural districts, sometimes called arts and culture districts, typically invite museums, historic buildings, art centers, galleries, performance venues, creative entrepreneurs, significant cultural features, restaurants, and lodging to participate. Through collaborations, cultural districts link resources for an exciting visitor concept, historic downtowns are renovated, and jobs are generated through the creative economy. Resources often available from state economic development, arts, and tourism departments provide a coordinated assistance effort.

The museum's role in restoring historic buildings, vital for preserving a sense of place, is another resource of high potential. Central to local identity and cultural retention efforts, these buildings are a source of "cultural memory," offering spaces to learn history and culture, vital to ongoing place-making. Historic buildings become resources that create a draw to cultural and heritage tourists as well.

In terms of audience development, revitalization surrounding history and the arts, plus the creation of itineraries, extends the amount of time a visitor spends in a locale. Cultural and heritage tourists are seeking to understand not only history but also the details of tradition continuity in a community visited.

PLANNING PROCESS

CONNECTING TO COMMUNITY

- What are beliefs uniting an understanding of local culture?
- How is history reflected in current art and culture offerings?
- Which historic buildings need restoration?
- What are the potential uses of these buildings (e.g. museums, classrooms, galleries)?
- How can a story be told through the unification of these offerings?
- Which messages will be conveyed throughout the district?
- Which themes will further convey our sense of place?
- How will the community connect to technical-assistance providers (local, regional, state, national)?
- How will we complete a plan for moving forward?

Local governments recognize the value of this unique opportunity to develop a market niche for the creative economy, as place-based economic development. For this reason, a museum clearly defining a role as part of an arts and culture district aligns with top local government priorities—usually centered on economic development. As described in chapter 9, "Connecting to Tourism," the museum can become positioned as a hub for the arts and culture vitality of a place-based economy.

PLANNING PROCESS

ORGANIZING A CULTURAL COMMITTEE OR BOARD

- How will partnership be developed to form a cultural district?
- How will different cultures be highlighted as an inclusive concept?
- How will full cultural participation and in-depth understanding of world-views be gained?
- Who will conduct an asset inventory to determine culturally related resources?
- Which electronic resources will be used to maintain connection of the partners?

Museum experiences based on cultural values and context offer a glimpse into another way of life or a different way of viewing the world. A cultural district is a specific area with a concentration of cultural facilities and activities. This experiential, unified visit is sought after by the national and international visitor. High in contemporary visitor interests are shopping, dining experiences, recreation, and opportunities to learn about environmental stewardship. The following chart illustrates a process for assessing and listing local cultural resources, then seeing clusters for an inclusive process.

With careful planning, decisions regarding information appropriate to share, balanced with cultural privacy, lead to the unique community-integrated visitation concept. According to the Americans for the Arts,[2] other terms for these clusters are used widely in the United States:

- **Cultural Compounds** are the oldest districts, primarily established in cities prior to the 1930s. These compounds are sometimes built in areas somewhat distant from the city's business district and may have large, open green spaces between buildings. Often included are major museums, large performing halls, theaters and auditoriums, colleges, libraries, planetariums, and zoos. Forest Park in St. Louis and the cluster of museums at the University of Chicago are examples.
- **Cultural Institution Districts** are often anchored by one or two major cultural institutions, such as museums or a performing arts center, which then

RESOURCE TYPE	Needs Business Plan?	Needs Renovation?	Needs Capital?	Wants Training?
Museums				
Cultural centers				
Historic sites				
Historic buildings				
Arts organizations				
Performance venues				
Galleries				
Shops				
Restaurants				
Lodging				
Cultural entrepreneurs				

Chart 8.2. Inventory Culturally Related Sources

attracts smaller arts organizations around it. Frequently these districts are located next to central business districts or near a convention center. The Pittsburgh Cultural District is an example.

- **Downtown Area Districts** may encompass the entire downtown area of a city. Designation is often tied to local neighborhoods and is common in small cities with downtowns conducive to walking. The Arts and Entertainment District of Cumberland is an example.
- **Cultural Production Districts** are comprised primarily of community centers, artist studios, and educational arts centers and media facilities. These clusters often exist in areas with affordable housing and commercial space. Such districts create a cultural hub and enhance city livability for residents of a neighborhood, rather than attracting tourists. The Warehouse Arts District in Tucson is an example.
- **Arts and Entertainment Districts** include more popular culture and commercial attractions and feature more modest-sized buildings with a bohemian feel. They include museums, small theaters, movie houses, private galleries, restaurants, and other entertainment venues. "The District" in Nashville is a well-known example.

The creation of a cultural district implies collaboration between the arts, cultural programs, and local community involvement.[3] Often the cultural district is a unique collaboration between local government and several partner organizations. District designation may be bestowed by a state program or a nonprofit providing technical assistance and access to new funding opportunities. Collaborations arising from the designation are a sign of a positive future for cultural retention efforts, visitor education, increased employment through the creative economy, and environmental stewardship as well.

PLANNING PROCESS

DEFINING A THEME

- What is the strength of the cultural cluster?
- How do local cultural resources weave a story?
- What is the central thread through the story?
- How can the theme be repeated throughout a unified concept?
- How will the theme be communicated?

There are nearly 900 Main Street programs in the United States unifying arts, culture, and tourism offerings.[4] The following diagram illustrates a four-part art and cultural district process developed by the MainStreet Program[5] under the New Mexico Economic Development Department. This program offers resources to grow a market niche in place-based economic development within a distinct boundary. Nationally, some Main Street programs function within state governments and others are developed by not-for-profit organizations.

Emphasizing the connection between historical and cultural strengths, while growing a creative economy, is a key strategy. With the aligning of multiple intentions, community momentum is strengthened. In partnerships with local governments, the National Main Street Center, Inc. offers assistance for the revitalization of traditional and historic commercial districts. Additionally, several federal and private foundation funders give priority to arts and culture district projects, realizing the strengths of collaborative institutions and the draw to tourism.

Buildings and their design hold cultural memory for bridging the past, present, and future of a community. Restoring historic buildings often represents a key strategy for arts and culture districts, for these are central to community identity and cultural retention efforts, as well as tourism development and creative economy. Improving building energy efficiency is an aspect of restoration amenable to funding. Consider the museum opportunity.

Networking cultural institutions, programs, and enterprises together can develop an arts and cultural district as a destination—if multiple-day itineraries are formed and customer service skills fostered. Developing culturally-related programs gives incentives for community members, especially youth, to learn

New Mexico Arts and Cultural Districts
Operational Components

Cultural Planning and Development
- Cultural Plans/Vision for District
- Cultural Facilities
- Cultural Entrepreneurs
- Cultural Activities
- Creative Economy
- Cultural Tourism
- Historic Preservation

Physical Planning and Development
- District Boundaries
- Master Plan
- Beautification
- Projects
- Dining/Lodging
- Physical Spaces
  - Theaters
  - Plazas
  - Studios/Galleries
  - Live/Work Spaces

Capacity and Sustainability
- Arts Leadership
- Org. Structure
- Volunteers/Staff
- Project Coordination
- Org. Planning
- Budgeting, Fundraising
- Financial Tools
- Public Relations
- Advocacy

Branding and Marketing
- District Image
- District Branding
- Org. Branding
- Cultural Events
- Promotions
- Destination Development

Chart 8.3. Stages of Cultural District Development

Source: New Mexico MainStreet Program

the history and local traditions. Teaching the arts to youth represents a way of nurturing focus and patience in many cultures.

Also, involving high-school and college-aged youth as tour guides provides valuable employment training while building a generationally connected future. Self-esteem benefits are a result as well. Intergenerational assistance in developing local stories and drawing upon traditional storytelling techniques provides a draw to visitors.

SENSE OF PLACE AND CREATIVE ECONOMY

Community participation initiated by local governments often identifies job creation as high on the list of desired outcomes. In both rural and urban areas, both high unemployment and underemployment are leading concerns. Why is this important to museums as cultural institutions?

The future of many regions depends upon developing local options for earned livelihood. When jobs are lacking, as is a growing trend, local residents move from rural to urban areas for employment and young people tend to not return after their education is completed. To stay connected to place and engage in cultural activities—while creating a means of livelihood compatible with culture—supports both community and cultural sustainability.

Typically, a museum store functions in isolation from the local economy. As the museum becomes part of a team encouraging discussions about local skills and small enterprise development, this process occurs prior to considering larger-scale ideas. When smaller, entrepreneurial businesses create products and services to feed into larger community businesses—rather than importing services and products from outside of the community—then tourism generates community referrals to the museum and develops in a way compatible with the culture.

The primary advantage of a network comprised of small-scale, linked enterprises—over an economy based on large-scale business—is the potential for authentic expression of local culture. Training to develop the skills of cultural entrepreneurs is basic to the success of small-scale and locally owned enterprises.

MUSEUMS AND THE CREATIVE ECONOMY

When community-integrated, a museum is an integral part of the creative economy. Participation is strengthened when this segment of the local economy is clearly understood. For example, expanding community integration leads to further support for a broad range of cultural entrepreneurs. Epidemics and the environmental crisis underscore the importance of such integration for job continuity. To understand the creative economy, distinguishing between economic development and business development is important, for these terms are often used interchangeably.

"Business development" is specific to individual enterprises. Business planning, capital, employee training, and marketing are all components of business development—which, in turn, contribute to a local economy. What is termed "economic development" refers to a whole system of interconnected businesses, entrepreneurs, and traditional economic activity. When the museum is envisioned as a hub, economic impacts will be far reaching.

The proactive museum's ongoing dialogue with local government keeps the creative economic sector at the forefront. Strategies or talking points are addressed in this section. One aspect of the creative economy related to the local business environment is the potential for the cultural arts to contribute those extra dollars from visitor experiences and tourism-related enterprises owned locally. These enable essential businesses and services, such as grocery stores, gas stations, lodging, and restaurants, to survive and thrive. This is an essential strategy for approaching local governments in terms of financial support for a museum.

A community's internal economy will benefit from the interest generated by entrepreneurial participation, and a broader range of fascinating, handmade or locally grown goods for sale. Cultural traditions are then strengthened, for economic development cannot be quantified in dollars alone. Assistance with product development is essential for maintaining quality: training topics were suggested in the next chapter.

In small-scale local economies, true economic development only occurs when specific factors work in unison—as economic multipliers increase, as leakages to the outside economy are reduced, as traditional items are produced, as traditional bartering and subsistence systems supplement cash income (thus reducing dependency on full-time employment), and as cottage industries flourish and support extended family units. This scenario is more culturally rooted and contrasts sharply with large-scale business development focused entirely on profit margins and the number of jobs created. Sustainable, flexible economy requires this long-term approach.

True economic development takes a great deal more time and effort than larger-scale business development. A solid yet flexible foundation is created through expertise expanding in local communities and diversification of the economic system. In other words, internal strengths or capacity of a community develop over time, while dependency on external development and management expertise is minimized. The smaller scale, strongly formed, is more sustainable and is longer-lasting through economic fluctuations.

Businesses that complement each other within a region form a strong economic system. An effective economic development planning process includes the creative economy and asks participants to look at both the economy of the region and their local economy. This analysis identifies the gaps, called business niches.

The hub concept for development—or a primary visitor intake point providing referrals to small-scale businesses—encourages local residents to see the niches available for entrepreneurship and to develop small businesses providing services and products. Strong networks based on cooperation, rather than competition, benefit from collaborative marketing and a consistent, friendly greeting.

As noted in previous chapters, the creative economy is often more sustainable than other forms of economic development.[6] Entrepreneurial businesses may withstand fluctuations in the economy with more stability than do larger enterprises. Given the high level of economic uncertainty globally, assisting entrepreneurs to grow and market their businesses and linking them together into a network provides economic resilience. And this is a very fundable service.

As the museum participates in local creative economy-building, assisting cultural entrepreneurs to develop product lines and services—cultural retention, employment, and income increase. An economic multiplier is the number of times a dollar recirculates in the local economy. In other words, economic multipliers increase in a locale as additional products are made within the region, rather than imported. Museums may not see themselves as an integral part of the economic system; however, with greater community integration, their role can be pivotal in the creative economy.

The challenge lies in finding the intersection between a cultural fit with museum visitors that also meshes well with local industries. Referrals to a community's businesses are another way of furthering the museum's community connection. For example, purchasing items or providing a recipe to bring home continues the experience and encourages word-of-mouth marketing and repeat visitation. Small "extras" with interpretation make a visit memorable.

Educating visitors about historical context, arts, artists, art-making processes, and other cultural traditions is an important role for the museum. This can be accomplished through exhibit interpretation, a changing exhibit for artists, sponsoring art shows or festivals, tours, and creating an exciting museum website.

Cultural tourists are seeking information about the artist, as well as authenticity of materials and the art-making processes. Providing referrals to entrepreneurs through the museum website is a possible strategy to increase community connection. Artist bios, artwork or product photos, contact information, and hours (seasonally) when businesses and artists can be reached are critically important. A listing on the website may be offered as a "perk" for advanced students.

Developing a vacation concept unifying arts and culture for the two-to-five-day stay increases overall expenditures into the local economy. For example, the concept could include the museum, shopping, dining, historic tours, art studios, cultural centers, and ecosystem tours. As a hub for tourism and art-activity referrals, a museum is in a position to initiate different modes of communication that create the tourism draw. Attracting repeat visitors is heightened by designing an exciting "experience," enhanced by the community's ability to vary the combination of amenities within the experience. Coupled with continuity and consistency from year to year, this caring approach encourages the return visit.

Cultural entrepreneurs are assisted through such unification. To increase sales from tourists, developing the capacity for mail order after the visit is a must in relation to job creation. Frequently, visitors wish they had purchased while on-site and want to order more for themselves, or as gifts. Ordering more of what the visitor purchased for the holiday season is an example. Friends who see their purchases may also wish to order by mail.

To increase expenditures, consider how items reflecting local culture might be combined in a gift box. For example, a handmade ceramic soup mug combined with a bag of chowder mix and a recipe is an example that draws upon existing local strengths. This is a creative product idea for the museum store.

By providing training and advertising support to local entrepreneurs, the amount of earned livelihood created through entrepreneurial activities is raised. In the next two chapters, training and assistance for local entrepreneurs are detailed. The cultural handmade item and traditionally based service draw visitors, building a market for the larger amenity businesses, such as lodging and food service. Expanding local opportunities and nurturing the sense of discovery increases interest in museum visitation. This is the link between museums, tourism, and local economy.

A WELCOMING UNIFIES

Consistent welcoming throughout the community unifies the visitation experience. The majority of cultures in the world have rich, traditional ways of welcoming. This oftentimes transcends a translation of the word "hello." Welcoming statements in the local language or languages, greeting songs, dances, offering of water or food all are ways of connecting, greeting, and caring for visitors.

Welcoming is the portal to another culture or worldview expressing that culture. Yet, museums often do not have a local or traditional way of welcoming. Most museums situate their entrance on a busy street, devoid of plant life and connections in nature. The entryway is designed to manage crowds and is usually quite empty. Brochure racks and a ticket counter tend to be the visuals. With a unique welcoming, the past-present-future continuum is reinforced with the message "we are still here."

Expressing aliveness, this is an invitation to enter a cultural worldview, a unique culture, or a different time period and a connection from object to people. Greetings set the tone of this emergence, this insight into new perspectives, a different way of being, or new learning styles. To this end, cultural expression embedded in a welcoming may communicate the following.

- You are invited in
- Experience interesting worldviews
- Learn from material expression of these worldviews
- If applicable, diverse languages are spoken here

One question to ask about the entry point: Is the entrance sterile or full of life and a reflection of cultures represented in the museum? Many museums experience shortages in staffing. For this reason, in-person greetings in a cultural setting may not be possible. A welcoming with a video kiosk is one option. Special events, such as opening receptions, arts shows, and festivals, are also greeting opportunities.

A welcoming is the bridge from community connection to increased cultural worldview understanding. Culturally specific greetings in museum entrances are one important facet of making the invitation to interact and learn from each other. In this sense, the museum greeting represents a respectful responsibility to the community. And local museum participants feel a sense of belonging.

THE MUSEUM GREETING

Audience development requires the merging of marketing techniques with relationship-building skills.[7] Visitors to museums enjoy personal interactions. Traditional greeting songs and dances—a part of the majority of cultures worldwide—may still be a part of community life. If it is not feasible to employ a greeter, consider other options. Recorded greeting songs and dances are interesting as part of a welcoming. Some communities ask elders to be greeters. Or staff at a front desk can learn a greeting for the museum. Hosting special events is another option for extending a traditional welcoming.

Greetings in the modern context take the form of the personal welcoming, in the language of the visitor, the traditional language, or both—as well as recordings, visuals, brochures, video viewing areas, and larger exhibits. When several languages are represented in the community, a bilingual or trilingual greeting enhances the authentic experience. Welcoming tradition and local language use, reflecting past and current practice, is an engaging topic to continue throughout exhibits. This illustrates the past-present-future continuum.

Consider greetings not only as important communications with visitors external to the community but also to the local community. Involving local residents for a consistent greeting increases cultural pride and community interest for cultural practice. Some museums coordinate with senior centers or youth groups for the presentation of a local greeting.

The language or form of a greeting reflects cultural continuity and language retention. When a traditional language or languages represented in the community are used, youth are inspired to learn a traditional language. Respect for elders is fostered. And cultural continuity is likely to be encouraged in households.

This is a serious issue worldwide, for of the 10,000 languages in the world, one is disappearing every two weeks.[8] Language communicates worldview, imbedded in structure—as illustrated in chapter 1. For example, the structure of many languages worldwide is more process-oriented than object-oriented. Process-oriented cultures tend to see interrelatedness in their worldview. If diverse languages do not continue, the means of cultural expression becomes severely limited globally. As language use is encouraged throughout community settings, cultural pride increases and is a stimulus to language learning. Recognition by visitors reinforces this process.

Many traditional cultures teach protocols, thousands of years old, for taking care of visitors. These protocols are imbedded in the use of a traditional language. Discussing these protocols for hosting visitors and deciding how to continue these traditions in current times delineates a contemporary way of addressing hospitality.

Welcoming within the expression of one's culture heightens the authentic experience. Examples from Native American cultures are the traditional greetings with water in the dry Southwestern United States, or the greeting songs sung by Northwestern tribes. Interviewing elders in a community, documenting hospitality traditions, and renewing these traditions assist a community with cultural retention. Traditional greetings are often extraordinary—from songs to dances or gifts, such as the welcoming lei, given in Hawai'i according to the Native Hawaiian tradition.

The absence of a welcoming is interpreted as rudeness in many cultures. For example, in Hispanic cultures, the greeting is tailored to the time of day. "Buenos dias" in the morning or "buenas tardes" in the afternoon are ways of being polite. These phrases are also an invitation to interact. Without these greetings, the encounter may be interpreted as hasty. A few moments of interaction sets the tone for learning receptivity.

DESIGNING THE WELCOMING

How people are greeted in a culture invites interaction. If the greeting is polite according to the culture, then warmth and the invitation to connect follow. Deciding collectively on a greeting style unifies participating arts and culture clusters.

PLANNING PROCESS

DISCOVER THE WELCOMING

- Which cultures of the community would be represented?
- What are the traditional forms of greeting in the local culture or cultures?
- Which languages are represented?
- How does the greeting connect to community and cultural values?
- How can multiple generations interact in the greeting?
- Are there cultural protocols to be followed, such as involvement of the political or spiritual leader?

A brief welcoming can communicate the cultural values considered important in the community. Making values visible fosters cultural understanding. To this end, an entrance full of life signals curiosity to experience a new cultural viewpoint. Greeting traditions signal an interesting cultural experience. Then, the welcoming content connects past to present and future.

PLANNING PROCESS

THE WELCOMING CONTENT

- What are important, yet brief, messages to convey?
- How does the welcoming connect to the museum's mission?

- Describe gestures that are important in a greeting.
- Are there welcoming songs or dances?
- Are there cultural boundaries on information appropriate to share?

Typical forms of saying hello or giving handshakes and hugs are quickly falling out of greeting practice due to pandemic times. Think verbal from a distance.

PRE-VISIT WELCOMING

A long-distance traveler's decision to visit a region is generally made well in advance of the actual vacation. Trip planning occurs from three months to a year ahead. For this reason, a strong welcoming statement is one persuasive factor indicating a pleasant stop ahead, as part of an interesting itinerary.

Technological options for inviting, welcoming, and sharing with visitors increase every year to include a multimedia approach, such as:

- A recorded greeting on the website;
- Apps;
- Electronic screen-video kiosks;
- Events calendar;
- Inclusion on in-room videos at local lodging; and
- Visitor guides and itineraries.

The effective welcoming orients the visitor to local cultures, signals an invitation, and serves as an introduction to the coming museum experience. A past-present-future connection is made by linking time-honored traditions to the present and fostering curiosity about connection to the future. Visitors appreciate this opening to the community!

CONNECTING VIRTUALLY

Extending the interpretive conversation on social media enriches the interpretative experience through interaction with museum visitors. The museum as a part of a unified community concept provides an experiential draw. Instant communication offered by social media is of immense benefit to developing a museum presence. Guiding potential visitors to the website or virtual museum is another essential benefit. Plus, nationally, tourism data from visitors to communities show a strong reliance on social media. As new platforms are developed, focus on the good platform match.

WEBSITE

Presenting a cohesive picture of history, arts, landscapes, and other offerings in a community heightens the sense of a cultural exchange. Options for promoting the museum as part of a larger, unified cultural experience include the following: historic tours, arts and culture tours, festivals, art shows, fairs, and cultural artist studio tours. These linkages contribute to community-wide interpretation. Options include guidance for exploring the multi-day stay on the arts and culture district website, the community's site, and a tourism website, plus the museum's website.

In chapter 9, options for unifying tours and promotion, readily available locally or regionally, are suggested. Overcoming museum isolation is a matter of collaboration for natural linkages. Market together and the cultural experience is born.

Social media suggestions in the next section are intended to apply in a general way. While new platforms may replace those mentioned, the basic functions of connecting with museum professionals, illustrating with video content, reaching individuals, and linking to the tourism market will apply into the future.

LINKEDIN

This is an ideal platform for networking with industry professionals and sharing new approaches for reaching the public, as well as for generating new strategies. More visibility for the museum facilitates inclusion in vacation-package concepts by interacting with tourism industry professionals—valuable for referrals.

Particularly, as an itinerary is developed featuring several museums, LinkedIn can be beneficial for connecting tourism personnel to local or regional offerings. European interests in travel tend to focus on: 1) education and culture, 2) community and relation, 3) nature and sustainability, and 4) body and health. In summary, the LinkedIn museum and travel marketing groups are important for networking, at no cost.

YOUTUBE

Potential culturally-oriented visitors want to experience contact with a local person representative of culture. For this reason, viewing a person welcoming on video holds a certain fascination. The direct interpretation possible with video is very appealing—as a glimpse of the "authentic" is highly valued with cultural tourists. Another benefit of video documentation involves creating an archive of seniors or elders speaking on traditions and the art-making processes. Community members speaking of the tie between exhibit themes and environmental preservation efforts will be a topic of growing interest.

Use of YouTube provides a valuable interactive opportunity. The following YouTube strategies are recommended to create an itinerary concept and to interface with offerings of the museum and visitor interests:

- An overview video featuring local activities and geographic features unifies a vacation concept. A story around historic sites could be included, as well as clips of arts and restaurants, local foods, and shopping to present the idea of a three- to five-day vacation itinerary with the museum as central.
- The museum seen as a history, arts, and culture "hub" positions the museum as a referral point.
- A video highlighting work of the museum relating to traditional arts and culture, particularly featuring interpretation, would be of keen interest to culturally oriented travelers.
- A recreational video could tie history, arts, and culture to geographic features. One example is a video tour of historic sites and trails.
- A storytelling video featuring traditional topics would interface with a storytelling program at the museum or cultural center.
- A video of the art-making processes emphasizes aspects of authenticity such as authentic materials, process, and maker. Such a video is prized by art collectors and would stimulate museum store sales or links to artists' websites through the creative economy.
- A video featuring an arts program and revitalization emphasizes the progress being made to bridge the historic to the contemporary. Cultural art interviews with instructors and students further their careers as artists and give them links to use on their websites. The virtual tour of an arts and culture district may provide the foundation for a later travel package, which could be further developed for travel agents to book.
- A video linking to the museum website and then linking that website to the local Chamber of Commerce website or the state tourism website plus social media is an effective way to gain inclusion on itineraries.
- A food video, highlighting foods available in local restaurants, could emphasize the unique options available, augmented by the museum's history of foods. Information on the cultural and nutritional aspects of local foods is value-added.
- If an arts and culture district develops with assistance from local government, an overview of businesses and activities can be featured.
- Traditional stories, music, and dances, as determined culturally appropriate, bring interpretation to life.

A well-sequenced video series is useful pre-visit to attract visitors as well as post-visit as a "souvenir"-type reminder for further learning. A common practice among cultural tourists is to host a vacation "show and tell" with friends post-visit. As tours sponsored by the museum are developed, a "preview" offered via YouTube is effective. When the museum applies for tourism-related grants, a video documentary can be written into the budget. Each video should mention the links to the museum website and local tourism-oriented websites of businesses.

FACEBOOK

Arts and culture district participants use Facebook effectively for posting comments and photos of events, inviting visitation. Often social media postings appear disjointed, not explaining the meaning or content of the event. Also, the intent of the content may be confusing—sometimes intended for locals and other times for tourists. Content needs to be sorted out and clarified, or another solution is two Facebook pages, with one for visitors to the museum and another for programs intended for local residents.

X (FORMERLY TWITTER)

The brief format is ideal for announcing activities available as they develop for the museum and an arts and culture district. These could include:

- Openings and art shows;
- Food offerings and menu specials;
- Sales of authentic and contemporary art items; and
- Invitations to art shows, dances, and other celebrations throughout the year.

TRIPADVISOR

Increasing the museum's presence as the hub for a local tour could further this important tourism draw factor on TripAdvisor. Positive reviews on TripAdvisor have become the most essential standard in the tourism industry for booking a vacation, which is an opportunity for a museum as part of an itinerary.

INSTAGRAM

Instagram usage is especially popular among millennials and Gen Z. This visually oriented site provides a means for museums to step outside their physical boundaries and attract visitors who otherwise might not travel. With 500 million Instagram users worldwide, at the time of this writing, the potential for connecting your museum to visitors with a broad range of interests is staggering—think virtual exhibits, tours of collection items, and the expression of community-connected missions. Photos of collections are an excellent way of sharing examples for cultural learning, if this route is appropriate to the community. Examples are the Field Museum in Chicago and the Museum of Modern Art in New York. The Art Institute of Chicago shares historic photos in a connective way to the present.

SUMMARY TIPS FOR SOCIAL MEDIA USE

Museums leading in social media use recommend the following practices:[9]

- Give exciting updates, keeping followers engaged in a continuing story.
- Stay current with cultural events, connecting your stories represented in exhibits and programs to widespread stories of local and regional interest.
- Highlight your community, furthering the community-integrated orientation, such as local events or including the artwork of your community and interfaces with other organizations.
- Cultivate pride in local history, sharing historic photos, major events through time, and showing the continuity of museum exhibit themes through time with images.
- Make the experience fun, combining storytelling with excellent visuals that encourage interaction.

Given the importance of virtual connection, museums need social media expertise on staff or on contract. Synergy between all outreach methods is essential to remember.

CREATIVE ECONOMY AND CULTURAL CONTINUANCE

The museum as part of a connected, local movement is a vibrant story. Cultural arts, food service, lodging, and entertainment are potentials for culturally meaningful sources of employment, resilient over time. Cultural survival often depends upon staying in the traditional geographic location, with access to traditional plants, animals, and sense of place.

For this reason, sustaining a cultural future based on history and tradition may depend upon generating cash flow through multiple income streams. When culturally based business ideas emerge, a unique network of institutions and businesses is created—far more exciting to cultural tourists than the larger-scale single enterprise that travel agents love to book, for profit and convenience.

Family involvement, or teaching the next generation, is essential for economic sustainability. Starting with families, encouraging intergenerational involvement builds upon cultural strengths. Community resilience is reinforced with such an approach by building upon traditional support systems. The tie-in between the arts and technology is key for a twenty-first-century concept, and increased Internet visibility is needed to expand local economic opportunity.

In summary, the option of full-time, large-enterprise employment in relation to quality of life is essential for a community to consider. A large number of immediate jobs from industry—highly susceptible to fluctuations in the national economy—does not necessarily translate to a long-term means of sustainable and ecologically sound earned livelihood. This is a consideration to bring up with local government in terms of tax support.

For rural and Indigenous communities in particular, there may be an expanded range of employment options that also sustain culture, family, community, and environment—while maximizing job creation. Local community needs may include learning and employment options that offer freedom of schedule to participate in the annual cycle of cultural activities critical to cultural survival in place.

Collaborative goals, creative problem-solving, and decentralized frameworks[10] lead to a more genuine, informal, and unified social network. This applies not only to museum structure but also to community dynamics. Unification, with all partners seen as equal players, leads to strengthening inclusivity. These are the foundations of community-building.

FURTHER READING

Redaelli, Eleonora. *Connecting Arts and Place: Cultural Policy and American Cities.* Switzerland: Palgrave MacMillan, 2019.

This book presents a unique approach to the arts and public policy through the lens of space. This analysis of five main concepts in the international discourse concerning cultural policy covers cultural planning, cultural mapping, creative industries, cultural districts, and creative place-making. The text highlights how each concept contributes to the understanding of ways the arts connect with place.

Francesconi. Alberto. *Advanced Cultural Districts: Innovative Approaches to Organizational Designs.* Bedford, MA: Palgrave Pivot, 2015.

This text explores organizational design issues within the cultural heritage sector, with particular focus on the advanced forms of cultural districts for local socioeconomic development. Covering eight Italian case studies, most of the literature concentrates on urban clusters plus cities of art and cities of culture, intended for local socioeconomic development. The book aims to extend the knowledge and understanding of cultural heritage under managerial and organizational perspectives.

Lorente, J. Pedro. *Public Art and Museums in Cultural Districts.* New York: Routledge, Taylor & Francis Group, 2019.

Presenting a history of museum/public art connections, the author includes sections on gardens as extensions of museums, open air museums,

museums of street art, and museum/public art articulation. International case studies are featured.

Means, Mary. *Main Street's Comeback: And How It Can Come Back Again.* Pennsauken Township, NJ: BookBaby, 2021.
  As founder of the Main Street program's national organization, the author chronicles its impact as an influential movement and describes why its principles and practices continue to be relevant today, especially given the economic challenges small towns face in the wake of COVID-19. The organization spawned a movement, helping bring thousands of small towns back to life.

NOTES

1. Basso, Keith. *Wisdom Sits in Places. Landscape and Language among the Western Apache.* Albuquerque, NM: University of New Mexico Press, 1996.
2. Americans for the Arts, "Cultural Districts Basics." www.americansforthearts .org/by-program/reports-and-data/toolkits/national-cultural-districts-exchange/ cultural-districts-basics.
3. Ibid.
4. www.mainstreet.org/mainstreetamerica/theprograms.
5. Note the spelling of the national movement Main Street differs from the New Mexico example without the space. Local areas may choose different spellings.
6. Markusen, Ann. "A Consumption Base Theory of Development: An Application to the Rural Cultural Economy." *Agricultural and Resource Economics Review* Vol. 36 (2007): pp. 9–23.
7. Walker-Kuhne, Donna. *Invitation to the Party: Building Bridges to the Arts, Culture and Community.* New York: Theatre Communications Group, 2005.
8. Davis, Wade. *The Wayfinders.* Toronto, ON: House of Anansi Press, 2009.
9. MuseumNext. "How Museums Can Use Social Media?" April 16, 2022. https://www .museumnext.com/article/museums-can-use-social-media.
10. Greer, Christian. "From Silos to Social Networks." In *Change is Required: Preparing for the Post-Pandemic Museum*, Avi Decter, Marsha Semmel, and Ken Yellis (eds.), pp. 165–69. Lanham, MD: Rowman & Littlefield, 2022.

9

Connecting to Tourism

Of the possible audiences for a museum, the connection to small-scale tourism is most often missed. When a museum's audience is comprised of local residents and tourists, the capacity for exhibits and programs expands. Post-pandemic challenges include rebuilding or stimulating confidence among both tourists and local people.[1]

Community connection plus authentic experiences enhance the sought-after visitor journey. A linked itinerary creates the sought after multi-day experience. Enter the possibilities of museum leadership presence in an arts and culture district plus participation in a local visitor's guide. Given the importance of connection to museum success, the marketing section of your museum plan will benefit from this interface.

Potential for future museum innovation is inviting! With recent travel limitations, communities are designing unique ways to reach visitors before the journey. Podcasts introduce aspects of interpretation and local history, not as widely available in a previous era. In addition to drawing a broader range of visitors, in terms of interests or regions, the museum refresh button benefits from an equitable exchange.

An opportunity for enhanced interpretation through inclusivity is furthered by stretching to understand the interests of culturally diverse groups. Linking to multiple worldviews is at the core of success in both audience and community building. An inclusive example of the exchange concept is gifting[2]—still prevalent in the majority of cultures worldwide. A small yet memorable gift as the museum visitor departs is a gesture of hospitality and generosity. For example, a small mesh bag with a few seeds accompanied by an information card is an opportunity to explain local related history. Or, sharing a local recipe either online or on paper is a small offer of hospitality. As mentioned in chapter 8 on arts and culture districts, the gifting tradition can be a collaborative effort among businesses and organizations. Increasing connection cannot be overestimated.

A COOPERATIVE CONCEPT

The tourism exchange is connected to an experience involving both tangible and intangible culture. Interfacing with the industry, developing visitor education, and becoming either a hub or a stop on an itinerary are all effective ways of expanding museum attendance while increasing earned income toward sustainability. Museum integration into local cultures, economies, and ecosystems requires connecting beyond museum walls as part of a cohesive network. Meeting shifts in visitor interest draws repeat visitation. To that end, keeping current with technological innovations furthers the ability to connect.

Museums, particularly rural ones, tend to work in isolation. Connecting to tourism broadens the museum's reach from local to regional and even further to a national level. As the museum becomes a resource for information, a link is formed in a museum and amenity network. The cooperative value produces the widest community benefit. This process is not only useful for attracting visitors but also for educating about a rich, regional cultural heritage. Additionally, museum participation enhancing the tourism draw to the local economy is a fundable project.

The interpretative story is continued not only from the museum locally but also to an entire visitor trip as well. Sharing with others after the trip is a significant part of the cultural tourism experience. As visitor surveys reveal, purchasing cultural arts and understanding cultural significance are a prime interest.

Cultural tourists are seeking authentic experiences and learning experiences to take home with them to show family and friends. An interesting story furthers their experience. And, important to the museum is the potential for support of cultural continuance programs.

In times of limited travel or epidemics, those seeking a getaway tend to perceive rural areas as safer from disease or violence. This value-added is an attractive factor in the desire to escape cities—an opportunity for rural museums. Small-scale tourism versus mass tourism attracting large numbers is a niche for museums to provide an in-depth experience.

Participating in the formation of local plans (see Appendix B) facilitates inclusion of the museum or cultural center in community-wide discussions—an effective way of furthering museum integration. This is an opportunity to enhance recognition of the museum's contributions. In particular, a specific connecting step is participation in tourism planning efforts, to learn details of the local tourism system comprised of attractions, services, transportation, information, and promotional efforts.[3] Opportune linkages and ways of working reciprocally then become apparent.

THE MUSEUM AS A HUB

A museum or cultural center is often the first visitor stop, particularly in a small community. As introduced in chapter 8, there are multiple ways for a museum to serve the important community function of visitor education. The foyer of a museum may serve an interpretive center function with visitor information. A video kiosk is an ideal point to introduce cultural and community context. Another ideal point for visitor information is the museum website for educating the visitor before arrival and encouraging locally respectful behavior.

Telling the community story begins by linking and communicating context. Providing visitor and interpretive information at this location is the ideal point for:

- Brochures;
- Visitor guides;
- Video kiosks for display of area attraction locations and services;
- Sample menus at local restaurants;
- Information on local businesses, artists, entrepreneurs;
- Interesting educational exhibits;
- Information on traditional arts;
- Explanations of desired visitor etiquette;
- Information on linkages to tourism websites; and
- Booking of guiding services.

Chart 9.1.   The Museum as a Hub for Tourism

A museum may be an ideal centralized point from which to manage and promote tourism, particularly for the small community. Referrals to other museums, local businesses, artists, guides, and entrepreneurs further regional benefits. Working with other local businesses for visitor education then becomes a unifying function of the museum or cultural center.

Information-added is a way of presenting community-based interpretation to complement an exhibit and other museum programs. In many cultures, this is considered treating an object with respect by imparting the cultural meaning. Beyond information conveyed directly in exhibits, informative interpretation continues with locally made products and foods.

LINKING TO THE TOURISM SYSTEM

Tourism participation often provides the added local stimulus for developing a museum or expanding existing programs. Successful audience development depends upon both local participation and visitors coming from other regional, state, and national locales. The opportunity for interrelated tourism and museum development is important for community presentation, as there may be mixed tourism receptivity in the community.

Tourism receptivity underlies potential for interface with regional tourism entities. Interfacing with local tourism planning efforts yields assessment data as to whether visitation is desired by the community and furthers inclusion of the museum or cultural center. Concerns for tourist health, safety, and security are elements of quality service. The World Tourism Organization (WTO) lists appearance of physical facilities, reliability, responsiveness, competence, courtesy, credibility, security, access, communication, and understanding the customer as the top dimensions of service quality.[4] Recommended topics for discussions include:

- The museum as a tourism intake point for visitor education;
- A cultural value-based approach to interpretation;
- Overview of the tourism opportunity;
- Planning for tourism and museum connection;
- Limiting and managing tourism congruent with community preferences;
- Developing a visitor etiquette, brochures, and websites, featuring inclusivity;
- Interface between tourism and cultural or local arts;
- Securing community input;
- Potential for a local souvenir line; and
- Linkages for collaboration (museum/tourism industry).

If the community shows hesitation to tourism, clearly defining the museum's audience and clarifying cultural boundaries for sharing—both for information and physical places—increases community receptivity. Finding the ideal tourism match is often a factor to receptivity, as cultural and heritage tourists tend to be respectful of local values. Starting with one market and increasing the markets targeted, particularly in small communities, is one approach used successfully as community capacity to accommodate visitors expands. Linking to broaden the experience is key for telling the story.

CREATING A NETWORK

Tourism works on the basis of cooperation. Referrals are readily given when a museum or an activity is interesting and offered reliably. To create strong tourism partnerships on both regional and community levels, consider potential collaborations between three sectors: government, businesses, and nonprofit organizations. Methods for planning, linking in a network, and developing a tour are presented in my book, *Sustainable Cultural Tourism: Small-Scale Solutions*.

Community benefits from participating in a tourism network include:

- Enhancing an understanding of local and regional history;
- Increasing the market for locally made arts, local foods, and services;
- Broadening skills with available training (in-person and online);
- Creating locally based employment; and
- Increasing cultural understanding among ethnic groups.

An initial step in the connecting process is assessing promotional and Internet resources already developed. This effort is useful for learning about your tourism partners, as well as securing existing materials for visitor education. The museum's role in visitor education is a central niche. Tourists generally plan a vacation in terms of the five- to seven-day experience, or for the shorter weekend trip. Tourists are more likely to visit a museum when the longer itinerary is easy to discover. The museum visit is commonly "a part of," not an isolated tourist draw.

A next step involves working with several sectors in the industry. Global, national, regional, statewide, and local tourism organizations assess the market through visitor surveys and market analyses, then promote tourism based on visitor interest and local offerings. These organizations include chambers of commerce, convention and visitor bureaus, welcome centers, cultural organizations, business assistance centers, and economic development corporations, as well as organizations dedicated specifically to tourism outcomes.

To become more involved in local tourism, host a tourism network meeting at the museum to highlight your offerings. Including tourism partners and tour operators during special events hosted by the museum demonstrates the potential for visitor education at the museum. One benefit of networking activities is restoring historical connections.

Services of tourism organizations benefit museums through visitor surveys, market analyses, insurance, training, and promotional opportunities, such as visitor guides, vacation planners, introductions in visitor guide articles or ads, calendar listings, social media, and the basic function of referrals. State tourism offices are main resources for these services, especially online business directories and itinerary builders. A fruitful partnership role of the museum is to provide history and art images of interpretive value to partners. Online training webinars are now offered frequently by tourism entities, broadening capacity to expand local skills.

Referrals to the museum result from the tourism organizations' interface with the hospitality industry and providers comprised of travel agents, tour companies, transportation providers, advertising companies, lodging, food service, and attractions, as well as other amenities and activities. Governmental agencies also participate in a tourism network, offering promotion (websites, visitor guides, brochures), data collection, conferences, and training. These agencies include departments of tourism, commerce, and economic development. Arts commissions and local organizations sponsor artist tours, art shows, and festivals.

Inclusion of the museum on a FAM, or familiarization tour conducted by a tourism entity, increases exposure. An organized FAM tour takes representatives from the hospitality industry to view different attractions and amenities in a region. Such a tour may be likened to connecting the dots on a journey. Which amenities are chosen relates highly to future itinerary building; therefore, museum inclusion enhances attendance.

Museum participation in a visitor's guide need not be costly. Articles telling a story—of the museum's history, collection, exhibits, interpretation, or connections to community—are free whereas advertising is expensive. Timing is key: Working with the visitor guide at least a year before the guide's release date is more likely to result in article inclusion. Plus, articles are more often read than advertising!

Museum connections to community needs such as economic development and job creation increase sustainability efforts. Tourism is largely an entrepreneurial industry. A total of 80 percent of US tourism is handled by small business, including guides, food preparers, artists, bed-and-breakfasts, storytellers, and vendors. To the extent that a museum offers opportunities to local entrepreneurs, museum income is increased while contributing to overall local needs. Through these connections, financial sustainability of the museum may be supported through:

- Local government support as a visitor information hub;
- Sales at the museum store;
- Tours (museum, historical attractions, local ecosystems);
- Food service featuring local specialties and cultural foods;

- Memberships and donations to cultural preservation efforts;
- Art shows and fairs; and
- Economic development and job-creation grants.

Tip: The stronger the link to tourism entities, the more opportunity for a cultural organization to suggest tourism survey questions. With this no-cost strategy, data are collected relevant to museum marketing and the development of visitor-relevant interpretation. Sharing data within a tourism network strengthens the ability to work cooperatively for studies, marketing, and funding.

FORMING AN ITINERARY

Telling a unified story with historic and cultural context for itinerary links is one possible niche for a museum. Visitors to a region seek interesting activities, regional foods, and unique experiences. When museums and heritage sites are viewed as part of a larger itinerary, museum attendance expands to a vacation concept in the eyes of the visitor. This depth of offerings supports learning about local cultures and history.

Creating a network with the region's museums, heritage sites, and tours brings the potential for the three- to seven-day vacation itinerary. Linking with the possibility of telling a story through historical connections, artistic traditions, and local food shapes the sense of discovery, or of the experiential. Studying visitor characteristics defined in tourism studies leads to a cohesive concept of local and regional visitor interests.

PLANNING PROCESS

LINKING FOR VISITATION

- Identify the potential partners in a tourism network.
- How will multiple views of culture and history be represented?
- Are local services adequate to address visitor needs?
- What other businesses must be created to provide adequate lodging, food service, or activities for visitors?
- How can a linkage of locally owned organizations and businesses strengthen the tourism network?
- What are collective ways of expressing interpretations of local hospitality?
- How can regional cooperation strengthen the museum's effort?
- How will cultural privacy be safeguarded?
- How will the environment be protected?
- What is the central role for the museum or cultural center?

Several museums in a community can link together for an attendance package or tour itinerary. The common features for forming an itinerary include the following: cultural similarities, historic interest, geographic proximity, or regional collaboration. This linking strategy may be marketed with a "culture pass." Drawing upon available visitor surveys is useful for linking visitor interests into an itinerary. The most innovative combination of links meets a balance of visitor interests. Several itinerary topics give choice for repeat visitation. A museum-centered vacation concept developed online effectively includes:

- Information about other museums;
- Historical sites and diverse interpretations;
- Ethnic foods;
- Culturally related attractions;
- Lodging;
- Services;
- Educational opportunities;
- Local ecosystems;
- Cultural landscapes;
- Tours available;
- Driving times;
- Transportation options;
- A map linking offerings; and
- A calendar of events.

Partnerships are key for enriching the museum's story. Including smaller-scale businesses that connect to local history and culture—such as bed-and-breakfast lodging or restaurants featuring local cultural foods—creates the experiential visit. Involving local community businesses in the museum's programs improves their ability to explain local culture and ability to provide informed referrals to the museum.

Information provided on local arts and artists—with biographical cards attached to items in museum gift shops, art shows, or outdoor markets—supports cultural entrepreneurs. Information increases visitor appreciation of the art and artist, in turn enhancing the likelihood of appropriate prices for handmade items. For example, hang tags telling of the historical importance of items and authentic materials add to the story. Demonstrations enhance the process of community connection. Such interactions representing local people's expression create the experiential.

Collaborating with local lodging is an enormous museum opportunity. An example of effective museum advertising that also educates visitors is the online or in-room lodging book in hotels, motel rooms, bed-and-breakfasts, or cabins. In addition to the standard lodging book information on services within the facility, lodging book content initiated by the museum can be customized by including sections on local history, museum exhibits, local cultures, cultural arts, information on shops selling locally made items, menus featuring restaurants serving local foods, and a calendar of events. The lodging book project initiated by a museum or cultural center is a service to community businesses and may be a project eligible for grant support as an economic-development benefit.

CULTURAL TOURISM TRENDS

The range of tourism market types reflects broad interest. Visitors interested in history and culture are the primary interface-market segment interested in museums. Cultural tourism offers the opportunity for an exchange of information on lifeways, customs, beliefs, values, language, views of the environment, and other cultural resources.[5] Heritage tourism implies a focus on history rather than cultures in the present and is a term sometimes used interchangeably with cultural tourism.

Agritourism involves the visitor gaining an understanding of growing practices, heirloom varieties, food traditions, and contemporary foodways. An overlap may occur with culinary tourism and the sampling of local foods. Creative tourism implies learning about art practices, the history of art traditions, and may involve hands-on demonstrations. These are markets of possibility for museum linkages.

Overlap of different types of tourism typically occurs. Eco-tourists are interested in learning about the local ecology and nature-based experiences. Geotourism refers to an overlap between cultural and nature-based tourism that sustains or enhances the geographical character of a place—its environment, culture, aesthetics, heritage, and the well-being of its residents.[6]

Knowing the characteristics and interests of cultural tourists is useful for program planning. The sense of discovery is appealing—from learning about lifeways, to tasting foods, to observing or participating in dance demonstrations, to hands-on creating. Cultural tourists are curious about contemporary life and efforts underway to preserve culture retention.

Trip planning for visitor vacations generally begins from six months to one year ahead of the trip, a key reason for museum planning of events, art shows, and festivals well in advance. Such advance marketing increases the audience draw, especially when dovetailed with new exhibits and other events in the community.

FINDING THE MARKET MATCH

The connection for focusing and increasing museum attendance from tourism is of high potential. Tourism is one of the leading US industries, at $1.1 trillion in travel and tourism total sales (2019), then dropping close to $355 billion in

2020 due to quarantine orders and travel restrictions.[7] The top international travel markets to the United States historically are Canada, Japan, the United Kingdom, Mexico, Brazil, China, and Germany. Throughout 2020, international arrivals decreased by 74 percent worldwide and started making a comeback in 2021. In 2022, the 22 percent increase in tourism and a forecast to exceed the 2019 peak in 2023[8] shows a bounce back in this industry. Women, young people, rural communities, and Indigenous peoples are impacted the most by loss of tourism due to pandemic conditions.

Cultural tourism is the leading interest of this international market segment, comprising 40 percent of all tourism worldwide. UNESCO reports the draw worldwide of heritage and religious sites, crafts, performing arts, gastronomy, festivals, and special events.[9] The tourism sector is estimated to contribute 330 million jobs, or one in ten jobs, around the world. Benefits of cultural tourism include encouraging traditional cultures, attracting talent, developing new cultural resources and products, and furthering creative clusters. UNESCO emphasizes the important role of museums through education about culture. Additionally, tourist interest stimulates the transmission of intangible cultural heritage practices to younger generations.

National, state, regional, and city data exist to identify tourism trends. Many of these sources offer data at no-cost, important for the museum with a limited marketing budget. Local sources of data include:

- Museum attendee surveys, in-person and online;
- Assessments conducted by area museums;
- Visitor surveys, in-person and online;
- Tourism business surveys;
- License plate surveys;
- Business records;
- Lodging surveys;
- Guest registers;
- Sign-in books; and
- Interviews with businesses.

A wide range of data sources is readily available for defining effective museum marketing. Access to a number of studies may be located free of charge online at state tourism offices. Chambers of commerce are the best local source, and they generally share their data, especially to members. Organizations providing data include:

- Museums;
- Cultural organizations;
- Museum organizations and conferences;
- Tourism organizations;

- Chambers of commerce;
- Convention and visitors bureaus;
- Tax and revenue departments (gross receipts reports);
- State or regional departments of tourism;
- Economic development organizations;
- National parks and national forests;
- National departments of tourism or commerce;
- Industry-specific state or national business organizations;
- Tourism trade shows (international);
- The World Tourism Association (international).

A profile of visitor interests constructed from market data may cover a large region, presenting the potential for drawing a museum audience. The more localized the data, the more specific questions can be tailored to local cultures, scenic attractions, or ecosystems. Both generalized and local data are valuable for planning museum programs. Look for the following types of data from each source.

- Visitor location, or "origin," as described in the tourism industry, shows where to market effectively
- Attraction, food, and activity preference
- National and regional differences in interests
- Age, indicating market segment
- Lodging preference, for identifying partners
- Products desired to buy, product selection and development and
- Income levels.

Collecting data from several sources is advised to allow for cross-referencing results. This practice yields a greater sense of accuracy in the plan market assessment. Those data sources containing specific information on referred activities provide the most effective way to interest cultural travelers.

FROM IN-PERSON TO ONLINE

Accelerated online participation stimulated by the COVID-19 pandemic facilitated a shift from in-person to a wide range of online visitation opportunities—out of necessity from closures and travel restrictions. Oftentimes, when multiple scenarios and conditions requiring closure were not anticipated, museums struggled to launch alternatives to the in-person visit. Museums, struggling for survival strategies launched online exhibit tours, webinars, artist interviews, auctions, art shows, and web-based stores. Screen tourism is a way to include tourism[10] experiences without the environmental impacts.

The online tour designed to peak visitor interest may serve as both an introduction to the in-person tour, stimulating pre-visit interest, or as an effective stand alone for times of closure. A museum tour linking to a community tour expands options to view cultural heritage—including outdoor spaces that are perceived as less vulnerable in health crises. Anticipating multiple scenarios in times of limited visitation leads to creative online option combinations.

For example, online evaluation using survey tools enables the museum to assess visitor satisfaction, both locally and far-reaching. This input furthers an understanding of visitor interest, invaluable for exhibit and educational program planning. Engaging the visitor nudges repeat visitation, beyond simply advertising, as participation signals that the museum values audience input.

Encouraging visitor interaction during webinars enriches interpretive interest. This moves the topic from a lecture to an interesting exchange. Surveys and chat functions are techniques for participation. Particularly in times of limited travel, mainly due to health or safety concerns and environmental crises, such interaction may relieve the loneliness that comes with isolation. Consider the opportunity of online connection and interaction for generating interest for in-person museum offerings.

Donors are now familiar with online resources used to solicit financial support. Using online tools for auctions and art shows provides essential opportunities for cultural artists to sell during closure times. By diversifying the base of financial support, artist, museum visitor, and institutional finances all benefit from the exchange.

A new array of social media options extends the educational experience and marketing opportunities, increasing the visitor draw. By tapping a multiple-scenario approach, organizational flexibility increases, and switching programmatic routes enables the museum to achieve stability and even thrive in crisis times.

TOURISM AND THE MUSEUM WEBSITE

The role of the museum in unifying local tourism elements creates a unique experience concept to capture visitor interest. Website content orienting the visitor to local values, history, arts, and entrepreneurs provides cultural context to the visit. Excitement about a destination motivates potential visitors to plan and go.

The tourism website must reach beyond lists and links to communicate a cohesive visitation experience. Photographs, graphics, and clips of traditional music enliven a website. Visitors are asking, "What new knowledge, understanding, or feeling will I come away holding from the visitation experience?" This is the memorable vacation concept. A new cultural appreciation of nature, a new interpretation of history, the feeling of contributing to a community effort, or the excitement of one-on-one contact with another cultural group are examples of the sought-after vacation experience.

A contemporary dilemma concerns how to transmit information in a digital age, or how to use the Internet in a culturally respectful way. Are stories on a website authentic when not told in a listening circle? Some communities may object to the Internet mode of presentation. Just explore locally.

Yet, the Internet is a primary venue for those not able to physically travel, or to prepare a traveler before the actual visit. Travelers provided with some depth on local initiatives feel connectedness; this is the experiential. Communities deciding internally on appropriateness of sharing information will reach a level of comfort with the Internet.

HOME PAGE INTEREST

As the number of websites for vacation options increases each year, so, too, does the competition increase for moments of visitor attention. Potential visitors tend to browse several websites quickly, spending less time per site than in prior years. For this reason, the home page must be both informative and inviting. Home pages need to be intriguing enough to reduce the bounce rate, or the number of people leaving early before exploring the entire site. The most frequent mistake made in website design is the assumption that visitors will stay and explore the entire site as a given. Increasing visitor time spent on the home page and continuing through the site is central to drawing the visitor into the experience concept and to the physical location.

Thinking creatively of the website as a visitation experience increases website impact beyond merely a way to post data. All the principles of hospitality should be applied, especially friendliness. Starting with a traditional welcoming or greeting is inviting, whether in the local language or in the visitor's language.

What are the community's offerings under the main categories? Pull-down menus will allow the visitor to navigate quickly. Travel tools include the weather, driving distances, and maps for all trip segments. The home page will communicate well with fewer words. Images or photographs rotating in a slideshow format are a way to communicate messages, authenticity, and adventure with few additional words on the page. Rather than paragraphs or long sentences, use keywords or phrases formatted for a quick visual scan.

When a website is effective, travelers will easily find the complement of activities and amenities—creating a vacation concept for themselves. Changing search or tag words and experimenting with effective topics makes a difference to success. Reassessing tourism market trends, both nationally and internationally, assists the museum, tourism program, or business to discover current visitor interests. Attending conferences, reading tourism reports, and obtaining information from the state tourism website are strategies for staying current.

Cultural tourism content for the museum website connecting to local tourism can include.

- Activities and exhibits;
- Brief history of the area;
- Overview of local cultures;
- Local cultural calendar of events;
- Location;
- Geographic features;
- Explanations of local cultural arts;
- Creation stories;
- Local cultural districts;
- Cultural teaching efforts underway in the community; and/or
- A vacation concept surrounding history, the museum, and the arts.

Keep in mind the tendency to consider this content as covered on other sites. Once potential visitors leave your site following a link, they seldom come back. Brevity of the vacation concept is easier to follow, building the local concept. By increasing the breadth of the website, the museum becomes a referral point to the broader, community-relevant experience. Exhibits then are understood in both community and cultural context, adding richness to the story and experience.

CULTURAL PRIVACY ISSUES

Limits to the sharing of information are important to define—particularly in communities with traditional cultures. Comfort with the intrusion of visitors increases as cultural boundaries are identified through the museum planning process. Cultural boundaries may reflect limits on the following types of information.

- Cultural knowledge to be shared
- Cultural meanings in symbolism
- Identification of gathering areas (e.g., food, medicinal plants, and raw materials for art-making)
- Location of sacred sites
- Fragile ecosystems

Limits on visitation times are critical to observe, such as the privacy required in Indigenous communities during ceremonial times or for the churches of some religions. Cultural resources may be impacted if cultural boundaries for the sharing of information—as well as physical boundaries for visitation—are not well-defined. Basically, visitors want to be respectful yet need to be guided with a visitor etiquette statement.

Setting cultural boundaries, such as which audience is allowed for specific topics, is frequently an outcome of defining key issues in traditional communities. Understanding different community perspectives is the starting place for bridging cultural gaps and creating an understanding of contemporary issues. The museum is often the visitor entry place into the community. Visitors feel more comfortable, even fascinated, when cultural boundaries are communicated. A statement of visitor etiquette provides a means of bridging the communication between community-determined policy and visitor education.

Many traditional cultures teach protocols, thousands of years old, for taking care of visitors. Discussing these protocols for hosting visitors and deciding how to continue these traditions in current times delineates a contemporary way of welcoming. Ideally, the online visitor orientation to local protocols occurs during the trip-planning phase.

Topics valuable for guiding the visitor include:[11]

- A welcoming statement (in several languages, if applicable);
- Clear definition of where community visitation is allowed and places that are off-limits;
- Boundaries on appropriate dress;
- Protocols on noise levels (e.g., silence during traditional dances, no applause);
- Protocols for being in natural areas (e.g., staying on the trail, not gathering or damaging plants, whether hunting or fishing is allowed);
- Photography regulations or fees;
- Events where visitors are welcome; and
- Thanking the visitor for coming.

As culturally-oriented tours develop, communicating visitation etiquette becomes ever more important. Either inclusion on a phone app, a brochure, or a rack card that could be given out on tours is important for creating a mutually beneficial visitation experience. Keeping the basic visitor etiquette concise facilitates visitor education.

Visitor etiquette created for educational purposes at the museum is a valuable way to convey those limits or cultural boundaries determined through community participation in the planning process. To bridge the cultural gap, training in local communities must also educate the receiving community on the values of their visitors. The museum can fill that role by working collaboratively with cultural groups.

Positive wording is welcoming to visitors. For visitors to behave respectfully and according to local cultural customs, guidance is needed. Phrase restrictions as positively as possible rather than the negative "Do not . . ." Including a symbol for a cultural trail or district will unify the message and the physical area concept. Navigation of historic sites is an example.

As a cultural institution, the museum can take a leadership role in developing these materials, along with community partners. Making visitor etiquette visible at the museum entrance and at other culturally related locations increases visitor ease while preventing unwanted environmental impacts in the area. To draw visitors, museum brochures and suggestions for courteous behavior should be distributed at information kiosks throughout the community and at other cultural institutions. Also, visitor etiquette may be included on the community's tourism website or in brochures. For a smaller community without a visitor center, the museum may be the ideal visitor intake point.

INSPIRING CULTURAL PRIDE

Visitor interest in local cultures tends to raise community appreciation. Particularly for youth, cultural pride raises self-esteem. Youth involvement in dance demonstrations, art shows, storytelling, and cultural art workshops encourages learning and cultural continuance.

Awakening cultural pride benefits community inclusivity in several ways.

- Furthering understanding of diverse worldviews complexity
- Encouraging traditional language learning
- Understanding multiple cultural viewpoints of historical events
- Educating on different perspectives regarding time (e.g., linear versus cyclical, as explained in chapter 1)

Museum programs involving youth at an early age in such activities as storytelling, art activities, and opening receptions encourage a pattern of participation. Classes for youth in middle school and high school in local history, language, or the arts open receptivity to multi-cultural views. Additionally, involving high school and college students as tour guides encourages all levels of cultural learning and sharing.

Cultural continuance is a precious heritage process. As a primary focal point for learning about history, art, and culture, the museum serves a pivotal function in community education.

MAINTAINING AUTHENTICITY

The boundary between sharing culture and over-commercialization of tradition is at the root of authenticity issues. Museum exhibits, interpretive guides, a speaker program, demonstrations, website content, and educational tags in the museum store are all means of educating the public on authentic art styles, techniques, materials, and cultural affiliation.

Why are authenticity issues so vitally important? In this age of imitations, consumers do not always understand the value of the handmade process and the traditions or stories connected to the cultural arts. Educational programs of the museum further cultural preservation through appreciation of traditional artists and time-honored traditions. This encourages more traditional art-learning and enables creative entrepreneurs to earn a living with their art.

To not exploit culture, yet to share; to sell, yet not change tradition; to give some information, yet respect cultural boundaries—these are the challenges of maintaining authenticity of both cultural arts and experience. Cultural arts are constantly evolving. Past, present, and future are considerations for traditional cultures, as a circle of continuity.

THE ONLINE MUSEUM STORE

Continuing the museum and visitor relationship after the physical visitation experience holds potential for continued visitor education, museum support, local job creation, and repeat visitation. (See prior chapters for inventory development.) With local items available online, museum visitors are likely to re-order after the visit—particularly for gifts. Visitors want to understand how cultural retention efforts are evolving and can feel supportive of these efforts knowing the positive effects on cultural learning and support of artists. Museum support is likely to increase with this extended connection to visitors. Consider discounts for museum members to inspire purchases.

Virtual exhibits combined with opportunities for online purchasing are a strategy for continued visitor involvement. A short virtual exhibit can function as a preview to the physical exhibit. As the learning experience expands, interest in local culture and community-wide benefits increase.

Success factors include:

- Workshops for artists in basic entrepreneurial training;
- Reliability of local artists in providing inventory;
- Adequate fulfillment of orders;
- Information regarding the art-making process;
- Explanations of the cultural meaning of the art (where appropriate);
- Artist bios for increased collector value;
- Guarantee of authenticity; and
- Follow-up, thanking the buyer for supporting the museum.

Most museum stores do not stock locally made products, citing the time and effort needed to work with local artists. Offering training in record-keeping, order fulfillment, preparing interpretive statements to offer with items, taxes, and additional small-business management topics increases local benefits in multiple ways. Not only does the museum become a catalyst for cultural learning but also a support system for youth staying in the area through job creation. Cooperatives and collectives may develop locally in addition to sales in the museum store. Grants for job training, marketing, tourism services, cultural preservation, and youth programs may then be tapped for museum support.

BEYOND THE VISIT

Cultivating repeat visitation with online updates and programming such as exhibit previews, speaker webinars, and changing inventory in the museum store furthers interpretation while increasing the visitor draw. The cultural and economic benefits of visitation can extend far after the visit. When a visitor understands local cultures and efforts underway to preserve traditions, eco-systems, and traditional economies, the desire to offer support is enhanced. Visitors offer support in the following ways.

- Museum membership
- Donations, particularly to specific funds
- Purchasing museum store items through online ordering capability on the museum website
- Volunteering for future programs
- Repeat visitation

Visitors, particularly cultural and heritage, are curious about local efforts to continue traditions. One of their interests is to meet and interact with people of diverse cultures. An experiential visit stimulates support of local efforts. And the museum provides an ideal way to facilitate this level of interaction. Thanking the visitor and expressing gratitude for their contribution's impact in making a community difference is an invitation for the repeat visit.

POTENTIAL FOR SUSTAINABILITY

Community sustainability depends upon the closely interwoven factors of culture, economy, and ecology. Culture is often the cornerstone of sustainability, for all actions are guided by beliefs. For this reason, a mutually supportive referral network is central to sustainability. Rather than seeing history and culture in isolation, integrating culture with local economy and ecology expands museum opportunities.

This integrative perspective of museum function opens options for increased attendance, participation, and financial viability. For example, eligibility for grants supporting a wide range of community benefits is increased. Often, tax dollars are available to support the valuable community function of serving as a point for visitor education and referrals. Support beyond the local tax dollar becomes available with a matching dollar approach, or leveraging.

Tourism, as a means of enlarging museum attendance, holds great promise for increased sales of local products in the museum store and admissions.

When interfaced with an overall community-wide tourism-planning initiative, a museum's role is defined and often supported. The museum can become the community "anchor," or a central draw for tourism.

A current challenge involves reestablishing visitor confidence, or "rebranding." Pandemic-oriented studies indicate that in addition to educational and entertainment preferences in trips, the well-being or safety perception is important in visitor decision-making.[12] Community integration of museums enhances the safety perception when the importance of safety is reinforced within a cohesive network. Other factors emerging as important to visitor destination choice are social justice and environmental responsibility. The inclusive approach outlined in this chapter generates visitor appeal.

In this age of shrinking resources, museums often struggle to keep the doors open. Seeing a multi-purpose vision, shifting beyond the object focus to a people focus, integrates the modern museum into the everyday life of the community. Offering this glimpse into the community connects visitors.

Community integration affords the museum an opportunity to participate in community-determined intentions. Recognition of the value of a museum is enhanced, and support is likely to follow.

FURTHER READING

Gowreesunkar, Vanessa G. B., Shem Wambugu Maingi, Hiran Roy, and Roberto Micera (eds.). *Tourism Destination Management in a Post-Pandemic Context: Global Issues and Destination Management Solutions*. Leeds, UK: Emerald Publishing, 2021.
    The era since 2020 has left an impact on the history of travel and tourism worldwide, leaving tourist destinations and amenities with long-term lessons to learn from the impacts of COVID-19. This text features new guidelines plus management solutions to deal with the challenges wrought by the pandemic.

Guyette, Susan. *Sustainable Cultural Tourism: Small-Scale Solutions*. Santa Fe, NM: BearPath Press, 2013.
    Small-scale tourism, rather than mass tourism, is more flexible to manage in changing conditions. Topics covered include a community-based and cultural-value approach to planning for tourism, conducting visitor surveys, analyzing the market, cultural centers and museums as a hub, creating jobs, the tour enterprise, and increasing sustainability. Key success factors, including using a regional approach to build partnerships and itineraries, are addressed.

Hargrove, Cheryl. *Cultural Heritage Tourism: Five Steps for Success and Sustainability*. Lanham, MD: Rowman & Littlefield, 2017.
    When stories and places are shared with visitors, this activity becomes what is known as cultural heritage tourism. Success and sustainability in this

growing industry segment requires careful planning and adequate resources. This text provides detailed instruction through a proven five-step process to help planners, managers, and community leaders attract visitors and their spending to cultural heritage sites, attractions, events, or destinations.

White, Chris. *Museums and Heritage Tourism*. New York: Routledge, 2023.
    This book features the symbiotic relationship between museums, heritage attractions, and tourism, using a range of international case studies. Divided into three sections, the author first outlines a theoretical framework for understanding the role of museums in heritage tourism before addressing practical challenges of interpretation, design, and pandemic response. Each chapter incorporates a key case study, with an international scope including examples from Hong Kong, the United Kingdom, Taiwan, Qatar, Dubai, and Kuwait.

NOTES

1. Lama, Rinzing, and Alka Rai. "Challenges in Developing Sustainable Tourism Post COVID-19 Pandemic." In *Tourism Destination Management in a Post-Pandemic Context*, Vanessa Gowreesunkar, Shem Wambugu Maingi, Hiran Roy, and Roberto Micera (eds.), pp. 233–44. Leeds, UK: Emerald Publishing, 2021.
2. Eisenstein, Charles. *Sacred Economics: Money, Gift, and Society in the Age of Transition*. Berkeley, CA: North Atlantic Books, 2021.
3. Guyette, Susan. *Sustainable Cultural Tourism: Small-Scale Solutions*. Santa Fe, NM: BearPath Press, 2013.
4. Wilks, Jeff, Donna Pendergast, and Peter Leggat, editors. *Tourism in Turbulent Times: Towards Safe Experiences for Visitors*. UK: Elsevier Science, 2006.
5. Guyette, Susan, and David White. "Reducing the Impacts of Tourism Through Cross-Cultural Planning." In *The Culture of Tourism and the Tourism of Culture*, Hal Rothman (ed.), pp 164–84. Albuquerque, NM: University of New Mexico Press, 2003.
6. National Geographic Center for Sustainable Destinations, http://travel.nationalgeographic.com/travel/sustainable.
7. www.statista.com.
8. World Travel and Tourism Council, www.wttc.org.
9. UNESCO. "Cutting Edge: Bringing Cultural Tourism Back in the Game." https://unesco.org/en/articles/cutting-edge-bringing-cultural-tourism-back-game.
10. Champion, Erik, Christina Lee, Jane Stadler, and Robert Peaslee, eds. *Screen Tourism and Affective Landscapes: The Real, The Virtual, and the Cinematic*. New York: Routledge, 2023.
11. Guyette. *Sustainable Cultural Tourism*.
12. Pereira, A., C. Frias, and A. P. Jeroonimo. "Falling in Love Again: Brand Love and Promotion of Tourist Destinations During the COVID-19 Pandemic." In *Pandemics and Travel: COVID-19 Impacts in the Tourism Industry*, Claudia Seabra, Odete Paiva, Carla Silva, and José Luís Abrantes (eds.), pp 227–42. Leeds, UK: Emerald Publishing, 2021.

10

Expanding Museum Income

Museum support from conventional sources is becoming scarcer. Rather than retracting services in a challenging economy, now is the time to look toward options that increase diverse public involvement—as well as bring more vitality to a museum. Often missed in project designs, inclusivity factors hold promise for bringing groups together. The community-integrated museum makes those inclusive connections, securing support for programs and activities, while generating a cohesive social equity benefit.

As a museum's mission for cultural education broadens, support options deepen. The people-focused museum responds to perceived equity needs, connecting to these new channels for support. Addressing inclusivity may require extra funding. For example, support for increased staffing illustrates the need for a diversified funding strategy. Funding for individual projects, the frequent piecemeal approach, often does not incorporate growing administrative needs such as training—a key barrier limiting inclusivity. Through a participative planning process leading to an organizational plan, project options identified can diversify sources of support, creating a "safety net" in times of economic uncertainty.

Funders tend to support specific projects defined with steps, timelines, and outcomes. Instead of viewing proposals as administrative drudgery, see the positive challenges of innovative project creation! Sources of data backing needs are often required, and even if not requested, they are powerful to include in applications. Review the cultural entrepreneur database in chapter 7, a valuable planning tool for demonstrating willingness to participate. Then, envision larger results in the context of documented needs. Diversifying sources of support through cooperative values is the effective strategy for the coming decades.

Using grant funds to "jump-start" museum income generators is one way of developing a structure for sustainability. By illustrating to funding sources the ways in which projects will become self-supporting or sustainable financially, the museum demonstrates continuity and a high likelihood of success with a range of topics from preservation to visitor education. A plan for project sustainability is increasingly being requested by funders when an application is submitted. Funders tend to look at the museum's website to scan prior organizational impacts, as a preliminary consideration in the application process.

FROM PLAN TO PROPOSAL

Funders like to see, or at minimum to know, that your organization has a long-range plan. In this new era, showing flexibility to shift has appeal. Best results with the planning process occur when the consultant or staff person completing the plan has a working knowledge of funding options (i.e., experience in development work). Moving from community participation to project design, to an evaluation framework assessing multiple benefits, then to the identification of funders in the plan is a successful approach.

Including a multi-scenario component in the thorough planning stage forms the basis for use in proposals or the securing of contracts for services. This is a very different approach from the plan that sits on a shelf. The following planning process can be used with museum staff or community groups involved in a project design.

PLANNING PROCESS

IDENTIFY PROJECT CONCEPTS

- See a desired result through the organization.
- How does a project idea support an equitable mission?
- How do the projects envisioned connect to all local cultures?
- Who would visit to achieve that result?
- Who in the community needs to be involved?
- How would accessibility be improved?
- Does the project embrace different worldviews?
- Are all aspects of viewing or discussing culturally appropriate to all groups involved?
- How do envisioned projects interconnect?
- Does the project have potential for flexibility in changing scenarios?
- Are staff members available with a good qualification match for the project?
- How will training and internships be provided to increase overall community-wide capacity for inclusive results?

All the groups who will participate in, or are affected by, the project can work toward agreement concerning project goals. Respecting cultural privacy in relation to who can view and who can learn are topics to discuss in the participative process.

PLANNING PROCESS

INCLUSIVE PARTICIPATION

- How can multiple community benefits be outcomes of planned projects?
- Are museum members likely to offer matching or in-kind support for an exhibit or other projects?
- How will modern technology be used to reach diverse groups across project ideas?
- Does this project fit into a larger community effort?
- Who are the partners for collaboration?
- How could partners contribute to inclusivity?

Unity at the initial project conception saves a great deal of time later, at the time of project start-up.

INCLUSIVITY AND PROPOSALS

There is a glass-half-full approach to proposals. Are you dreading the work involved? The cure lies in seeing the proposal as a project design, or a "blueprint," for the museum and community to follow once the project is funded. Creating a team to work on the funding effort broadens the range of skills available to design a thorough project idea. Diverse input strengthens community ties. If proposal sections are assigned to team members, a timeline for the completion of steps furthers a coordinated effort. Keeping focus on the people served turns the funding process into a heartfelt activity.

Although a proposal is generally written to gain funding for a project, a well-written proposal will also serve the museum as a plan for carrying out the steps and gain an optimum result from the funding. A new museum staff member, volunteer, a consultant, or a community member involved should be able to pick up the proposal, read it, and use it as a guide for implementing the funded project.

The starting place for the project idea lies with the museum planning process. If there is general agreement that a project is needed and that the project fits the long-range plan of the museum, then the development of a proposal can begin. In traditional communities, there is cultural appropriateness to also consider. If the community does not back the concept, a great deal of energy can go into the development of a project idea, but the plan may not go further than the paperwork.

Community planning meetings, events, and needs assessments are good techniques for determining the nature of the project and the size of the project. For example, is there community interest in developing an interpretive guide, a museum tour, or a program to teach local traditions? These are examples of projects on a size continuum, from small to large.

Designing a focused, realistic project is the most important start. A frequent error in the small museum is designing a very large project, beyond available staff capabilities or not suitable for one single funder. Large ideas are reachable but often on a step-by-step basis, applicable for a series of funders.

PLANNING PROCESS

PLAN AN INCLUSIVE PROJECT

- How will diverse worldviews and messages be conveyed by the project?
- How does the project interface community needs with collection access (in-person or virtual)?
- What documented content is available for interpretation and what new research will be conducted?
- Are experienced staff members or consultants available to carry out the project?
- What are their qualifications?
- How will training to community participants be included for diversity and capacity-building?
- Will additional technical assistance or contractors be needed? What are their qualifications?
- What steps are needed to carry out the project, including adequate compensation for community participants?
- What will the project cost to carry out?
- Are adequate resources available, or will additional sources be secured?
- Is there documented community, local government, or tribal support for the project?
- How does the project link to other community priorities?

Taking the larger idea and breaking it down into smaller projects over time, as outlined in an earlier planning chapter, gives the museum staff a series of successes to build management skills and a track record. For example, the Museum Store Association recommends starting with a smaller number of inventory items and phasing up, particularly for managing online stores.[1] Funders are very astute at assessing the capabilities of an organization to carry out a project.

SUSTAINABLE FINANCIAL SUPPORT

Museum sources are essential for museum-specific functions, such as exhibits, interpretive programs, cataloguing, and curation. Yet, other related community projects and support for the start-up of income generating enterprises become eligible for resources that tie directly to a broader funding strategy. And funders respond well to evidence of local inclusive participation, assured of the increased likelihood of ongoing project involvement.

In these uncertain times, reliance entirely on grants and government tax revenues increases risk, for one source may decrease suddenly. Projects now supplement the more common sources of museum income—such as admissions, memberships, donations, and support from local government or tribal taxes.

Crowdfunding is another productive way of raising matching funds for projects, enabling fundraisers to collect money from a larger number of people via online platforms. Emphasizing need and specific projects is aligning. A platform fee is charged by a crowdfunding site, taking a percentage of all the money raised, typically from 5 to 12 percent. Highlighting equity and inclusion intention is a plus.

The successful museum budget utilizes these resources as matching funds to other sources, thus leveraging the basic museum budget. In the current economy of shrinking resources, earned income is becoming a budget essential. This chapter outlines a multi-pronged approach to sustainable support.

Considering multiple income streams for a museum budget (see Chart 10.1) expands the scope of services offered. Projects, as defined in the planning process, are fundable by grants and contracts for services such as workshops, lectures, or tours. Earned income carries the advantage of creating jobs or earned livelihood for community members while generating museum support. For example, available sources already discussed include a museum store or art gallery, a museum café, tours (museum, nature, historical), traditional meals and regional cuisine, or training programs offered to community members.

Online tools for offering valuable programming and soliciting support are particularly productive

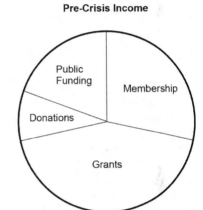

Pre-Crisis Income

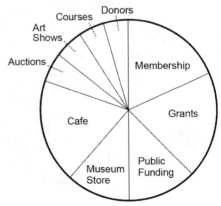

Diversified Income

Chart 10.1. A Fundraising Shift

when linked with compelling program ideas. In this new economic era, signing up for a broad range of electronic funder newsletters is helpful for staying informed of new opportunities.

While staffing may be the most urgent need, this usually is not a basis for funding. Rather, funding is secured to carry out a project, and staff time may be included to carry out the tasks. For this reason, a good project design—with a detailed workplan to carry out project steps and qualified staff—is essential to construct a good proposal.

Diversifying income sources provides alternatives for multiple scenarios, plus it connects to multiple community needs. Operating budgets tend to expand with this approach.

REGIONAL NETWORKING FOR COLLABORATIONS

The benefits of regional networking include creating context for historical and cultural topics, as well as forming partnerships for collaborations—a current trend appealing to funders. The same strategy applies for expanding resources. Funders are looking for larger or widespread results. While this directive can appear to be a barrier to the small museum with limited staff, larger results may become the most important asset for a small community to create and hire additional staff. Regional linkages are valuable to smaller communities as a way of expanding resources in the following ways.

- Inclusion in a larger project initiated by an urban community
- Linking smaller communities together to create a museum itinerary or a cultural pass concept and, therefore encouraging more visitation and job potential
- Serving as an outreach site to larger museums, particularly for inclusive, regionally oriented exhibits
- Engaging in higher education, with collaborative development of courses
- Developing a virtual exhibit to complement other regional exhibits
- Creating a mobile museum
- Offering discounts for tours
- Developing traveling exhibits

Partnerships are important for securing mentoring relationships, matching resources, and gaining regional historical understanding—thus creating larger results from a project.

PLANNING PROCESS

SEEING LARGER IMPACTS

- How can an interpretive program promote cultural understanding?
- Could an exhibit idea be multi-museum?
- Which community organizations link together to form a visitor experience?
- Is there a volunteer base in the community to assist with expanded programming?
- Is interpretative material needed for network partner websites or virtual tours?
- How does collection access further learning and interpretive programs in the community?
- Where is a technological upgrade needed to accommodate distance learning, webinars, and virtual tours?
- How can the museum link to arts in public places projects?
- Are collaborative "Research and Demonstration" projects with a local university or college possible?

The larger the project impact, the greater the benefits and the more interest will be gained from funders. This strategy is key for securing the larger grant. Although the track record nationally (in the United States) of proposals funded is at 35 percent success, there are techniques for approaching the proposal with skill and optimism. Increasing your track record to 80 percent or even 90 percent is possible with the tips in this chapter.

Thorough planning of projects—with both inclusive participation and input from project partners—gives an applicant a distinct advantage. Success in generating funding is directly related to thoroughness in the planning process and a practical approach from project concept to fundable outcomes. The staff members of a funding agency readily recognize a well-conceived project with local involvement and a solid evaluation plan.

FORMING FUNDING RELATIONSHIPS

The process of contacting funders, discovering opportunities, and learning about a funder's goals for assisting communities is strongest when organizational relationships are already formed. Culturally diverse groups generally know solid relationship-building skills within their family-based knowledge and experience. Listening to participants' cooperative project ideas may become a strong inclusivity point for your funding efforts.

Often not realized by applicants, funders have internal agency goals for results with communities served—usually imbedded in the guidelines. Approaching staff well ahead of the deadline, learning about the agency's internal priorities and goals, networking with other communities that have worked with the agency, and communicating how you are connecting with your region all are strong points for beginning the relationship with a funder. Conversely, an ineffective approach is treating the funder like an ATM with last-minute submissions!

In-depth partnerships are becoming increasingly essential. Forming alliances with partners demonstrates less duplication of efforts to funders, more cost-sharing, and the strength of a network possible with coordinated programs. The potential for technical assistance between partners is an appealing part of this approach.

Funders are usually interested in specific projects rather than basic administrative support. With nonprofit status, a negotiated indirect costs agreement can be used to support "overhead," or administrative costs. Once the museum has project success, a good relationship with the funder can lead to additional grants or contracts in future years. Best to have more than one idea ready when contacting a funder, in case the first idea isn't an appropriate match to the funder's priorities.

The detailed, yet concise, proposal is a must step. An established working relationship with the funder can guide you to the formation of a thorough community-integrated proposal. Study the proposal guidelines carefully, noting word or character limitations. For electronic uploads, the attachments are an opportunity to include more detail, such as examples of collection items or data on museum impact.

A well-written museum plan describes needs and exhibit or project descriptions, the basics for good proposal design. Qualifications of the project director count heavily. This chapter contains methods for linking to expand resources, designing a community-based project, preparing a proposal, and locating and approaching funding sources, as well as leveraging resources. Funders have commented to me, "You are so organized, we already know you would do well overseeing the project." Confidence in the grantee is an invaluable success factor.

BROADENING SUPPORT

Given this era of scarcer financial resources, museums and cultural centers must think in a broader sense to find support. Small communities often attempt to develop museums primarily with volunteer resources. Although local involvement is a critical element to developing museum programs—adequate resources to cover the costs of teaching, exhibit development, collections care, and staffing are vitally important. Gaining access to resources is generally an increasingly challenging step for both museum development and operations. Inclusivity factors in relation to fundraising are central to community benefits.

1. Fundraising is often seen as a board of directors' responsibility. In affluent communities, the board members tend to be key donors. In organizations working with low-income populations, the board of directors is not likely to be affluent. A more diversified fundraising strategy not only increases income but also diversifies ethnic attendance as well. All too often, fundraising training offered to a board of directors comes from an elite perspective: ask the wealthy. One size does not fit all.

2. In some cultures, charging an admission fee runs counter to traditional hospitality values. Voluntary donations are more acceptable in these situations. Sometimes a small gift accompanies the donation. Particularly for cultures where generosity is a primary value, a museum may not feel comfortable charging an admission fee, considering admission as a part of traditional welcoming and hospitality. Sensitivity to local views is vital to explore.

    Admission fees are frequently a stable part of the museum budget, yet they usually generate less than 10 percent of that budget. This income type is of significant value as a matching source to leverage grants or larger amounts from other sources such as donors. In those communities where charging an admission is acceptable, appropriate pricing can be determined by assessing admissions fees of culturally similar and regional museums.

    Pricing also relates to cultural values. For example, family rates, adult group rates, senior rates, reduced fees for members, and school group rates reflect values and generosity. Consider packaging an admission plus a tour at a discount to increase income. For communities where aversion to paying exists, there are cultural solutions—such as a free pass for community members, while visitors pay. Tour companies prefer to book a half-day or full-day "package" for a unique experience, easier than assembling several parts.

    Competition for membership dollars is increasing as other sources of income decrease. While membership programs are a standard component of museum support, valuable in leveraging for furthering cultural and interpretive programs—potential members are asking for more—particularly learning and experiential opportunities.

    Recognizing changing trends in charging for admissions is essential for projecting a realistic operating budget. In *Museums and Millennials*,[2] Jaclyn Spainhour points out the "affordability" factor—or the difficulty in finding full-time jobs with benefits leading to an adequate income with enough surplus beyond basics, with surplus income for luxuries such as admissions. Take into account the needs of Generation X, or young people born from the late 1990s through the current era. High unemployment or underemployment in the pandemic era underscores the need for keeping current with museum visitor trends. Look for funding to address special needs due to unemployment.

3. Launching a "Friends of . . ." organization and distributing an e-newsletter are two ways for the museum or cultural center to inform members locally, nationally, and internationally. Not all small or ethnic museums use this technique to broaden participation. Keeping member events and potential activity attendees informed about the museum's expected goals, programs, and results attained is an aligning approach. In the twenty-first century, inclusivity is often a supportable goal of the museum.

    A "Friends" membership program created in conjunction with a virtual exhibit generates connection—particularly when a special "page" is created for use with a member code. Heightening awareness through direct member involvement is a way of creating a meaningful cultural education experience for the public. Members become part of a living history process through support of cultural education and retention programs. Point out the importance of your museum's work in relation to preserving the vast pool of cultural knowledge as a resource for solving worldwide issues.

4. Encouraging ongoing community participation via an electronic newsletter, outlining progress on inclusivity intentions, educational programs, teaching of arts, and cultural revitalization efforts, is the usual incentive for keeping members involved year after year. This may be brief, with photos showing classes or events. In times of forced closure, these routes are vital to keeping interest and involvement levels high.

    Create interest with messages on the importance of preserving and restoring traditions, supporting local conservation and cultural revitalization efforts—as well as progress on creating local employment. Adding an update on exciting programs, by podcast or a special bulletin, is a stimulus to attend and give. A list of member email addresses keeps the museum in touch; send out notices about new programs and when new membership fees are due each year. Museums representing culturally diverse groups are sometimes reluctant to reach out in this way.

DIVERSITY INCREASES OPPORTUNITY

Expanding outreach to a broad range of ethnic groups represented in the community requires several approaches. Connecting or integrating the different approaches to fundraising "brings along" the donor base. And each group is likely to benefit from the infusion of new generosity strategies. New directions in membership programs include:

*   Using online donation platforms such as crowdfunding for ideas engaging the public in new, exciting ways;[3]
*   Virtual programming, including recorded interviews;

- Direct member interaction with artists at openings in-person or online, relating to collections, exhibits, or training programs;
- Web visibility (e.g., virtual bricks with names engraved), if desired by the member;
- Educational lecture series;
- Online content for schools;
- Developing topics of increased public interest, such as climate change or racial issues;
- Volunteer opportunities and recognition; and
- Cultural interpretations of generosity.

Remember to point out membership benefits, covering a year of education and activities possible for the entire family—a true bargain. As many households are experiencing budget limitations or limited outings, reminders of benefits, both on-site and virtual, will increase incentive to join. A key draw for most ethnic groups is food. Rather than paying caterers, involve local cultural entrepreneurs.

Include a schedule of memberships with benefits on the museum or cultural center's brochure, program materials, website, and on social media. Repetition of messages integrating these resources is key. Special programs offered to members leave opportunity for innovation. Note: There is a temptation to raise membership rates as other sources of funding are decreasing. Carefully assess whether raising rates will affect the number of people who join. This may not be a winning strategy in your region, depending on the economic profile.

WORKING WITH DONORS

Donors are looking for an interesting experience while connecting with giving. The more exciting electronic newsletter creates a sense of involvement. Links to the organizational website expand information options. Consider an overview of organizational successes, interviews with museum participants, storytelling events, virtual tours, webinars, and electronic auctions.

Donations are an effective way to benefit from both museum visitation[4] and tourism community-wide. Informing visitors of projects in need of support, as well as a museum's recent track record in service delivery, creates alignment with donors interested in supporting local cultural retention efforts.

Networking with potential donors in the region and donors who visit from national and international locations is part of a diversified support strategy. Community-wide benefits accrue when members gain an awareness of the local history and local cultures. Reaching donors is easier via the Internet than in prior decades, and connecting your museum to national or global issues may easily result in memberships from other regions. The saying "think globally, act locally" takes on increased relevance every year. Using a multi-scenario approach instills donor confidence in the organization's ability to "switch direction" if an unforeseen event carries heavy impact.

Involving museum members is the first step toward securing larger donations. A brief, completed plan is invaluable for aligning donors. A clear executive summary, mission, goals, and projects including timelines and evaluation criteria inspire confidence. Using a multi-scenario approach is now more important than ever in this era, to draw donor confidence.

A donation draw, based on community-generated cultural goals, is a tool to establish an endowment for long-term earnings on investments. (Note: The word "campaign" carries the battle over the conquered connotation for colonized groups and should be avoided). Endowments then can fund general operations or support specific projects, such as construction or classes, and create long-term stability to the museum budget. Short-term funding may support classes to address cultural retention or for preparing artists in the business skills necessary to be a part of job creation through a museum store or an outdoor market.

Fundraisers, such as small events to interact with artists or traditional feast meals, frequently are planned to further donor involvement. These special events for donors may be low cost, yet informative. For example, in a Native American community, a trip to see the buffalo herd, a hike on an historic trail, or an outdoor camp in a tipi and eating a traditional meal are precious experiences for heritage-oriented visitors. Remember, the donor likes an experience or to feel special, appreciated, and included.

Educational events, exhibit development, interpretive programs, or cultural retention efforts are topics to emphasize with donors. For large donors, a museum may consider the idea of small, special events not only to keep these donations coming in but also to inspire large donors to tell their friends about ongoing work in teaching the cultural traditions or heightening awareness of environmental connections. These may include pre-opening receptions, talks by local artists or historians, gifts, classes, or recognition plaques.

Many types of available funding, such as construction, exhibit development, operational costs, and teaching grants, require large matching amounts. Donations are flexible funds, ideal for use in matching fund requirements. Benefits to the community increase by involving visitors.

Small offerings of thanks—such as a special place on the website—appeal to donors and create the connection of relationship. Many museums offer gifts, depending on the membership category. When training in the cultural arts is part of the museum's offerings to the community, then items made by the learning artists are a potential resource for member gifts. The more integrated the programming, the more the options for support expand.

Although contributing to good is the primary function of donations, mainstream donors also focus on the tax deduction. Providing a letter of thanks—along with the amount donated and the museum or cultural center's

IRS 501(c)(3) identification—is a must to insure continued donations. The majority of donors need this documentation for tax deduction purposes. While a form letter with the amount recorded at events, or the letter sent afterward, is sufficient, including a sentence or two about your current accomplishments is aligning and feels like a heartfelt expression of gratitude. If your museum does not have nonprofit status, finding a fiscal sponsor with that status can move along the process of establishing a donation structure. If operating within a tribal programmatic structure, utilize the tribe's nonprofit status letter for taxation purposes.

EARNED INCOME AND THE AUTHENTIC EXPERIENCE

The business model of earning income is becoming ever more popular and necessary to supplement the conventional sources of museum income. Museum enterprises include the museum store, an art gallery, tours, restaurants, art shows, festivals, and providing services for a fee—such as serving as a visitor center. To leverage funds, triple or quadruple annual income by expanding the experience. The most effective use of earned income, memberships, and donations is for matching funds for a grant or a donor-related challenge since these are "unrestricted" funds. Also, seek out challenge grants, invaluable for leveraging with matching funds.

Although the gift shop is a common museum enterprise, consider upping the sense of the experience to a museum store, a continuation of the learning opportunity. When regarded as a way to meet multiple equity needs, the enterprise form of support fits logically within a museum's community-integrated mission while providing a substantial amount of the museum's budget in times of decreasing grant resources. For example, if the museum taps micro-loan programs available to entrepreneurs for start-up, these products may provide inventory into the museum store or art gallery enterprise. Different ways of "framing" projects to broaden funding applicability expand options for inclusivity in museums and cultural centers.

Community-integration furthers the ability to broaden sources of income. Contracts to provide specific community services are becoming increasingly feasible for museums and cultural centers.

- As an example, in some communities, museums earn extra income serving a tourism-related function (see chapter 9) by providing referrals or leading interpretive tours. Local governments and economic development grants are sources for this income.
- Working with schools opens doors to contracts as well as to youth grants. Look at art program funders, education sources, and school budgets to create both in-person and online projects.

- Retirement homes and senior housing offer programs for residents. Cultural and history-based programs fit well with a museum's mission.
- Demonstrations are possible to offer for a fee, particularly in conjunction with festivals and art shows. This type of income is also valuable to cover the demonstrator's fees and travel. Think beyond the museum walls to art shows, events, and even private parties. Interpretation takes the demonstration to another level.
- Cultural art demonstrations at conferences are popular.
- Apprenticeships in the cultural arts are available through art funders.
- For Native communities, casino funding or "giving back funds" often support both tribal and local school projects. Hotel or casino demonstrations, e.g., the cultural arts, can be pitched as a draw.

Think community need, then the culturally based solution. Participating in community networks opens the way for innovative partnership. If the entrepreneurial database (chapter 7) includes a question on willingness to demonstrate, then the museum has the option to match artists or storytellers with events for a fee. Hands-on projects, if culturally appropriate, add the experiential dimension while encouraging cultural retention. Small projects as incremental subprojects in a larger project design provide valuable-measurable results, such as audience development.

WORKING WITH DEVELOPMENT PERSONNEL

If the museum is large enough to afford development staff, or contractual assistance, here are tips for the best outcomes. Constant deadlines faced by development personnel are stressful. Working ahead of deadlines is a compassionate stance. Encourage a team effort with staff to develop a fundraising plan. Even a one-page chart outlining funding source, contact info, deadline, project topic, and persons working on the proposal helps the team effort.

If writing a proposal on your own, these points become even more salient.

- Let development staff know about your planned projects at the beginning of the year.
- Deadlines tend to cluster in the spring and fall. Working well ahead and with a timeline for tasks alleviates the tension of a deadline pileup.
- Outline your proposal sections, and create a team approach.
- Leveraging with matches tends to be more successful when planned for a year.
- Show development personnel your long-range plan, as content becomes available to proceed.
- Point out demographic and needs assessment data supporting your request.

- Attend conversations with the funder, as you are the program's expert and capable of adding valuable information.
- Avoid last-minute changes, as aligning all the proposal parts in a consistent way at the last minute is difficult.

In the twenty-first century, online submissions are almost always the case. Working ahead of the deadline is recommended since online systems can malfunction just before and during the deadline.

EXPAND YOUR CONCEPT

A common challenge to securing funding for museum projects is finding the appropriate topic fit with funding opportunities. Museum funding can be difficult to find, and grants tend to be small. For this reason, structuring a museum project to interface with priorities of the community is a successful way to expand opportunities for museum funding. Presented in Chart 10.2 are a few examples of "framing" or shaping a project idea. A community-integrated, multiple-benefit approach expands positive outcomes.

Within the common mission of a museum exists a variety of ways to creatively frame a project for funding, including visitor education, children's programs, teaching cultural arts or language classes, a lecture series, cultural preservation skills workshops, special events, festivals, and art shows. Other outside-the-box thinking of common categories include the following: a traditional foods learning program; cultural stewardship practices; job training; tours; tourism support for a small visitor or interpretive center in the museum foyer; entrepreneurship classes; job creation through a museum store; an art gallery; an online museum store; membership drives; creating an endowment; capital campaigns; capacity-building; and contracts for services.

The process of creative framing involves conceptualizing the ways in which conventional museum topics overlap with other funding descriptors. Partnering with other community organizations not only expands the possible inclusivity benefit outcomes from a project but also opens the path for collaborative larger grants. Funders tend to require partnerships to be documented with letters of commitment.

Request a one- or two-page letter of commitment from partners, since a limited-space electronic upload is likely. In prior years, a "letter of support," or generalized endorsement, was sufficient; in this era, the letter should be specific as to the partnership offer—e.g., use of a building, hours of time donated, or cash—and the dollar value of the commitment. Work with partners several months ahead of the deadline to build relationships and secure letters of genuine commitment, emphasizing both quantitative and qualitative benefits. A strong letter also reflects the funder's priorities and a direct statement of how

FUNDING DESCRIPTOR	MUSEUM RELATED PROJECT
Museums	Museum planning Exhibit development Collections management Collections acquisitions Interpretation
Arts	Art classes Business of art classes Cultural preservation Arts demonstrations Art shows Festivals
Training	Museum skills Cultural arts Entrepreneurial skills Customer service
Youth	Cultural arts Youth business club Substance abuse prevention Language Tour guide/ docent
Business Development	Tours—historical/art/ecological Museum store enterprise Art galleries Entrepreneurial job creation
Economic Development	Museum networks Sales for local people Organizational development Marketing Tourism function

Chart 10.2. Increasing Funding Options

the partnership contributes to the project concept. Communicating with the partner on these topics gives the lead for letter specificity.

Creative framing expands not only options for funding but also potential project impacts. Ideas for diversifying topics frequently are generated in the participation process. Careful listening and creative project design with multiple outcomes is the creative process for crafting a winning project. Uniqueness of the concept, community need and interest, equity outcomes, and a plan for determining effectiveness through evaluation and broad population-support reach are appealing points for the proposal review process. Think overlap of project ideas.

In the contemporary funding setting, a first question asked by the funder in this era is "Did you secure community participation in defining the project?" When a museum project benefits one or more of the topics, broader impacts are perceived by the funder, which is a positive. A balance between broad impacts, yet designing a project focused enough to be considered feasible, is the key to successful project and evaluation design.

When an organizational plan is completed, use this plan to approach the funder. As funders see a long-range strategy to carry out a vision—coupled with qualified people to implement the projects—their confidence increases in granting funds. A museum plan should outline the projects that will contribute to the long-range cultural goals of the community and identify a broad range of funders.

The plan is a reflection of a well-organized local effort based on agreement. This collaborative factor is the most critical for carrying out museum projects. For this reason, the planning steps are very convincing to a funder. Once a well-written plan is completed, many sections can be used directly in other proposals to save time. The organization's history, organizational chart, project descriptions, and service population statistics are examples.

LEVERAGING FUNDING

Larger projects need a fundraising strategy to identify a range of funders, a sequencing for applications over time, and needed matches. When approaching local or tribal governments for a matching funds commitment, a strong approach is leveraging—or using one source of funds to match and generate a larger amount of funds for the same project. A condition of receiving a grant may—but not always—require a certain match amount to be raised before the grant funds are released. Matches are required for most funding applications, whether the source is private or federal. Examples of possible resources for leveraging funds are:

- Local tax dollars;
- Local government funds;
- Another grant;
- Earned income; and
- In-kind (e.g., staff time, volunteer time, operating expenses).

Federal sources (in the United States) often require non-federal funds as matches. In-kind matches, although allowed by some funders, are generally not as strong in the review process. A balance of in-kind and "cash match" usually works well. Effective documentation of in-kind resources is specific, including a letter on letterhead stating the type of service to be donated and the value—e.g., the number of hours times an hourly wage, or detailed publication costs. Most funding sources often require that a specific match not be used for more than one proposal request.

Challenge grants are based on the principle of leveraging. Typically, a challenge grant offers a dollar amount contingent on the grantee securing a two- or three-times match per dollar. The main point of a challenge grant is to provide incentive for donors.

Once the commitment is made on the part of the federal grant, private foundations and donors are more likely to commit their matching funds when a target or goal must be achieved. The challenge grant application may specify the subsequent use of the funding, such as a new exhibit or construction of an addition to the museum—depending on the requirements of the funder. Or, often, a challenge grant is used to create an endowment that will yield ongoing support.

FUNDING MUSEUM ENTERPRISES

Nonprofits are eligible to operate enterprises under certain circumstances—usually if the profits are used to cover the operating expenses of the nonprofit. Using a nonprofit approach expands funding opportunities to create an enterprise, depending on the funder and how the project is framed. Income-generating ideas are appealing to some funders as part of a project grant when framed as a sustainability plan—carrying project results into future years.

Government Internal Revenue Service (in the United States) publications explain the allowed income and reinvestment for enterprise arms of a nonprofit. The nonprofit route offers tax-exemption benefits. Some larger organizations use parallel nonprofit and for-profit structures if the income generation is quite substantial. Consulting a tax attorney is recommended here for determining the ideal organizational structure.

Using a nonprofit approach is useful for creating a museum store, webinars for fee, courses, art shows, auctions, tours, and other events. A five-page minimum business plan and, in most instances, a maximum of twenty-five pages is essential to show the funder and to track results. Chapter 11 explaining evaluation, presents key guidance for assessing success. Setting goals or targets for generating income will be essential to demonstrate. After funded, tracking income and expenses, with an attentive eye to the bottom line is essential. Funders want to know your reinvestment strategy and are aligned through creative project ideas.

Financial planning to determine community needs and museum ways of maximizing earned income is fast becoming an essential skill of the museum, cultural center, or art program. Income generating ideas are appealing to some funders as part of a project grant. Receptivity to this type of project varies from funder to funder; therefore, checking in the initial stages of an application is wise. Just be certain to emphasize the reinvestment of profit into the nonprofit operating budget.

While overreliance on too few sources is risky in uncertain times, organizational readiness to expand must also be a consideration.[5] Gradual enterprise development usually takes three years to the break-even point, where income at least equals expenses. Grant assistance is valuable yet must be adequate for the type of project; for example, a speaker series is low cost compared to the more expensive museum café. A multi-year grant may be necessary to achieve the larger result. Ask experienced business personnel to review and observe carefully whether the projections are realistic for your organization.

LOCATING FUNDING SOURCES

Planning a project first and then finding the funding source with a correct fit helps ensure that the project will not be skewed to meet funding source criteria rather than community needs. Designing the project, learning the funding agency's requirements, and forming a proposal well in advance of the deadline are steps for funding success. Involving and aligning the community for future participation is certainly an invaluable step in the process, since failure to meet stated targets after funded closes the door for future applications.

There are several methods for finding funding sources. The best place to start is by utilizing directories created to identify federal agencies and private foundations. Several expensive software purchases, such as Candid (https://fconline.foundationcenter.org) or the Grantsmanship Center (www.tgci.com), are available online or for community access through city libraries, state libraries, state agencies, or colleges. Some are free, such as the online guide to US federal funding.

Although Internet searches are useful for identifying funders, databases contain condensed information useful for narrowing down options. The next step is then studying the funder's website to learn detail on funders' preferences and to obtain guidelines. Funder priorities change over time, highlighting the value of staying current. Understand the funder's goals—or specifics on results they promised to their source. This information is usually found between the lines in the request for proposals. If it is not obvious, ask about the outcomes important to the agency or foundation.

A second strategy for locating funding is to network with individuals and museums with experience carrying out similar projects. These sources may advise on who is likely to fund a similar project. Connecting with technical assistance resources (i.e., courses on proposal writing or organizational development) is useful for advice on potential funders. Since some foundations are not included in the foundation directories, this is a good strategy for discovering lesser-known funders, such as local family foundations.

Sources to search for museum-appropriate projects include the following.

- Federal/national (i.e., in the United States, there is www.grants.gov.)
- Private foundations (www.foundationcenter.org)
- Regional
- State
- City
- Individual donors
- Corporate sponsors
- Small business sponsors
- International sources

Smaller private foundations or local government grants are valuable for matching larger grants, for an effective leveraging strategy. Mapping out a leveraging framework, along with deadlines to assist a staff or volunteer team with coordination, maximizes funding potential. The next planning process further develops the project design idea in a community process from chapter 2, expanding an initial idea to a complete project design.

PLANNING PROCESS

THE SUCCESSFUL FUNDER MATCH

- Does the project align with the funder's current goals?
- Is the priority to address underserved communities recognized by the funder?
- Is need for the project well-documented, including diverse groups?
- Does the project align with the organizational plan?
- Are partners located to enhance the services delivered in a network?
- Does the project design include specific steps and outcomes?
- Do accessibility factors match the requirements of the funders?
- Are multiple scenarios defined?
- Is an evaluation plan in place to assess outcomes?
- Is there a means of feedback to the community identified?

Showing the funder your plan for shifting to another scenario—sometimes called a contingency plan—builds funder confidence. These are appropriate to address in the approach, timeline, and budget sections of a proposal. Culturally based evaluation criteria and success points demonstrate an implementation process congruent with the values represented by diverse ethnic groups in the community.

AN EMPHASIS ON PROCESS

Community-shaped projects and exhibits excite not only the museum audience but also donors and funders. Opportunities then open. Involve local groups, connect to relevant issues, and address culture as an evolving process—and funding will follow. Beyond just surviving, the museum will thrive.

Foremost, persistence is a key characteristic of successful development. Funders perceive whether passion and caring for people are guiding the process. Shifting from the ends goal of a dollar target to the means goal of service to others is aligning. And if not funded, remember the important option of revising, requesting comments, and resubmitting.

As museums seek relevance in the unfolding challenges of the twenty-first century, engaging in reframing and reshaping museum activities with positive energy leads to transformation.[6] Multi-scenario thinking is a productive starting place. In the next chapter, discover the nuts and bolts of evaluating progress—now essential for demonstrating accountability.

Shifting the focus off the money to people and inclusive, beneficial results is a winning approach.

FURTHER READING

Alexander, Brian. *Museum Finance: Issues, Challenges, and Successes* (American Alliance of Museums), 3rd edition. Lanham, MD: Rowman & Littlefield, 2023.

This book's purpose is to help museum leaders at all levels recognize and avoid certain financial minefields and realize that while there are financial hurdles in the museum world, they are solvable. Featured are numerous examples illustrating the range of challenges faced by museums and how institutions met these challenges, along with advice on how institutions can be successful in the face of difficult financial times.

Decker, Juilee, ed. *Fundraising and Strategic Planning: Innovative Approaches for Museums*. Lanham, MD: Rowman & Littlefield, 2015.

Strategies museums employ to raise funds tend to include admission prices, membership categories, donor groups, and specialized event-driven efforts. Innovative twenty-first-century approaches include crowdfunding, rebranding, a membership program, and capital campaigns. The importance of strategic planning and concept development is emphasized.

Catlin-Legutko, Cinnamon, and Stacy Klingler, eds. *Financial Resource Development and Management. Small Museum Toolkit, Vol 2*. New York: AltaMira Press, 2012.

Providing guidance for small museums to adopt policies for sound financial management and stability is essential to survive and thrive. This text offers sample fiscal policies, guides for fundraising plans, and budgeting templates to help small museums manage their money effectively. Also detailed are fundraising methods available to small museums and steps for measuring progress toward funding goals. Legal issues pertaining to financial management are covered.

Walhimer, Mark. *Museums 101*. Lanham, MD: Rowman & Littlefield, 2015.
    In addition to starting a museum, this book includes text on understanding how museums work, how to set up an exhibit, and funding programs. This easy-to-follow text includes sections on completing the museum feasibility study, museum finances, museum marketing, and museum evaluation.

NOTES

1. Museum Store Association. *Museum Store: The Manager's Guide, 4th edition*. New York: Routledge, 2016.
2. Spainhour, Jaclyn. *Museums and Millennials: Engaging the Coveted Patron Generation*. Lanham, MD: Rowman & Littlefield, 2019.
3. Decker, Juilee, ed. *Fundraising and Strategic Planning: Innovative Approaches for Museums*. Lanham, MD: Rowman & Littlefield, 2015.
4. Catlin-Legutko, Cinnamon and Stacy Klingler, eds. *Financial Resource Development and Management. Small-Museum Toolkit*, Vol 2. New York, NY: AltaMira Press, 2012.
5. Alexander, Brian. *Museum Finance: Issues, Challenges, and Successes* (American Alliance of Museums). Lanham, MD: Rowman & Littlefield, 2023.
6. Anderson, Gail. *Reinventing the Museum: Relevance, Inclusion, and Global Responsibilities*, 3rd edition. Lanham, MD: Rowman & Littlefield, 2023.

11

Evaluation and Resilience

Sustainability is more than financial stability. Considering historical context in relation to human survival, that rich pool of knowledge available through cultural diversity is critical for museums to define, include, and support. A changing cultural context includes adapting programs to diverse cultural priorities, technological advances, educational needs, and global interaction. This underscores equity.

The evaluation section of a plan is a foundation for data gathering along the way, leading to a solid evaluation process useful for redirecting later. Both internal museum and visitor/participant evaluations are needed. To be adaptive, museum management strives to understand whether current strategies are working to meet inclusivity needs. Example criteria to look at include the following.

- Were cultural considerations incorporated in all aspects of planning?
- Is the collection being adequately curated, documented, and shared?
- Is proper collections storage provided, addressing special needs for access?
- Do museum education programs complement or fill gaps in community educational programs?
- Are online programs developed for times of restricted visitation to broaden reach?
- Do staff members need additional training in museum skills or new technologies?
- Are funding sources adequately diversified and sufficient to meet changing needs?

Improving community participation in evaluation efforts not only addresses inclusion goals but also improves the sampling needed for a diversified perspective. Online polling and survey tools now complement the in-person visitation reach. And, asking inclusive, community-relevant questions is vital.

Evaluation is a basic step for improving museum programs—essential to sustainability. In addition to securing community input for cultural relevance, other stages of participation yield information valuable for improving programs. Five foundational questions create an optimal evaluation process:

1. "What are our intentions?" Goal formation in the planning process provides a solid basis for evaluation, addressing the question.
2. "Where did we start from?" Collecting baseline data determines the starting place in relation to goals.
3. "How will we assess progress along the way?" Collecting data over time and with data-collection options enables a comparison on progress toward reaching goals.
4. "Where are we now in relation to our intentions?" Measuring progress on achieving goals assesses success.
5. "How can we improve services to meet ongoing needs?" Redirecting as necessary improves museum performance and community connection.

Chart 11.1. The Evaluation Process

Evaluation ties back to the planning process as reflected in Chart 11.1, with the evaluation process guiding redirection. Value-based goals and objectives developed in the planning process provide the foundation for an inclusive evaluation.[1] The museum plan developed with adaptive intentions will reflect criteria for changing course as needed. Community-based criteria for success, as well as museum standards, are important for resilience. To be useful, specific and measurable objectives for each goal are needed.

DEAI AND EVALUATION

The diversity, equity, accessibility, and inclusivity (DEAI) movement indicates a broad range of questions to address in the evaluation process. The findings of an invaluable report produced by the American Alliance of Museums (AAM) in 2022 identify four core concepts related to these issues: 1) DEAI is the responsibility of the entire organization; 2) DEAI is an ongoing journey without a fixed end point; 3) DEAI demands an ongoing commitment of resources; and 4) DEAI work must be measured and assessed. The report defines equity as "the guarantee of fair treatment, access, opportunity, and advancement while at the same time striving to identify and eliminate identity-based disparities within a museum and in the broader community."

Key indicators identified in *Excellence in DEAI*[2] recommend the following:

- Adopting equity as a cornerstone of the museum's mission, strategy, values, management, and culture.
- Embedding responsibility and accountability for implementing DEAI policies and process into operations, job descriptions, and performance reviews at all levels of the institution.
- Taking a holistic approach, integrating DEAI into all aspects of the museum's operations through a process of assessment, reflection, capacity building, iteration, and measurement.
- Publicly committing to the ongoing work of transforming organizational culture and dismantling systems of inequity within individual museums and the communities they serve, the museum sector, and society broadly.
- Allocating financial resources in the budget for staffing, and capacity building in internal or external DEAI expertise.
- Dedicating ample time for DEAI work, including individual and collective reflection, trust, and relationship building.
- Measuring and assessing DEAI work.
- Defining the museum's equity goals as the elimination of identity-based disparities.
- Measuring progress by disaggregating data by identity over time.

Indicators of progress for each point are suggested in the full report, readily available on the AAM's website. Integrating these indicators into the evaluation framework of your plan and sharing these indicators with other museums are adaptive steps.

CONCEPTS OF SUCCESS

Defining success is multi-dimensional. In relation to the national museum standards now developed,[3] success in curation and basic museum operations can be determined. Going beyond earlier standards may be necessary as a means of assessing progress in meeting urgent diverse needs. A community-integrated approach looks at the museum's connection locally and assesses both visitor and community satisfaction with museum programming.

Sustainability is about community vitality. For this reason, museum success defined from *internal* to a community or a culture looks very different from measures defined from *external* to the community. Evaluation criteria are often provided from sources external to the community, such as funders. The proactive community-based museum benefits by developing an internal evaluation framework based on inclusivity and communicating these to funders—in addition to meeting national-level criteria.

In *Measuring Museum Impact and Performance*, John Jacobsen broadens consideration of museum impacts and benefits for a community-integrated approach.[4] These include impacts that are public, private, personal, and institutional. The following represents a partial list.

- *Broadening participation* addresses the benefit of increased understanding of worldviews, social justice, and inclusion.
- *Preserving heritage* includes caring for and interpreting our past, both physically and culturally, to include stewardship of collections, historic sites, and cultural neighborhoods.
- *Enhancing public knowledge* indicators through documentation and research contributes to public and professional information.
- *Serving the educational system* addresses museum impacts to formal education (schools) and museum professionals through student programs.
- *Advancing social change* assists communities to make changes determined beneficial by the community—such as addressing social problems, health initiatives, global environmental conservation, education initiatives, social justice, anti-discrimination, and poverty, as well as others determined locally.
- *Communicating public identity and image* efforts assist a community or individuals to develop and present a desired identity and image.
- *Contributing to the economy* includes participating in the local tourism draw, providing jobs, and developing the workforce.

Museums that plan, evaluate, adapt, and redirect are more resilient over time. Throughout this text, the theme of connection is illustrated through a planning framework that connects to all aspects of community needs—cultural, economical, and ecological. Assessing direction and staying in alignment with contemporary concerns and trends brings relevance to museum programs.

In relation to sustainability, avoiding isolation leads to an increased network of resources. This book emphasizes two-way benefit results from being part of a network. The museum benefits by increased participation, increased resources, and community-relevant programming. Other museums, tourism entities, and community programs become aware of the museum's mission as a result of interaction, with increased capability to link and create an experience.

Small communities sometimes develop a theme, such as history, that is reinforced throughout the community's businesses and public programs. When a museum stays connected to all community segments, plus tourism and museum networks, the net impact of museum programs grows.

Assessing the benefits of community-wide linking during the evaluation process addresses community depth,[5] to include:

- Mentoring and professional development;
- Sharing assessment data and participating in larger studies;
- Collaboration to save costs and extend outreach, such as advertising;
- Gaining financial support, in the form of government allocations, grants, donations, joint fundraising, and referrals to museum enterprises;
- Supporting collections documentation, such as shared public catalogues;
- Creation of a community-wide visitor guide—online, print, or both;
- Developing new forms of access, such as media presence, through collaboration; and
- Raised "community-esteem" and cultural pride by honoring and valuing all cultures.

As resources become scarcer, trends in funding emphasize accountability and the measuring of success. Such an approach is beneficial for monitoring progress and redirecting to new circumstances, be it environmental, societal, or community-wide. Yet, evaluation is susceptible to bias. Techniques in this chapter will pinpoint bias tendencies and offer suggestions that work across cultures.

SETTING EVALUATION INTENTIONS

Staying on an inclusive path involves articulating the initial questions reflecting different worldviews and then including in-depth questions relating to the involved cultures at each stage of the evaluation process. The *Practical Evaluation Guide*[6] asks these relevant questions in the initial stage:

- What is the purpose of the study?
- Who is it for, an internal or external audience?
- Who will undertake the study?
- What is the budget of the study?
- How will you share the results of the study?

Starting out with these questions creates focus to the study. Keep in mind that if a funder requires an evaluation, costs of the study may be included in the budget.

FORMATIVE AND SUMMATIVE EVALUATION

Consistent recordkeeping is the key to a successful evaluation, the foundation to measure goals in relation to the before and after comparison. A *formative evaluation*, aimed at "forming" the programs of a museum to maximize the use of resources and improve results, is conducted by program staff at the six-month interval. This intermediate evaluation is not only used to monitor progress on objectives but also to redirect program activities when off course.

Summative evaluation at the end of the year or project examines the broader status of collections, exhibits, and programs. Topics may include diversity needs met, community feedback, museum visitor satisfaction, jobs created, fundraising targets, and encouragement of cultural activities and retention, as well as positive liaison with other programs. Assessing results assists the museum to redirect as necessary and to document achievements in a format desired by funders, as well.

The formative evaluation is useful for progress reports whereas the summative evaluation is invaluable for redirecting, as well as for preparing final reports to funders and board members.

BIAS IN EVALUATION

Who asks the evaluation questions and how they are structured affects responses. To prevent bias, use a culture-value based approach to both earlier goal formation and evaluation criteria. Often, in practice, the questions asked are not related directly to the museum's goals.

Equity representation in the evaluation process is gained by considering:

- Age and gender range;
- Cultural and linguistic identification;
- Worldview differences;
- Socioeconomic factors; and
- Rural/urban location.

Ethical criteria are directly related to cultural worldview. Factors to keep in mind when designing a balanced evaluation design include:

- Protection of cultural privacy, as indicated by different cultural groups;
- Attention to documentation not only for exhibit interpretation but also for future teaching efforts; and
- Adequate representation of all, or specifically indicated ethnic groups.

The natural tendency to the bias of one's own culture illustrates the need for a participatory process to create community-based measures of success. Choosing an evaluator familiar with the cultures involved, using a team approach, is critical for reducing cultural bias. Include qualifications of the evaluator in a funding proposal—strengthening the workplan. Tip: Including your own evaluation outline in the funding proposal—even if not required—is a proactive way to further inclusivity, or being evaluated by culturally relevant criteria.

QUANTITATIVE AND QUALITATIVE APPROACHES

Both quantitative and qualitative measures are essential to understand museum performance. Quantitative approaches gather numerical data to answer highly structured questions. Measureable objectives are stated at the beginning of the year and data are collected to assess whether the target was reached.

The object-oriented museum may be over-reliant on quantitative measures such as museum attendance and the number of curated collection items, rather than on the visitation experience. Quantitative views represented in the scientific orientations very seldom lead to an understanding of the whole. A strength of the historical and cultural contexts represented in most museums is the potential for interpretation on a broader, connecting scale.

When cultural appropriateness and connections underlie motivation in a community, then the museum may become a trusted location for teaching and retaining culture. Including the entire community in assessments of needs and progress sustains a community-supportive effort.

Qualitative approaches invite discussion, identify desired directions, note opinions, and allow a broad range of information and cultural views to be discovered. Qualitative methods provide context for interpretation, tend to be process-oriented rather than goal-oriented, and are useful for building consensus. Qualitative methods elicit inclusive data and support participation that is contextually relevant.

An emphasis on quantitative measures in the short term becomes problematic as the sole emphasis, to the neglect of those qualitative indicators that support long-term outcomes necessary for cultural retention or community revitalization. Funding sources, particularly for grants, tend to focus on the one-year outcome, and numerical targets are often required by the funder. This factor can lead to a disjointed and hurried project approach, as well as an over-emphasis on quantitative measures. An example is a class to teach the cultural arts. Grant sources tend to emphasize numbers of individuals trained in a "class;" whereas, learning an artistic skill may take a series of classes, in levels, in order to develop expertise for one art.

Using several approaches captures the most representative views in both the planning and evaluation processes.[7]

Qualitative methods emphasize:

- Focus groups with five to ten people per group, inclusive to the different views or ethnic representation locally;
- Visitor-generated comments, either unstructured or prompted by a question; and
- Open-ended, unstructured interviews.

Quantitative methods include the following when numerical data result:

- Online or in-museum surveys, asking a set of questions, either at a computer station in the museum, phone apps, or as an online perk for after-visit response
- Intercept interviews asking a series of questions
- Observations, watching visitor behavior

People-focused museums play a strong role in community sustainability. The power of actions that have worked well over time and come from wisdom passed down for several generations sit at the core of sustainability. Each culture has these traditions, although high-tech cultures may not seem to pay attention.

Even in cultures where culture change is occurring at a rapid pace, museum education programs making past-present-future connections will serve to remind a community of underlying cultural values. The museum that stimulates discussion about cultural change and retention— i.e., cultures evolving—will stay at the forefront of visitor interest.

PERFORMANCE MEASURES

Yes, evaluation is worth the effort. Defining performance measures ahead of time in a strategic planning process or to a funder is valuable for:

- Ensuring a balance of qualitative and quantitative measures, in relation to museum mission;
- Increasing visitation;

- Assessing the adequacy of museum activities in relation to goals and objectives;
- Determining repeat visitation;
- Setting realistic targets for an annual workplan;
- Allocating resources to balance priorities; and
- Increasing staff job satisfaction by understanding progress of the museum team;

This chapter is intended to enhance the ethical responsibility issue by illustrating other qualitative measures that extend museum inclusivity, such as:

- Historical and cultural documentation completed;
- Diversity in staff members in relation to community representation;
- Increased public understanding of historical contributions;
- Quality of outreach to community programs;
- Museum operations in coordination with community programs;
- Opportunities for entrepreneurial employment developed;
- Appreciation for, and understanding of, local ecosystems;
- Degree of cultural retention enhanced in the community;
- Satisfaction with museum services; and
- Raised community esteem.

An evaluation framework is vital to guide the planning, implementation, and redirection process. Other criteria are recommended, with specific targets for project periods to be added as adequate resources are secured, supporting an expansion of services to the resilient museum. Examples of longer-term topic areas are:

- Curation of the current collection;
- Collections storage developed;
- Social media and online platforms utilized to broaden reach;
- Online programs offered to the community;
- Mentoring relationship and reciprocal interactions with three regional museums established;
- Interpretive materials developed, to include an exhibit guide;
- Annually changing exhibits;
- Demonstrations; and
- Special events.

Topics for quantitative measures include:

- Museum admissions;
- Ethnic representation in museum programs;

- Attendance at museum events;
- Participation in online programs;
- Educational program attendance;
- Trainings delivered;
- Number of new exhibits per year;
- Number of items registered and catalogued;
- Increase (accession) in the number of collection items or decrease (deaccession);
- The number of collection items housed in a new storage area;
- Increase in the number of traditional language speakers;
- Jobs created; and
- Progress providing entrepreneurial opportunities, training, and access to resources.

Examples 11.1 and 11.2 illustrate specific measureable outcomes for quantitative variables.

EXAMPLE 11.1.   MEASURABLE OUTCOMES

Several example priority targets for a small inclusive museum can be recommended for a five-year period:

- Update the catalogue by 50 percent;
- Increased attendance (online and in-person) by 30 percent;
- Increased cultural arts and language classes by 50 percent;
- Increased operating budget by 50 percent in five years and 100 percent in ten years (of current levels);
- Increased earned income by 200 percent;
- Increased diversification in staff member composition by 100 percent; and
- Establish a membership program, with 250 members.

EXAMPLE 11.2.   ADDITIONAL MEASURABLE GOALS

Representative outcomes for a small museum might include:

- Documentation on eight storyline topics, including video and audio recordings of elders to present in exhibits;
- Completion of twenty-four bilingual labels;
- Completion of a ten-page interpretive guide and posting on the website;
- Completion of three video documentaries, using existing footage plus new footage;

- Increased exhibit visitation by 1,000 community members, including 300 youth; and
- Exhibit visitation by 5,000 tourists.

The most frequently used measure of museum progress is annual attendance. For this reason, keeping ongoing and accurate records is essential for measuring benefits. Once the museum takes care of this bit of recordkeeping, then the more innovative ways of defining success can be addressed.

Ways of measuring attendance include:

- The sign-in book;
- Counting attendance at events (easier when you know the amount of seating setup);
- Electronic counters; and
- Social media or website visits for virtual sharing.

Museum visitor surveys are useful for indicating topics of interest and frequency of mention. Progress on qualitative variables can be measured in a variety of ways: 1) a three-point satisfaction scale (e.g., high, medium, low), as in the Appendix C survey example, or 2) a five-point scale (e.g. low, somewhat, medium, good, very good), 3) yes or no agreement, or 4) a ranked scale of one to five. Open-ended questions are useful for eliciting comments directed at improvement.

It is useful to develop your own evaluation framework questions, and then draw from other surveys in the museum field as necessary for examples. The comments and questions of museum visitors are invaluable for shaping future evaluation criteria. Asking front desk staff to record comments is useful for producing narrative to interpret attendee satisfaction results.

Depending on the commitment of the community to historic preservation and ongoing heritage teaching, the cultural future of community members can be continually expanded through museum activities. A high level of staff dedication to both community and public programs indicates a positive direction for the future of a museum. Gradually securing additional resources and increasing earned income will lead to a sustainable future.

EXHIBIT EVALUATION

Evaluation affords an opportunity to test content and exhibit designs in the development process, supporting the gathering of input and improvement as the exhibit progresses. Three phases of museum exhibition evaluation are useful for developing and redirecting[8] a community-relevant process.

1. **Front-end:** Audience research is conducted at the beginning stage of exhibit development to determine how their interest shapes the conceptual stage by defining objectives, themes, and worldviews represented—with input from representative museum participants. This stage is valuable input to the concept design and interpretive plan.
2. **Formative:** During the design phase, tests of planned design and text understandability are often prototyped to obtain audience and staff feedback.
3. **Summative:** Once the exhibit is complete, a test is conducted with an actual audience. This process can lead to the improvement or "tweaking" of the exhibit and suggestions for inclusive or additional interpretation. The results improve exhibition success.

As a process, exhibit evaluation contributes to planning, development, and improvement. Particularly, when community segments reflect different worldviews, evaluation input enriches and assists with accurate interpretation. Innovative exhibit ideas emerge in this context.

COLLECTING EVALUATION DATA

The thoroughness of an evaluation depends upon the adequacy of data collected during the year. Maintaining rapport with the community encourages participation in the data-gathering process. Keep in mind the opportunity value of a survey conducted during a local event or training session.

Evaluating impacts and redirecting as necessary are essential steps for keeping in close communication with local government and organizations, as well as the community with:

- Community surveys conducted;
- Visitor surveys updated to determine trends;
- Public meetings held;
- Increased cultural retention;
- Tracked reduction in environmental impacts;
- Job creation documented;
- Number of people trained; and
- Unemployment rates reduced through locally owned businesses.

Regarding evaluation as an outreach and improvement process focuses the activity on people. Taking into account local participation styles is essential for inclusivity while gathering input. Remember this guideline: in many cultures a meeting without food lacks "warmth" and is not likely to draw participation.

RESPECTFUL CHANGE

The call for museum change is at the forefront, as the field is recognizing the need for a shift from objects to community priorities, connection, and inclusivity. Piotr Bienkowski and Hilary McGowan, in *Managing Change in Museums and Galleries*[9] use the term "rebalancing"—a term accurately describing redirection with inclusivity.

When the impetus for change is financial and not tied to a redefinition of purpose, inclusivity is not likely to be a guiding factor. Rebalancing connotes a true interest in more effectively reaching the interests, worldviews, and learning styles of diverse groups represented in the community or region. Evaluation methods frequently tend to focus on interests. As explained in chapter 1, worldviews and learning styles, in addition to topics, are essential for assessing the inclusive visitor experience.

Such factors are rarely considered in the evaluation process and inspire change in an inclusive, culturally meaningful direction. From previous chapters, inclusivity considerations such as access to collections and interpretation from more than one worldview are examples for essential rebalancing shifts. Honoring the environmental and social contributions of diverse cultures in the evaluation steps is critical to an inclusive process.

Inclusion of these values and worldviews is respectful to the cultures involved. Rebalance and meaningful participation will grow.

THE EVALUATION REPORT

Reporting in a way that fits funding requirements yet reaches community members requires skill. Here is a suggested outline:

- Executive summary
- Evaluation intentions
- Evaluation objectives
- Evaluation design
- Inclusivity factors
- Methods
- Techniques used for data gathering
- Suggestions for redirecting
- Distribution strategies to reach community segments
- Funding needs to support redirection
- Proposed timeline for implementation

A separate evaluation summary posted on the museum website or inclusion in the museum's newsletter is a way of providing feedback to the community. Keep in mind flow; the thorough evaluation report provides a solid basis for the next funding proposal.

MEASURING RESULTS FOR GRANTS

Learning how to develop an excellent evaluation plan is one vital success factor for securing grant funding. Funders want to know "What are the project intentions?" "How many people will you reach?" and "How will success be measured?" Results are then part of the final project report.

Here is one pitfall of tailoring a museum project to grant funding. The one-year timeframe of the majority of grant sources tends to obscure long-term targets in museums (i.e., beyond the next exhibit and the next year of programs). Be careful not to limit thinking toward longer-term results that are sustainable in the community.

As a solution, develop long-term goals and nest objectives within those goals suitable for adapting to annual targets. You can expand project results by:

- Developing a traveling exhibit;
- Partnering with community organizations to increase outreach involvement in museum programs, such as field trips (in-person or virtual);
- Linking museum exhibits to local events;
- Sponsoring a speaker program related to exhibits;
- Utilizing the website and social media to extend interpretation and an invite to museum programs;
- Developing a model or success story from your project and then distributing the success story through newsletters, newspapers, journal articles, museum associations, on-line; and
- Networking with other museums for collaborative projects.

Grants often require creative thinking about project impacts, and this can be a positive benefit to the museum. Funders like to see large numbers of museum visitors benefiting from new projects developed. All of these activities extend museum benefits and broaden possible sources of funding.

REBALANCING AND RESILIENCE

Sustainability is about interdependence and balance. Museums, history, and culture do not exist apart from community; therefore, the museum that demonstrates connectedness to all aspects of sustainability is likely to be seen as valuable and supported in these times of rapid, societal, and economic change. The following are potential actions for a museum to support the three sustainability variables—culture, economy, and ecology. These criteria are also valuable to consider when revising mission statements, goals, and objectives in the cycle of planning, implementation, marketing, and evaluation.

CULTURAL

- Increase diversity in staffing;
- Preserve and interpret collections from inclusive worldviews;
- Include elder wisdom in interpretation;
- Exhibit the connection between past, present, and future;
- Teach cultural history and arts intergenerationally;
- Integrate traditional language use in exhibits and classes;
- Encourage learning of the arts by youth;
- Increase family activities; and
- Share successes and challenges with other communities.

ECONOMIC

- Encourage a broad range of museum services to connect to the local economy;
- Create the maximum number of jobs through direct employment and indirect employment;
- Support locally owned entrepreneurial businesses;
- Integrate business skills into art class content;
- Increase marketing linkages to a respectful audience base;
- Assist entrepreneurs with marketing; and
- Encourage multiple income streams both for the museum and for community members.

ENVIRONMENTAL/ECOSYSTEM

- Target a specific museum audience, e.g. culturally-oriented (cultural tourists, heritage tourists) and environmentally-oriented (geo-tourists, eco-tourists, recreational tourists);
- Less people equals fewer potential impacts;
- Use visitor education and online resources to increase appreciation of the interrelationship of history, cultural arts, traditional practices, and local ecosystems;
- Manage the flow of visitors and carry out periodic assessment of environmental impacts; and
- Protect environmentally sensitive areas through educational efforts.

A resilient community draws upon strengths developed in the past, integrating knowledge with present challenges, to forge a positive future. A cultural future may be at stake with a museum's success in teaching culture and integrating language, as well as providing programs to the public. With public interest comes support for local artists, income for community program support, and enhanced cultural pride through cultural sharing and understanding. All of these factors encourage interaction with museums and cultural centers in the community setting.

PLANNING PROCESS

EVALUATING IMPACTS

- Have museum project goals evolved in tandem with community goals?
- Was access to collections improved?
- Did exhibits tell stories important to the community?
- Which arts and culture workshops or classes are still needed?
- Were youth engaged and cultural pride enhanced?
- Were entrepreneurial skills integrated into the educational curriculum or other programs implemented to benefit the local economy?
- Is there an effective link between museum enterprises and local cultural entrepreneurs?
- Are features of the building serving local cultural needs?
- Does the museum building need expansion to serve new programs?
- How effective are rebalancing efforts?

Evaluation is about nurturing the maximum benefit through museum programs. By assessing effectiveness, the path of improvement to better serve community is guided. Deciding on desired outcomes to meet community needs, then fine tuning with each evaluation, keeps the museum rebalancing and evolving. Through this pattern of adaptive change, service to people remains central while flexibility increases. Chart 11.2 describes potential sustainability impacts for an integrated concept.

THE RESILIENT MUSEUM

Cultural/Social Access	Economic	Ecological
• Following diversity, equity, accessibility, and inclusion guidelines, as these evolve • Increase of historic and cultural understanding through interpretive programs & tours • Documentation of traditions and skills valuable to thriving in a changing world • Increase in awareness of local events open to the public • Increase in cultural participation for cultural and language programs • Reinforcement of cultural knowledge through mentoring and storytelling • Progress on furthering inter-cultural collaboration with direct community relevance	• Increase in financial potential by developing museum enterprises • Increase in culturally-based community employment opportunities such as cultural and contemporary arts • Increase in market niche identification, leading to new product development • Increase in promotional links to entrepreneurial businesses • Increased purchasing opportunities for the visitor • Increase in tourism benefits through art shows and sales • Increase in financial sustainability measures for the museum through earned income, plus donations and membership programs	• Renewal of traditions surrounding ecosystem connections • Increase in awareness of ecological practices through storytelling tours • Increase in connections to local ecosystems through tours • Increase in awareness of diverse agricultural practices, preserving knowledge • Increase in cultural interpretation of spiritual relationships to animals, plants and ecosystems • Communicating highly interrelated, cultural, ecological, and economic messages to the general public–important to current global issues and the protection of Earth.

Chart 11.2. Potential Sustainability Impacts

STAYING AT THE FOREFRONT

Museums tend to become stagnant when operating with outdated goals and annual targets. In contrast, developing flexible goals in the planning process allows for the setting of annual targets that keep up with changing public needs. Then, evaluation and redirecting keeps museum activities in tandem with the changing conversation.

The wealth of knowledge present in the world's archive of diverse cultural wisdom—including environmental—provides the basis for solutions to coming challenges. Diverse language structures represented by the 10,000 languages worldwide are essential for expressing the worldviews of this cultural wisdom. For intercultural sharing to occur, cultural and language preservation are essential.

A coming trend will be discussions concerning connection in local and global ecosystems. Explore issues drawing from worldwide knowledge of animal and plant diversity—within the context of worldviews that foster reciprocal relationships between humans and these resources. These are central to the future of our species.

Nature is the highest level of sociocultural context. Public education concerning environmental issues and direct links to local ecosystems bridges knowledge from the local to global.

FURTHER READING

Bienkowski, Piotr, and Hilary McGowan. *Managing Change in Museums and Galleries*. New York: Routledge, 2021.

The authors have direct experience of leading change, running change programs, and advising on change in more than 250 museums and galleries. This book identifies the various problems, issues, and challenges that any professional in a museum or heritage organization is likely to encounter and provides advice on redirecting. The book's six parts treat change holistically and help the reader understand what change entails, preparation for change, and lead redirection, ensure that everyone in the museum is involved, plus understand what can go wrong and evaluate and learn from the experience.

Catlin-Legutko, Cinnamon, and Stacy Klingler, eds. *Reaching and Responding to the Audience, Small Museum Toolkit, Vol 4*. New York: AltaMira Press, 2012.

This volume of the Small Museum Toolkit encourages small museums to examine their audiences and make them comfortable, program to their needs and interests, and spread the word about the museum's good work. It also features several case studies of successful evaluation programs, sample press releases, accessibility checklists, visitor experience checklists, and more.

Jacobsen, John. *Measuring Museum Impact and Performance*. Lanham, MD: Rowman & Littlefield, 2016.
This museum-specific guide for assessing museum value and performance addresses museum impact—particularly in relation to purpose, museum value, community impacts and relevance. Ways of broadening impact and multiple purposes are emphasized, with a process to determine, measure, and compare your museum's key performance indicators. An accompanying MIIP database presents an analysis of indicators based on direct data collection with museums.

Diamond, Judy, Michael Horn, and David Uttal. *Practical Evaluation Guide: Tools for Museums and Other Informal Educational Settings, 3rd Edition* (American Association for State and Local History). Lanham, MD: Rowman & Littlefield Publishers, 2016.
Administrators of museums and other informal-learning centers often need to demonstrate, in some tangible way, the effectiveness of their institutions as teaching tools. The *Practical Evaluation Guide* discusses specific methods for analyzing audience learning and behavior in museums, zoos, botanic gardens, nature centers, camps, and youth programs.

NOTES

1. Guyette, Susan. *Planning for Balanced Development*. Santa Fe, NM: ClearLight, 1996.
2. American Alliance of Museums. *DEAI Report*. 2022. www.aam-us.org.
3. Ambrose, Timothy, and Crispin Paine. *Museum Basics: The International Handbook, 3rd Edition*. New York: Routledge, 2012.
4. Jacobsen, John. *Measuring Museum Impact and Performance*. Lanham, MD: Rowman & Littlefield, 2016.
5. Klingler, Stacy, and Conny Graft. "In Lieu of Mind Reading: Visitor Studies and Evaluation." In *Reaching and Responding to the Audience, Small Museum Toolkit, Book Four*, Cinnamon Catlin-Legutko and Stacy Klingler (eds.), pp. 37–74. New York: AltaMira Press, 2012.
6. Diamond, Judy, Michael Horn, and David Uttal. *Practical Evaluation Guide: Tools for Museums and Other Informal Educational Settings*. Lanham, MD: Rowman & Littlefield, 2016.
7. McKenna-Cress, Polly, and Janet A. Kamien. *Creating Exhibitions: Collaboration in the Planning, Development, and Design of Innovative Experiences*. Hoboken, NJ: John Wiley & Sons, 2013.
8. Hansen, Beth. *Great Exhibits!: An Exhibit Planning and Construction Handbook for Small Museums*. Lanham, MD: Rowman & Littlefield, 2017; Lord, Barry, Gail Dexter Lord, and Lindsay Martin. *Manual of Museum Planning*. Lanham, MD: Rowman & Littlefield, 2012.
9. Bienkowski, Piotr, and Hilary McGowan. *Managing Change in Museums and Galleries*. New York: Routledge, 2021.

12

We Are All Related

Cultural resilience is the increased capacity for adapting to changing conditions. The museum integrated with local values, cultures, and pressing community needs increases adaptability. To cultivate empathy for others in the planning process, rather than acting out of a "duty" to be inclusive, enriches the two-way learning process. Building trust is about museum methods that work across cultures, encouraging the sharing of information while protecting what is not to be shared.

By using participative processes, museums and cultural centers can redirect, becoming a community resource for fostering continuance of the knowledge and beliefs reflected in worldviews. These nurture youth and families. Reinforcing the positive role culture plays in guiding youth by continuing time-honored and proven traditions strengthens cultural resilience.

Be creative with the process, listening to multigenerational participation. Then, you can adapt the planning processes in this book to your community. Starting the discovery hones these questions to a good community and cultural fit. In many cultures, a cultural center or museum connects by providing several functions—from welcoming to providing visitor information to telling stories new and diverse.[1] Options for financial support expand in tandem.

Community-integrated museums are places for cultural learning and gathering, rather than facilities with a primary emphasis on objects. While objects may be important to learning, they are not the main issue for improving inclusivity. Access to collections, critical for learning traditional designs and symbolism, tends to be an inclusivity concern. Diversity, equity, accessibility, and inclusivity (DEAI) variables were discussed chapter by chapter.

Museums that connect to every aspect of community reflect culture. In addition to furthering cultural understanding, integrated museums connect to the community as a whole—to pressing issues such as cultural retention, job creation, and restoring ecosystem relationships. Seeing ways of connecting is central to this expanded role. *Museum Resilience* had chapters on learning programs, creating employment, and tourism, in addition to arts and culture districts, emphasizing practical methods for making these integrative links.

The recognition that cultural identity is a source of strength[2] is important for self-esteem building. For example, shared core values, beliefs, and behaviors related to resilience include: foodways, spirituality; childrearing and extended family; veneration of age/wisdom/tradition; respect for nature, generosity, and sharing; cooperation and group harmony; autonomy and respect for others; composure and patience; relativity of time; and non-verbal communication. These aspects of culture are highly interrelated. Traditional values of diverse groups support not only social and cultural needs but also economic and ecological relationships, forming the web of life.

MOVING OUTSIDE THE BOX

In a rapidly shifting learning environment, museums may access a wide range of learning and experiencing styles to broaden their mission. Several of these multimodal options cost less, reach thousands more visitors, and open avenues for linking museum programs. For example, defining directions for use of a collection to increase teaching of the cultural arts not only increases cultural retention through the skills and intergenerational interaction but also encourages traditional language retention and the imparting of leadership skills as well.

Why is reviving the traditional arts of importance to the current global crisis? These art forms tend to be integrated with everyday life and cultural continuance, connected to our ecosystems. Characteristic of these arts, function and aesthetics reveal cultural symbolism and values. Seen in the broader perspective, the contemporary arts reflect a past-present-future continuum.

One difference between the mainstream Western/European view of the arts and many culturally diverse groups exists when the arts are separated from other aspects of daily life. A hierarchical approach often found in Western culture frequently regards the arts as a separate, higher form of culture. The disconnect that is a result of this approach is now being evidenced in isolation and alienation, apart from the richness of everyday life.

A community-integrated approach emphasizes the meaning of the art-making process and interpretation rather than art as objects. This view integrates art with all aspects of everyday life. Interpretation becomes a cultural and local story—with less emphasis on the individual. Contemporary art may tend to place more emphasis on the individual than does cultural art. Knowing the distinction, while encouraging individual expression, is central to designing culturally relevant classes while avoiding cultural appropriation.

Cultural pride inspires retention. Seeing the arts integrated with all aspects of everyday life shifts the focus and value of the arts. Teaching styles are often different in cultural ways, emphasizing the need for a community-based program. For example, the process of family collaboration in art-making and teaching are predominant in many cultures. In rural communities, arts such as quilt-making and pottery-making are collaborative—with shared interaction as cultural items are made.

Why is teaching at a museum or cultural center beneficial to a community? Language preservation efforts are encouraged with art-making, particularly when vocabulary is integrated into the classes. Access to collections to study designs and materials, combined with informal gathering spaces for discussion, are more conducive to the learning process. The connection to history tends to inspire cultural pride and fosters enthusiasm to learn. School environments are most often designed according to standard mainstream classrooms, removed from cultural context.

Cultural institutions exploring the relationship between exhibits—at the museum and virtual—to community issues and needs to cultural retention are exciting to visitors. Connecting to environmental concerns, global warming, and health issues necessary for our very survival as a species is a fundamental ethical direction.

Integrating topics for a more inclusive definition of culture serves a broader audience while increasing options for financial support. The current trend of decreased museum member support indicates a pressing need for museums to reinvent their missions in sync with twenty-first-century interests.

ADAPTIVE PLANNING

Adaptive, value-based museum planning examines the scenarios of possible futures, given the unknown direction of the economy, environmental conditions, and popular interests shifted by cultural change. For this reason, an organizational foundation is created that encourages resilience, or the ability to improve decision-making, adjust, and be sustainable in times of change. Central to adaptive planning is an analysis of current trends and strategies for alternative scenarios. The strengthening of a local network is another outcome of linking through adaptive planning.

In summary, adaptive scenario planning:

- Sees inclusivity as foundational to every aspect of museum management;
- Examines multiple scenarios;
- Uses participatory approaches, necessary for representing multiple viewpoints and multigenerational interests;
- Sees the museum plan as a management tool;
- Furthers connection, forming a community network for ongoing participation; and
- Provides a means of feedback to the community.

Such an approach goes beyond inviting communities to programs. Estimated directions determined with participation further an interface with other community programs. In turn, the community connection integrates cultural richness into museum programming. Yet, this is more than just an invite. Rather, it implies that the museum will use resources (e.g., human, collections, space, etc.) to support the goals of the community. In relation to a school, this might involve offering interpretation for children, classes in the cultural arts, or an exhibit of children's art in a changing exhibit space.

UNIFYING PAST, PRESENT, AND FUTURE

As a museum moves into a next phase of development, the balance between urgent museum needs, such as cataloguing and curation, and community needs, such as cultural arts and programs for youth, may be central to meeting the museum's goals. Linking cultural entrepreneurs to tourists and local visitors is another significant opportunity. Reimagining a museum is possible with a *community listening*; participation is essential to determine the ideal balance of services.

Rural community museums as well as neighborhood urban museums engage in the vitally important function of fostering identity and cultural pride with youth. Cultural arts classes plus events honoring master artists and those who take the time to learn are among the unique priorities of the community-focused museum. Balancing community learning and general public education creates a high level of community satisfaction.

The benefits of linking together small museums—or large museums to small—include a strong regional referral network. The advantages of multi-community collaborations also accrue to the individual community. Within the museum context, tourism is a likely rallying point for other types of collaborative action, such as artist cooperatives. Well-planned linkages between communities may stimulate knowledge-sharing collaborations for similar traditions, resulting in success at "bringing back" traditions nearly lost.

In renewing community relevance as times change, integrating community priorities of cultural retention and economic revitalization are important to keep in mind while moving forward. The museum's role as a community hub is ideal to integrate public programs, cultural retention efforts, environmental education, and job creation through tourism linkages. A museum fully integrated into the local economic system is moving toward increased community relevance.

Staff training in museum and administrative skills is essential to a positive future for the small museum. Training needs to be tailored to local culture to be effective—to not skew cultural values. Working with trainers in advance to orient them on the uniqueness of your community museum, local values, local history, environment, and the local economy will be important for a favorable training content outcome.

This book recommends balancing specific museum topics with community and culturally based projects. How they support each other will evolve the uniqueness of exhibits and interpretation. Synergy between projects is important to consider. For example, curation of the collection is important to cultural arts classes—both in the short-term and the long-term. For widespread and long-lasting results toward cultural retention and employment generation, interfacing these projects will achieve the optimal result.

Youth carry the future of the culture. As these elements of a successful program work together, a positive cultural future is created, youth are inspired to learn, and families cooperate from a common historic connection. This rich tapestry of cultural knowledge is interwoven with everyday life activities, forming the uniqueness of each community.

To reshape with new concepts requires funding and resourcefulness. The challenge at a planning point is to move the museum to the next level, integrating solutions that address a broad range of community needs. Using new technologies for cataloguing and curation makes the collection more accessible to the community—now and in the future. Interpretive projects and tours educate community members on local history and increase cultural pride, as well as further cultural understanding by visitors.

Challenging economic and ecological conditions are stimulating cultures worldwide as they move into an era of adaptation. During this process, opportunities to present culturally-based solutions increase with collective wisdom. And community-determined messages to share in relation to sustainability will stimulate innovative intercultural cooperation.

Global resilience in the future depends upon preserving the cumulative, bio-cultural knowledge base developed over the past several thousand years. Numerous answers are already here, ready to be recovered and shared. The compacts made between the first humans and animals to take care of each other show us how to live respectfully and wisely on Mother Earth. For this reason, retaining cultural diversity is of far-reaching importance.

NOTES

1. Murawski, Mike. *Museums as Agents of Change: A Guide to Becoming a Changemaker.* Lanham, MD: Rowman & Littlefield, 2021.
2. Heavyrunner, Iris, and Joann Sebastian Morris. "Traditional Native Culture and Resilience." *CAREI Research/Practice* Vol. 5, No. 1 (1997).

Appendix A

Community-Integrated Definitions and Concepts

Access: Permission guidelines for viewing and/or handling objects, including cultural affiliation, gender, or religious considerations.

Archive: A space with environmental controls dedicated to the storage of historical and interpretive records relating to objects (physical or electronic) in a collection.

Business: The selling of services or products to produce income for the support of museum programs and local livelihood.

Business incubator: A start-up program, usually featuring small spaces for production, such as studios), joint access to office equipment, and business coaching assistance. This is a possible approach for securing a local, culturally based inventory for a museum store while encouraging cultural retention.

Business plan: A document showing projected expenses and income needed to cover museum operations and services to the public as a cultural institution. The museum business plan reflecting cultural values will become more community-relevant.

Collection: A group of objects representing a specific topic determined to be of value to the history or cultural continuity of a community.

Collections audit: An assessment of the collections held by the museum.

Community: A group of people living in a particular area or having common cultural interests, sub-interests, values, and stories to tell.

Conservation: The activity of preserving or restoring objects and cultural meanings regarding beliefs, uses, and cultural importance.

Conservator: A specialist with training in the scientific area and treatment of collection objects, including cultural knowledge of the proper handling of objects.

Context: An expression of the relationships between the elements of an exhibit project and the worldviews of the cultures represented.

Cooperation: Seeing other museums as part of a larger network, all working together to attract a larger percentage of potential museum visitors or telling a collaborative story.

Critical path: The pathway showing the progression of a project, correlating work directions with a project timetable. Key milestones are featured, supporting evaluation steps and switching points to different possible scenarios.

Cross-marketing: Marketing several museums at once in a way that creates synergy in learning experiences between the museums.

Cultural affiliation: The culture represented by the object or design, especially in terms of historical ownership or cultural use.

Cultural tourists: Travelers seeking to understand other cultures by observing customs or lifeways or purchasing items representative of that culture.

Customer satisfaction: The level of museum participant value from services, determined by obtaining customer feedback, useful for subsequent improvement and design of additional services.

Customer service: Providing educational experiences, meaningful interactions and basic services to visitors in relation to local hospitality and cultural styles.

Dehumidifier: Equipment functioning to decrease the level of relative humidity when environmental conditions at the museum are excessively damp.

Destination: An area offering a series of services or experiences for attracting non-local visitors with the intention of enriching the visitor experience through collaboration between local programs and other museums.

Development: Bias in the assumption of growth as the primary economic intention. The term "sustainable development" implies culturally appropriate program form, scale, and timing.

Diagram: A drawing showing basic shapes and the placement of elements in telling a story with objects.

Diorama: A three-dimensional scene capturing a moment in time. Adding cultural interpretation, demonstrations, and vocal interpretation brings life to this historical form of exhibit.

Eco-museum: A museum relating to and explaining ecosystems or landscapes, documenting, interpreting, and encouraging conservation of both natural and cultural heritage.

Economic multiplier: The number of times a dollar recirculates in a local economy, therefore preventing economic leakages. Museums selling locally-made goods contribute to a higher economic multiplier in the community.

Eco-tourists: Travelers seeking a nature-based experience. Linking exhibit topics and tours in nature expands scenario possibilities.

Ecosystem: A community of living organisms, including plants, animals, microbes, air, water, soil and people, interacting in an interconnected and supportive way.

Evaluation: The process of assessing and determining progress in relation to goals, objectives, and timelines, as well as making recommendations for improvement.

Exhibit: A physical or virtual means of presenting and interpreting objects, with visual interpretation through design, text, graphics, and video recordings.

Exhibit plan: A scaled drawing showing layout arrangement as structure to communicate objects, meanings, or interactions.

Floor plan: A technical drawing reflecting a "map" of a floor area showing the arrangement of spaces and structures, including use for interactive exhibits.

Formative evaluation: A periodic assessment of progress on program goals, used to shape, "form," or redirect as necessary.

Front-end evaluation: Testing the effectiveness of ideas generated during the planning process before the start of exhibit or project initiation to determine if re-direction is needed.

Geo-tourists: A new concept with overlap between cultural tourists, eco-tourists, and heritage tourists, connoting concern for local people and their environments.

Heritage tourists: Visitors interested in local history, museums and historic places.

Humidifier: An electric equipment item designed to increase the relative humidity when conditions are overly dry.

HVAC: Acronym for a physical system controlling heating, ventilation, and air-conditioning.

Interpretation: An explanation of an object, place, or landscape in relation to historical or cultural significance.

Inventory: A list of objects to include type, cultural affiliation, and special considerations (both physical and cultural) for handling.

Itinerary: A linkage of possible stops on a trip, in the form of a museum website, a printed brochure, or a section of a visitor guide: travel times, information on where to visit for experiences plus obtain food, service and lodging, and maps are included in an itinerary to guide the visitor on a journey.

Label: Brief text and possible illustrations to explain an item on display—monolingual, bilingual, or multi-lingual, depending on the cultures represented.

Lifeways: The customs, beliefs, values, language, views of the environment, and other cultural resources representative of a people or a community.

Managed visitation: Development that defines allowed areas of visitation and prohibited areas, provides a balance of activities, protects culture, and educates visitors about people, places, and access.

Market: The overall potential interest groups that can be drawn by the museum to include both the local community and tourists.

Market analysis: An assessment of the structure, composition, and preferences of potential museum attendees, useful for determining topics, themes, activities, and interpretive projects.

Market niche: An opportunity for a unique, unfilled experience or product line or service.

Market penetration: The extent to which a museum succeeds in attracting participants from the market as a whole by diversifying with different market segments.

Market segment: A part of the total possible market, with a particular set of characteristics, such as heritage travelers or eco-tourists.

Market share: The portion of the overall possible market attracted by the museum; increasing market share is a step toward increasing museum income.

Marketing: The process of reaching out to potential audiences and participants through a broad range of advertising techniques, including the Internet.

Mission: A statement of purpose of a museum or an exhibit, or an educational intention, representing a past-present-future orientation of cultural groups and the community involved.

Model: A scaled three-dimensional representation of an object, a group of objects, or an exhibit.

Multiple income streams: Earning a living through several different types of income or jobs, pieced together to form an income.

Object: A three-dimensional representation of cultural beliefs and uses.

Outgas: The process of emitting toxic gas from an object or display material, possibly affecting the health of museum employees or visitors.

Paradigm: A set of beliefs shaping a situation. A paradigm shift occurs when one set of beliefs loses its influence and another takes over.

Performance Evaluating progress attained on goals and objectives, with **measurement:** community and visitor input, and considering changing external conditions to assess whether redirecting to another scenario is needed.

Person-trips: An indicator of tourism volume used in the tourism industry; the number of one-way trips between two points, at least fifty miles away from home.

Point of origin: Place where the visitor lives or starts the trip, useful to know for marketing purposes.

Product development: Matching the existing skills (or desired skills) in a community with ideas for products that are in demand by visitors to a specific area.

Promotion: Media distribution on activities and services, given free of charge to the potential visitor(s) on their journey.

Regional approach: Including museums in both urban and rural areas and linking them together in a larger geographical area.

Relative humidity: RH is the ratio of water vapor in the air compared to the amount that the air can hold if fully saturated, expressed as a percentage.

Repatriation: The process of returning an item of symbolic value to its owner, whether to a culture or to an individual.

Research: Documentation of a subject, including a review of scholarly work and interviews with people representing the cultures involved—for culturally relevant and contemporary interpretation.

Saturation: The ability to absorb.

Scenario: A possible future outcome.

Schematic phase: The initial planning period.

Scriptwriter: The person responsible for researching and writing interpretive text, including outreach to community members.

Souvenir line: A lower-end line (in price, not necessarily in quality) purchased to remember the trip or to give away to friends and family; souvenirs are generally defined as costing $30 or less.

Specialist: A knowledge keeper, either in museum skills or cultural knowledge.

Stakeholders: Groups with a special interest in the museum's activities, including the local community, keepers of cultural knowledge, museum members, sponsors, as well as the regional museum network and visitors coming to the local area.

Study collection: An assembly of items, often replicas by cultural experts, for use in cultural art learning classes.

Summative evaluation: An assessment conducted at the end of project completion or at the end of the year for the total of museum activities in order to determine overall success.

Sustainable tourism: A managed approach taking into account the preservation of local resources, cultures and long-term self-sufficiency.

Technical drawing: Two-dimensional representations developed for an exhibit area and structures.

Terminology: Words related to a specialized activity, considering cultural uses and diverse interpretations.

Tourism draw: A pull of visitors created to a visitation offering through targeted marketing efforts.

Tourism market: The potential people who could be attracted to a specific area as tourists.

Traditional: Peoples who pass down specific cultural practices and languages for generations.

Value chain: Products pass through all activities of a chain in order, and at each activity the product gains some value. The chain of activities gives the products more added value than the sum of the independent activities' values.

Visitor: A participant in the museum's offerings and experiences. A visitor who travels fifty or more miles is considered a tourist. Fewer miles and they are considered local.

Visitor education: Providing information to the potential or actual visitor on local peoples, history, cultural values, foods, etiquette for behavior, the local environment, and other topics of local interest, for the purpose of enhancing the visitor's learning experience, while reducing impacts on the local community.

Visitor etiquette: Guidelines developed by a community to describe culturally appropriate or respectful behavior according to the viewpoints of a particular community.

Visitor guide: A publication, usually printed in color, with maps, a calendar of events, itineraries, articles on local activities, places, cultures and arts, as well as advertisements showing visitors shops, lodging and eating places. Guides are promotional and given free of charge; inclusion in an itinerary increases visitor attendance.

Visitor profile: The demographics and interests of the museum's visitors or potential visitors in relation to local residents and tourists.

Visitor survey: A survey distributed to a sample group of museum visitors to determine information such as where they are from, educational topics of interest, the activities desired, planned length of stay, item interest for purchase, and food interests.

Voice: An interpretive and communicative style reflecting the worldview of the people in a cultural story.

Work plan: A list detailing each task in a project, including community outreach and review.

Appendix B

Community Plans Valuable for Museum Interface

Taking the approach of community integration furthers coordination with other local or regional programs and affords the museum an opportunity to encourage consideration of cultural issues in the formation of policy. A proactive approach keeps the museum visible and increases the likelihood of funding connected to new innovations.

THE COMPREHENSIVE PLAN

The comprehensive plan covers a broad range of community topics or elements, with a brief overview of each program or governmental unit, goals, and future directions, as well as an integrated approach for coordination. A community may or may not have completed a comprehensive plan, and often, the cultural element is omitted. An important role of the museum is to remind the community-wide planning process of the inclusion of the cultural element or section.

The inquiry is worthwhile since this type of plan serves as a summary for museum linkages. Comprehensive plans typically cover these topics, known as plan elements.

- Community vision
- Demographics
- Culture
- Education
- Natural environment
- Economic development
- Health services
- Land use
- Housing

- Utilities
- Transportation

Regarding community sustainability is only possible with a comprehensive approach. Museums fit into the cultural element, integrating their resources and directions into the overall community vision.

CULTURAL PLANS

Culture forms the basis for the uniqueness of a community. Beliefs guide actions toward economy and ecology; therefore, culture is the cornerstone of sustainability. As the relationship between cultural diversity and the preservation of biodiversity comes to the forefront of global discussion, so, too, is the awareness of the urgency to preserve the vast body of planetary knowledge that is rapidly disappearing. Cultural plans identify:

- Cultural groups within the community;
- Characteristics and organizations of groups;
- Art programs;
- Other cultural programs;
- Languages spoken;
- Needs for language retention;
- Goals, programs, and activities offered;
- Art and culture district potential;
- Potential for historic tours;
- Gaps in services; and
- Strategies for moving forward individually and collaboratively.

Cultural plans encourage understanding of diversity, knowledge held, and intercultural sharing. As the museum seeks to develop interpretive programs inclusive of diverse worldviews, languages, and desired directions, the process of developing a community cultural plan provides a strong interface. Broadening museum services to become more community-relevant can include activities such as hosting cultural learning or language classes. The museum is a likely catalyst and contributor to this valuable plan relating to cultural continuance!

ECONOMIC DEVELOPMENT PLANS

High on the list of municipality priorities is the local economy. Frequently, the focus of economic development is attracting large corporations that contribute heftily to tax income for the local government's budget. In small towns, the pattern of attracting the "big box" stores carries the impact of driving small, locally owned businesses to closure.

When this happens, local artists, food providers, service providers, and other entrepreneurs are forced to close shop—resulting in a loss of "local flavor" and ethnic expression in the local economy. What municipalities often fail to recognize is how the corporatizing of the local economy leads to cultural loss.

When locals lose their opportunity as cultural entrepreneurs, cultural practice tends to decline, as well as cultural styles of doing business. Even products needed to support cultural artists and entrepreneurs disappear from the shelves, impeding the continuation of traditions.

Topics expanding economic development with cultural considerations may include:

- Descriptors of the local economy;
- Cultural groups and their economic contributions;
- Values reflected by cultural groups;
- Needs for entrepreneurial support services;
- Local activities serving as a draw for economic activity;
- Low-cost and no-cost marketing opportunities;
- Economic projections; and
- Planned infrastructure to support economic development.

Cultural styles for business may have served a community's ethnic groups well, for centuries. The local economy as a whole is enriched by preserving and fostering a diverse range of options for earned livelihood.

The museum can serve as a catalyst for economic opportunity in many ways. For example, information on the cultural arts supports cultural entrepreneurs. Providing space for brochures in the museum foyer (see chapter 6) or information on the community's cultural entrepreneurs on the website furthers linkages for earned livelihood. Purchasing locally made items for the museum store and providing information on authenticity often occurs in conjunction with an exhibit. Sponsoring art shows and festivals at the museum is another opportunity.

Keeping the local economy and cultural retention efforts at the forefront encourages creative solutions to economic challenges. Particularly in small communities, the museum's resources represent one of the few opportunities available to cultural entrepreneurs.

EDUCATIONAL PLANS

Educational institutions complete plans for curriculum, school activities, administration, and budget projects. These institutional plans may fit into an overall community education plan. Frequently, in this era, the arts and cultural activities are overlooked due to budget cuts—presenting an opportunity for museums to fill this need. The museum's 501(c)(3) status may open new funding doors. Topics frequently include:

- Educational approach;
- Educational goals and objectives;
- Course outlines;
- Bilingual education;
- Support services;
- Extracurricular activities;
- Evaluation methods;
- Home schooling liaison;
- Career development strategies;
- Parental involvement; and
- Community liaison.

The museum, recognizing the value of cultural retention in the community, is in a position to offer guidance on cultural programs and to share information or identified keepers of traditions. In turn, outreach to schools and in-depth collaborations are likely to follow. If the museum offers to participate in these planning processes, interpretation of history, language, and culture are likely to be integrated, enriching educational plans. Bringing museum programs into the schools is another possible outcome.

THE LAND USE PLAN

Yes, museums impact local land use, both through the museum facility and the visitors that come to the museum. Physical impacts are essential to assess.

The land-use plan assesses the physical qualities or characteristics of land and demographics, as well as defines use needs, including acreage and location. Topics often included are population, agriculture, archaeological and cultural sites, boundaries, buildings, fishing, flood control, forests, lakes, rivers, timber, historic sites, housing, irrigation ditches, landscaping, land status, minerals, roads, sacred sites, sewage lines, sewage treatment, soils, topographic data, traditional use areas, vegetation, water lines, water rights, water supply, and water quality.

Benefits to museum coordination with the land-use plan include:

- Viewing the museum beyond its walls;
- Connection to the impacts that museum visitation may cause and collaborative efforts to prevent negative environmental impacts;
- Location of additional public lands that might be utilized by the museum for expansion or use for new functions;

- Gaining an understanding of local ecosystems and possible connections for interpretation; and
- Establishing collaboration with local government.

How many visitors can a community's infrastructure (water, sewer, environmentally sensitive areas, etc.) sustain? Land-use planning and environmental impact studies are tools for considering the extent of visitation regarded as sustainable and ways of containing visitors—or managing away from ecological and culturally sensitive areas.

For the museum to engage in environmental education effectively, ecosystem understanding must be in place. A sense of place connects the museum to its surroundings, creating environmental and cultural context.

HEALTH-CARE SYSTEM PLANS

Community services of vital interest include the provision of health-care and emergency services. Generally, these services are delivered according to mainstream, Western culture modalities rather than offering alternatives that draw from the traditional healing practices of ethnic groups. Integrating cultural knowledge and the need for access to healing-plant sources is one topic to look for when reviewing the plan. In the following outline, culture is integrated to demonstrate the potential for museum involvement.

- Identification of community diversity and needs
- Different healing modalities appropriate to include
- Health-care organizations
- Provision of services
- Prevention programs with a cultural basis
- Emergency services
- Coordination of services
- Future directions

The museum addressing cultural diversity issues is in a position to recommend specific needs of cultural groups and needs for access to local plant-gathering areas—i.e., land-use plan considerations.

TRANSPORTATION PLANS

As public interest shifts to a lowered carbon footprint, the necessity of public transportation is at the forefront. Museums attract visitors, and visitors need transportation to reach the museum. Coordinating with local and regional transportation entities ensures the museum's inclusion. Topics that are likely to include the museum cover:

- Local transportation and tourism trends;
- Connection to regional, national, and international systems;
- Transportation systems comprising the local network: road, rail, air, water-borne, transit, and non-motorized (bicycle, pedestrian, etc.);
- Public transportation routes;
- Gaps in transportation service;
- Signage;
- Parking; and
- Landscaping (connections to local ecosystems).

Efficient transportation links to regional, national, and global markets are essential to the maintenance and growth of the community's educational and economic base. If the museum develops interpretive tours as a diversified means of support, cost-effective transportation is essential. The museum is also in a position to serve ethnic and underserved neighborhoods, facilitating visitation and participation in museum programs. Make certain the museum is on that planned route!

TOURISM PLANS

Visitors, particularly cultural tourists and eco-tourists, come to a community seeking to understand history, culture, the arts, and local ecosystems. Often, particularly in rural areas, an influx of visitors contributes to the mainstay of expenditures sustaining the local economy. Understanding the demographics (point of origin), age range, educational level, income range, and interests is essential for developing museum programs and exhibits that connect to the visiting public. If a tourism plan exists, either regional or local, examine content for topics indicated by visitors.

If no plan exists, museum presence on the planning committee can guide visitor surveys to include educational interests. Tourism topics to watch for include:

- Market size;
- Seasonal trends in visitation;
- Visitor demographics (e.g., age range, educational level, income range);
- Transportation used;
- Point of origin;
- Cultural identification;
- Specific interests;
- Whether the museum is on the itinerary;
- Connections to visitor amenities (e.g., lodging preference, food preferences);
- Suggestions based on the visitation experience; and
- Intention to return.

When a museum contributes to the design of local visitor surveys, topics of cultural interest are more likely to be included. Knowing a visitor's point of origin, where they live or start their trip, is valuable for inclusion in marketing efforts. Visitor interest often sparks local cultural pride, inspiring residents to learn history, the cultural arts, and entrepreneurial skills.

TECHNOLOGY PLANS

Reaching an expanded audience in the rapidly changing weather, epidemic, and workplace conditions requires equity in access to modern technology. Outreach through the Internet requires access to broadband and mobile phone applications, as well as use of new platforms and emerging technologies for physical distancing. Participation in forming a museum technology plan component and then interfacing with the community's technology plan, furthers connecting potential.

SUMMARY

Staying connected community-wide multiplies museum benefits. Participating, or even initiating the idea of these community plans, furthers input on cultural issues, concerns, and resources. When considering a broader range of potential contributions and partnerships, funding options open for the museum. Being an integral part of a network furthers museum survival.

Appendix C

Sample Visitor Satisfaction Survey.

MUSEUM VISITOR SATISFACTION SURVEY

Date:

Before you leave the museum, please help us to improve visitor services by taking 5 minutes to complete this short survey. Those responding will receive a one time 10% discount in the museum store.

1. Primary residence:
- ❏ City/Town: _____
- ❏ State: _____
- ❏ Out-of-country
  Country:_____

2. Age (check one)
- ❏ under 15   ❏ 30-44
- ❏ 15-19   ❏ 45-59
- ❏ 20-29   ❏ 60+

3. Return visitor?
❏Yes ❏No

4. Number in party:
Adults ___ Children ___

5. Interests while visiting community: (check all that apply)
- ❏ Learning about history
- ❏ Eating local foods
- ❏ Learning about local cultures
- ❏ Demonstrations
- ❏ Learning about local arts
- ❏ Museum   ❏ Local agriculture
- ❏ Tours   ❏ Other _____

6. How did you learn about us? (check all that apply)
- ❏ Website/ social media
- ❏ Visitor Guide
- ❏ Brochure
- ❏ Chamber Commerce
- ❏ Newspaper/ magazine
- ❏ Atlas/ maps
- ❏ Family or friends

7. Which of the following topics interest you? (check all that apply)
- ❏ Educational experiences
- ❏ Learning about local ecosystems
- ❏ Cultural retention efforts
- ❏ Family activities
- ❏ Current local issues
- ❏ Website
- ❏ Virtual museum
- ❏ Newsletter
- ❏ Local events

8. Your occupation? (check all that apply)
- ❏ Retired
- ❏ Professional
- ❏ Technical
- ❏ Student
- ❏ Unemployed
- ❏ Other _____

Appendix CSample Visitor Satisfaction Survey.

9. Which of the following interest you for purchase?
(check all that apply)

☐ Books   ☐ Paintings

☐ Scarves   ☐ Music

☐ Food products   ☐ Toys

☐ T-shirts   ☐ Jewelry

10. Are you interested in becoming a museum member, receiving the newsletter & discounts?

☐ Yes   ☐ No

Email:_____

11. Please rate your satisfaction with exhibits.

Permanent exhibit	☐ high	☐ medium	☐ low
Changing exhibit	☐ high	☐ medium	☐ low
Exhibit guide	☐ high	☐ medium	☐ low
Exhibit labels	☐ high	☐ medium	☐ low

12. Satisfaction with tours:

Museum Tour	☐ high	☐ medium	☐ low
Nature Tour	☐ high	☐ medium	☐ low
Art Tour	☐ high	☐ medium	☐ low

13. Satisfaction with customer service:

Admissions desk	☐ high	☐ medium	☐ low
Other museum staff	☐ high	☐ medium	☐ low
Museum store	☐ high	☐ medium	☐ low
Tours	☐ high	☐ medium	☐ low
Café	☐ high	☐ medium	☐ low

14. Overall quality of the museum experience?

☐ Excellent   ☐ Very good   ☐ Good   ☐ Adequate   ☐ Disappointing

15. Was the speaker series informative?   ☐ high   ☐ medium   ☐ low
     ☐ not applicable

16. Rate the cleanliness of our facility: ☐ high   ☐ medium   ☐ low

17. Were restroom facilities adequate and clean? ❑ Yes ❑ No

18. Is more visitor information needed at this site? ❑ Yes ❑ No

19. Is parking adequate?   ❑ Yes ❑ No

20. What is your combined household income?

❑ less than $20,000   ❑ $50,000 to $74,000
❑ $20,000 to $29,000   ❑ $75,000 to $99,000
❑ $30,000 to $39,000   ❑ greater than $99,000
❑ $40,000 to $49,000

21. Comments or suggestions regarding your experience:

Thank you!
Please return this form at the museum front desk or electronically.
(address of where to return form)

Index

Index

About the Author

Susan Guyette, (Ph.D. Cultural Anthropology, M.A. Urban and Regional Planning) blends both academic and planning careers with culturally diverse communities, lending a practical aspect to the discussion of the adaptive planning process. She is of Native American heritage (Métis—Mi'kmaq Indian and Acadian French) and utilizes many Indigenous examples to illustrate contrast in worldviews, values, and community priorities. Currently an Adjunct Professor at the Institute of American Indian Arts—teaching in the Masters degree program in Art Administration—she utilizes four decades of direct experience working with cultural centers and museums, as well as tourism and economic development with Indigenous and rural communities.

Her life project is assisting the development of the Harvard award-winning Poeh Cultural Center at the Pueblo of Pojoaque in New Mexico, where she has served as planner, development specialist and program evaluator. Experience includes completing over 50 long-range plans with Native American, Hispanic, and mixed-ethnicity communities, including several statewide plans with state agencies. Additional experience was gained by serving as a technical assistance provider for the arts-and-culture integrated MainStreet program in New Mexico and conducting national level training for the Smithsonian Institution as well as state agencies.

This text further develops these culturally-based planning techniques, building upon her prior books—*Sustainable Cultural Tourism: Small-Scale Solutions*, *Planning for Balanced Development: A Guide for Native American and Rural Communities*, and several texts for American Indian Studies—*Issues for the Future of American Indian Studies* and *Community-Based Research: A Handbook for Native Americans*. She is also the co-author of the award winning book on environmental issues, *Zen Birding: Connect in Nature* and a newspaper columnist, writing "Everyday Green" for the *Green Fire Times*.

Her work continues as a consultant through Santa Fe Planning & Research in New Mexico (USA). She cares deeply about the future of cultures, communities, and Mother Earth.

www.susanguyette.com